Human Relations for
Emergency Response Personnel

Human Relations for Emergency Response Personnel

By

HERMAN J. BANKS, M.P.A.

and

ANNE T. ROMANO, M.A.

Instructors
Social Science Department
Police Academy
New York City Police Department
New York, New York

CHARLES C THOMAS • PUBLISHER
Springfield • Illinois • U.S.A.

Published and Distributed Throughout the World by

CHARLES C THOMAS • PUBLISHER

2600 South First Street

Springfield, Illinois, 62717, U.S.A.

© *1982 by* CHARLES C THOMAS • PUBLISHER

ISBN 0-398-04555-0

Library of Congress Catalog Card Number: 81-9232

Printed in the United States of America

CU-RX-1

Library of Congress Cataloging in Publication Data

Banks, Hermon J. and Romano, Anne T.
  Human relations for emergency response personnel.

  Bibliography: p.
  Includes index.
  1. Police communication systems--New York
(N.Y.)--Case studies. 2. Telephone operators--Training
of--New York (N.Y.)--Case studies. 3. Assistance in
emergencies--New York (N.Y.)--Case studies. 4. Crisis
intervention (Psychiatry)--Case studies. I. Romano,
Anne T. II. Title.
HV7936.C8B36   362'.0425   81-9232
ISBN 0-398-04555-0   AACR2

PREFACE

LARGE urban settings, such as New York City, continue to experience crisis situations in which the victims walk away from their crisis, having experienced further victimization, if not fatality. Municipal services have increased training by adjusting and responding with more and more advanced technology, and the concentrated efforts on the part of the municipal employees to become "technocrats" has failed to prepare emergency operators adequately in responding to the human trauma.

The accuracy of programmed technology oftentimes fails to address itself to human needs. In fact, the natural process of technology widens the existing distance between those responding to the emergencies and those calling for assistance.

Technology may improve efficiency, but there is more needed than advanced technology to capture effectiveness. To be effective in responding to the citizens at large calling for assistance, there must be not only efficiency but also effectiveness. During many emergencies, such as crimes in progress, serious illness on the street, or serious illness in the home, advanced technology has proven its efficiency by quick response time of emergency personnel, but, because these personnel were not sensitized to the human side of the crisis, they have not been truly effective.

Perhaps, if at this point we cite a few examples, the problems we have been addressing will become clearer. The following situations are true, though the names have been changed to disguise the people involved. They have been selected from incoming calls into New York City's 911 Communications Division, in order to convey some of the main ideas of this book.

Friday, 0900 hours, April 1978: Operator No. 000 is on duty and receives a call from a very excited citizen, stating that a female was being dragged into an alley by a man with a gun. The caller was so excited that the police operator could hardly determine exactly what was going on. The operator did get the location,

v

however, which the excited caller stated as being 110 Greene Street. The operator confirmed the address with the caller, asking whether it was 110th and Greene, to which the caller in the excitement of the moment responded affirmatively.

Having been caught up in the excitement by the caller, the operator was part of the confirmation of a wrong address, and the police officers responded to 110th and Greene Avenue instead of 110 Greene Street. Meanwhile, the female was being fatally wounded at the other location. The operator did not use the kind of precautions necessary to prevent this kind of error.

Wednesday, 1900 hours, October 1978: Operator No. 000 is on duty and picks up a caller stating very quietly in a controlled and calm voice that her husband is in the bedroom with two friends of theirs, trying to stop their male friend from slitting his girl friend's throat. She said very calmly, "Please hurry."

The operator takes the information, but discusses her doubts about the true emergency nature of this call with her supervisor, at which time they both decide that this is not a real emergency call. However, a car was dispatched anyway, but with disbelief and without the proper priority code. The supervisor decides to call back the woman caller, asking her to once again explain the situation. The woman repeats the story, again in a calm, controlled voice, showing no excitement. Due to the lack of fear or excitement in the woman's voice, the supervisor decides that this is truly not a real emergency call. She scolded the caller, telling her, "We don't have police cars to waste sending on prank calls lady, and if you want to be an actress you should consider going to Hollywood." In the meantime, when the originally dispatched car finally arrived at the scene, the officers found the victim with her throat slit.

Information was out in adequate time, enough for the police to respond in the first situation, however, because of the contagious nature of crisis, the operator failed to be explicit and accurate with emergency information, therefore dispatching assistance to the wrong location. In the second situation, the operator failed to recognize any crisis quality present in the caller's voice. The caller's voice and behavior did not meet the expectations of the operator's guidelines of what a crisis caller should sound like. The operator tended to fix on excited behavior as an indication of a crisis occurring, and this caller's voice and behavior were without excitement, was calm, and well articulated, which did not fulfill the operator's expectations of what a person calling in an emergency should sound like. Therefore, the operator and her supervisor did not believe that this was a true emergency call.

On the one hand, the operator got caught up in the contagious nature of crisis calls and placed erroneous information into the terminal. On the other hand, the operator didn't believe it was a crisis, because the caller didn't meet her expectations of what a crisis victim should sound like.

New York City has approximately 10,000 coin phone booths, which permit free dialing of 911. From any telephone in any home, store, or pay booth anyone may call direct and free of charge to police headquarters. The phone rings more than 1,000 times an hour, twenty-four hours a day at the 911 emergency number. During the winter, 17,000 calls are normally logged daily, and in the summer of 1980 the number rose to approximately 25,000 calls a day. The average call is answered in four seconds.

The 911 operators take an avalanche of calls, in the millions annually from people seeking police assistance. These operators are the sounding boards from which hysterical voices bounce off of 365 days a year. They are the catalyst which initiates the chain of events that will eventually lead to emergency assistance for those people in crisis. It is the information that the operator gleans from in as short a time as one minute from conversations with perfect strangers that determines what type of action will be taken to assist the caller.

Each call that comes into 911 signals a potential crisis on the other end. Many of the callers are hysterical, some are calm, some speak in foreign languages or accents, some are frightened children, and some are the frightened confused elderly. Some are intoxicated or incoherent from drugs, and some are extremely angry at what they perceive as bureaucratic inefficiency, because their call was not responded to quickly enough.

It should be apparent that the important link between the public in need of assistance and the attaining of this assistance is the emergency operator, and it also indicates the awesome responsibility that each operator faces as he sits down at his console at the beginning of this shift.

Prior to the implementation of this particular program, the training for this extremely important link consisted of two weeks technical training of both in-service and classroom instruction. The curriculum consisted of a concentration on increasing typing speed and skills, familiarity with the eighty-two different input messages, the ability to interpret as many output messages or formats, instructions on which types of calls to screen, instruction on gathering of important information (such as address, names, telephone numbers, and descriptions, where indicated), and directions on the use and operation of the computer terminal as part of the SPRINT (Special Police Radio Inquiry Network) system. At the conclusion of the two weeks training, the operator was given a multiple-choice written test, and, if it was passed, the operator was ready to take emergency calls from the citizens of New York City.

In terms of its advanced information-processing technology and equipment, the system worked well. However, in terms of its sensitivity to the human element, the system was a total failure. Under continuing severe criticism from the public and the media of its handling of recent emergencies and because of the increasing number of civilian complaints being lodged against New York City and its 911 operators, a second look was taken at the training program for emergency operators.

The complaints centered around the problems of "poor attitude" and the "insensitivity" of the operators. There was a clear indication that a solution must be sought to this problem. The problem and the need for its solution was directed towards the social science department at the police academy and placed in the hands of Detective Hermon J. Banks. This book and the program presented within its pages is the result of the search for an answer to this problem.

Since the program's development, inception, and inclusion in the training, the curriculum for all potential 911 operators, the overall number of civilian complaints lodged against 911 has been noticeably reduced by one half. However, the training programs proven success is not in the reduction in the number of civilian complaints, but in the improved services provided to the citizens of New York City, which is rightfully theirs. This program stresses that the human element involved is as important as the technical procedure of recording the information and dispatching help.

Since it is virtually impossible to train an entire urban setting of 8 million people, this program focuses on those persons responding to crisis situations with needed assistance, giving them insight into the behavior of the caller, and an analysis of their own responses to the crisis situation. It further develops mannerisms and language conducive to the successful resolution of a crisis situation. Since the ultimate success of any police agency depends largely on the nature of its police-citizen contacts, this program will be of valuable assistance. What we hope to do is to prevent the further victimization of crime victims and to promote harmonious resolution of crises.

Our intended audience is varied. This is by no means a book only for police emergency operators. It is our hope that this book might be of some value to anyone interested in crisis behavior and the appropriate intervention into crisis events. Therefore, it will be helpful to not only police emergency operators, but also emergency medical operators, paramedics, ambulance attendants, telephone operators, city complaint operators, nurses, those in the medical profession especially emergency rooms in hospitals, firemen, instructors of police science, social work and related disciplines, and anyone finding themselves involved in intervention and resolution of crisis situations.

This book doesn't waste the trainer's time on the generalities which so often permeate police-related materials. This program not only analyzes the crisis and those in it, it also analyzes the behavior of the respondent and indicates clearly and specifically how they affect and are affected by the crisis situation. It further makes specific recommendations as to the avoidance of further victimization and gives advice on promoting the relief of physical and psychological trauma.

The underlying theme of this book is that the emergency operators position is not only oriented towards information gathering, but that it is also people oriented. Many of the calls that emergency operators respond to are stressful events for those involved. Knowing what to say, understanding the person and his predicament, and knowing how to respond effectively as well and efficiently can make the operators job more self-satisfying and rewarding.

Each chapter also includes a section of role plays, with suggestions on simulating calls for training purposes. The participation in these simulated calls will further enhance the operator's competence and improve self-confidence and their abilities to make prompt and proper judgments during crisis situations.

H.J.B.
A.T.R.

INTRODUCTION

IT should be apparent that initial inputs into the communications system from an operational viewpoint are telephone calls. Most emergency requests for assistance from the public come to the communications center via the telephone. Therefore, the telephone provides the primary means by which the public can contact the police department.

The first contact a person in distress makes is with an emergency telephone operator. The nature of that important first contact and the way in which it is handled can either lead the caller to state that the municipality is indeed concerned with their problem, leaving the caller with a sense of satisfaction of having the emergency dealt with properly, or the caller can be left dissatisfied and have the city in court as being held liable for negligence.

The deciding factor that determines whether a caller is satisfied or dissatisfied is the manner in which the emergency operator handles the interaction. This book isolates and articulates all possible human dynamics between the operator and the caller and explains how these human qualities either continue victimization or how they reverse crisis behavior towards a successful resolution. However, prior to our description of the contents of this program, we would like to present a brief description of a typical large, urban setting communications division and a description of the process that a call for emergency assistance initiates.

For example, the Communications Division of the New York City Police Department has the function of directing and coordinating activities occurring in one of the largest population centers of the world. New York City proper has over 9,000,000 inhabitants, with the metropolitan area having a population of approximately 13,000,000. New York's communications system is the largest of its kind in the country. The center is operative twenty-four hours a day, and the phones ring more than 1,000 times an hour from both emergency and non-emergency calls coming in. Ninety-eight percent of calls are handled within thirty seconds, and the average call is answered within four seconds.

The ability of the Communications Division to effectively and efficiently monitor the pulse of New York City is a tribute to the extensive research and unbelievably complex array of the most sophisticated communications and data processing equipment ever designed by man. The Center directs and coordinates the operations of approximately 24,000 sworn personnel in the department.

Annually, the Communications Division completes more than 10 million calls. Part of its critical responsibility is the job of relaying a daily average of 1,100 reports of fire to the fire department and hundreds of calls for ambulances directly to the Health and Hospital Corporation — a separate city agency for sick and injured citizens.

In addition to serving as a police and ambulance emergency number, 911 also has a "conference" capability on fire and ambulance calls that brings the fire department and especially trained health and hospital personnel into a 911 conversation as a third party.

In 1970, SPRINT (Special Police Radio Inquiry Network) became operational. The SPRINT system utilizes two IBM 360 computers and sophisticated telecommunications hardware to keep the entire system efficiently operational to handle the massive volume of calls for police assistance that come into the Comunications Division daily. Each of the emergency operators has a SPRINT terminal, which is the operator's link with the SPRINT computer and the radio dispatcher, who will ultimately assign a patrol unit to investigate the complaint. Resembling a typewriter, the terminal, surmounted by a TV monitor, instantly reproduces the typed message on its monitor.

Police emergency operators have been trained to use the coded language of the computer as they are feeding information from a received phone call. There is a regular computer format to follow when entering information. Any incident requires the entry of four fields. For example, upon receipt of a call, the information is translated into computer-coded language, and the operator may encode a message as follows:

1/3/2854 W. Lake/54/Cardiac Apt 5-OX REQ(S).

This message translates /1/ emergency, /3/ in Bronx, at 2854 West Lake, ambulance sent (10-54 code) oxygen required, /S/

Safety Emergency Division. The operator then strikes the enter key, whereupon the data is sent to the computer. Within three seconds, the information is processed and routed to the proper parties, be they dispatcher, complaint desk, notifications, fire, etc. The computer will automatically select those who need to receive the message and route accordingly. The information in this example would be displayed upon the dispatcher's terminal.

All data entered subsequent to an operator's signing in at a particular terminal will be identified with the operator's tax number. This identifies him to the system and, in so doing, provides a measure of security by allowing restricted access to information stored and compartmentalization of data, which is retrievable by only certain individuals. The computer will not accept any input of information from an operator until he has signed in.

As stated previously, each operator has learned eighty-two different coded input messages and has learned to interpret as many output messages, or formats. Certain code signals, when formatted into the computer, have automatic priority. Thus, a robbery in progress, a homicide, a riot, or an assist of officer will get immediate attention. One of the operator's responsibilities is to be able to determine the urgency of the call and code it appropriately, prior to entering the information into the terminal.

Considering the complexity of the SPRINT system, and its demands for technological skills to be developed by the operators of the computer terminals that activate this system such as priority formats, incident codes, tax registry numbers, abbreviations of street names, and names of hospitals and other landmarks in New York City, and other important components of computer language, one can understand the difficulty of retaining human skills in the process. It is easy for the 911 emergency operator, in his quest to gather information and to satisfy the needs of the information-processing technological equipment, to lose sight of the fact that there is a human being in distress on the other end of his headset.

In addition, even with the most advanced, sophisticated telecommunication hardware ever designed, there is still the possibility of human error because of the nature of crisis behavior on the part of both the caller and the operator. An investigation of recordings of incoming calls to 911 revealed this alarming information. Observations indicated that when the operator responded to the caller in crisis, the operator's behavior was such that as a result of their interaction one could not help but see continued victimization. The process of technological advancement promotes distance and an insensitive response by operators. The satisfaction that one gets from mastering the technology of the machine is conducive to reducing the desire to contact human qualities and satisfy the emotional needs of the victim caller.

As human skills developers, we are ever mindful of the importance of integrating the human and the technological whenever and wherever possible. The intent of this book is to present a training process that integrates the two: technology with human needs in an effort to sensitize the operator to the point of reaching the human side of the crisis victim in spite of the maze of technology.

The style of this book utilizes two modes of teaching: lecture for content and role play for process. The process of human dynamics is demonstrated through role play. The most effective training programs include role play or experiential training, permitting the student to actually experience crisis calls and to have the opportunity to practice intervention roles and responses in the laboratory setting.

Chapter 1 deals with an explanation of human styles of communication and hard communication systems and the difficulties involved when you integrate the two. It also explains how the communication procedure is in conflict with basic human needs. A number of practical methods are employed to improve communication skills. Basic flow charts are introduced to enhance the student's ability to conceptualize the complexity of the communication process and to avoid the pitfalls inherent in communication. Loaded words and phrases that tend to break the human communication system down are isolated and identified. Chapter 1 also establishes the kind of information necessary for it in order to be an emergency. It also explains the conflict that is caused by the need to gather information on the part of the operator and the opposing need of the caller to tell the operator something else.

Chapter 2, by way of "Transactional Analysis," explains why a person tends to select a particular mode of communication. It analyzes and feeds back to the student how that mode of communication affects the entire system. It further teaches the student how to diagnose communication modes on the part of others and suggests the appropriate mode for the operator to use in response. It explains the probability of conflict and continued victimization if the inappropriate mode is selected.

Chapter 3 focuses on communicating with victims. Victimology, the study of victim's behavior, is outlined in a practical, observable fashion. It focuses on the victim's behavior, their attitude about what has happened, and the resultant behavior of that attitude. It differentiates between various types of victims and the intensity of the trauma. It further explains how this trauma affects the psychological and emotional stability of the victim. Chapter 3 also illustrates how society shows a reluctance to believe the innocence of the victim; therefore, an explanation for society's introducing the blaming element when communicating with the victim is presented.

Chapter 4, under the umbrella of understanding crisis behavior, is an explanation of the behavior associated with various communication modes and categorizes that behavior in ways that explain whether the behavior is supportive of a successful resolution or whether the behavior is supportive of continued chaos. It also offers a quick and practical way to recognize behavior as a result of a crisis situation. This quick analysis is explained by way of a two-dimensional table with five categories of behavior: tone of voice, verbal expressions, physical movement, decision-making ability, and display of confidence. Within these categories, Chapter 4 will analyze and explain the mode of communication and the associated behavior that tends to resolve crisis or continue victimization.

Handling problem callers such as suicide callers (i.e. those callers contemplating suicide), child callers, elderly callers, and intoxicated callers in need of police assistance are discussed in Chapter 5. The suicide caller is a unique problem to the emergency operator, and, in a section of this chapter, we explain the nature of a person contemplating suicide and their behavioral tendency, their modes of communication, and their behavior patterns as a result of this contemplated act. This section also makes practical suggestions on the mode of communication that should be selected in order to communicate as effectively as possible with this person.

The common thread that runs through the other four types of problem callers is a childlike communication quality, i.e. the quality of communication that is exhibited by a child. For example, the child himself has not established a mature frame of reference in order to communicate effectively. The intoxicated person's frame of reference has been impaired to the point of their acting like a child in communication. The elderly may communicate in a childlike way because of senility. The tourist is like a child in that they are not familiar with their surroundings, therefore in a crisis situation they cannot communicate reference points that would be helpful to the operator offering assistance.

In Chapter 6 we integrate the five previous chapters. Communication theory, victimology, crisis behavior, and techniques for handling special callers are all integrated with transactional analysis (T.A.) in a way so as to simplify the application of T.A. to the operator's role.

As if the complexities of mastering technology and integrating human skill were not enough, the process by which they get integrated is done under severe time constraints. This produces a pressure on the operator, which generates an inflow of at times overwhelming anxiety.

In Chapter 7, we discuss the effects of this anxiety on the operator, including the effects of a seemingly constant influx of hysterical voices battering the operator's eardrum. How does all this affect the operator's ability to communicate effectively in his interactions with the caller? Stress.

After each of the first six chapters, in order to reinforce the principles that were covered within the chapters, one can actually observe whether or not the principles covered are being integrated into the individual's communications modes through hands-on role playing. Further, through the use of these role plays, one can observe and analyze how the computer console either creates more distance between the caller and the operator, or one can observe how the operator integrates technology with his human qualities, in order to be more effective in responding to crisis situations.

ACKNOWLEDGMENTS

WE have been influenced by many people. To acknowledge by name all those who have contributed to the substance and content of this book would be to list most of our colleagues, students, and former teachers. We are initially grateful to all of those students in all of the 911 classes we have taught at police headquarters. Their readiness and willingness to learn, their acceptance and interest, and their helpful feedback and suggestions have smoothed the rough edges of this program. It has indeed been a rewarding experience for both of us.

We must satisfy ourselves with mentioning just a few particularly influential people to whom we owe a special debt. We wish to thank Inspector Robert J. Houlihan, commanding officer of the New York City Police Academy, for placing his trust in the social science department that this program would be handled correctly. We are most grateful to Sergeant Peter J. Mancuso, Jr., chairman of the social science department, for the expression of confidence that he had in us in addressing these training needs and for the latitude he has given us in developing this program.

We wish to thank Lieutenant Ray Sherwood, commanding officer of Communications Training Unit, and his training staff for giving us carte blanche in analyzing the existing tapes, so that needed human skills could be detected, isolated, and articulated. Also, for allowing his staff to be readily available to integrate the technical skills with the human skills, so that proper relationships could be addressed in training.

We express our thanks to Lieutenant Dick Koehler, director of Communications Division, for establishing work policies supportive of an environment receptive to this type of training and establishing guidelines for continued motivation and implementation.

Finally, we wish to thank our families for their tolerance, patience, and understanding. We apologize for not being there when you needed us, and we thank you for continuing to be supportive and giving of yourselves, even in spite of our absence. Thank you, Katie, LaShawn, and Sadiqa Banks, and thank you Annette and Patricia Romano. A special thanks to Barbara Romano Vitello, for shouldering an additional responsibility of typing our manuscript, and to her husband, John Vitello, for his sharing of her presence and talent with us.

CONTENTS

Human Relations for
Emergency Response Personnel

Chapter 1

COMMUNICATION

THE daily activities of an emergency operator are many and varied, but most importantly the activities require the application of a communication skill. An effective emergency operator must be able to communicate well with people on many intellectual levels, from the well-educated to the illiterate; this could very well extend to the mentally retarded and verbally handicapped as well. People who call for assistance are of all ages. They come from a variety of cultural backgrounds and may speak only a foreign language, or a difficult-to-understand combination of a foreign language and English. The operator must be able to overcome language barriers, calm the fears of the emotionally upset caller, talk to the very young child in need of help, and understand the speech of the elderly.

The manner in which the operator speaks — softly, firmly, friendly, or authoritatively — provides the atmosphere for communication with others. The caller responds to many of the hidden meanings of what is said; that is, attitudes, tone of voice, and symbolic meanings of words, in terms of his own background and previous experience. For example, consider the tone of voice: a person responds in a warm, friendly way to a speaker who uses that tone of voice, but the reverse, a tone revealing fear or distrust, may invoke an aggressive reply. In addition, a poor choice of words or phrases reflecting symbolic meanings might well result in the creation of a psychological gap between the operator and the caller.

Communication is the transmitting and receiving of information. We usually take for granted our ability to initiate and understand communication and give little thought to its nature and function. It is not surprising, therefore, that we overlook the great influence of communication on the normal functioning of society. We can communicate with each other in many ways, e.g. the smoke signal of the Apache Indian, the starter's pistol in a track race, the sign language used by the deaf, and the Morse code are all variations of com-

3

munication. We also all engage in a variety of communication processes.

Intrapersonal communication involves one individual as he thinks or talks to himself

Interpersonal communication involves an individual with another individual

Group communication involves an individual with more than one person in close physical proximity.

Mass communication involves a communicator with large numbers of people

Within these processes there are different modes of communicating. Communication may be:

Verbal: to talk and to listen

Non-verbal: how we use body movements, hand gestures, facial expressions

Written: to read and to write

In one simple personal interaction, we can and do make use of all these communication channels. For example, when interviewing a complainant of a past burglary, you probably would *ask* questions and then *listen* to the answers to get information to *write* a report of the incident. Both you and the complainant would automatically use expressions, gestures, and other non-verbal techniques to enhance your communication. At the same time, some other message such as *nervousness* or *displeasure* may be expressed by the complainant, or *empathy* or *professionalism* may be expressed by the operator. When giving a summons for a moving violation, a police officer *verbally* informs the violator of the infraction and *requests* the information necessary to write a summons. The violator may politely reply verbally and provide the information necessary, but he may convey a different message *non-verbally* through glaring eyes of displeasure. The police officer writes the summons and verbally informs the violator where he is to respond to answer the charge. The violator may respond with a verbal "thank you" and a non-verbal expression of anger.

One useful way to analyze communication is to develop a model of the process. We can better show the dynamic, ongoing, ever-changing aspect of the process if we diagram it, the same as a football coach would diagram a football play. Such a diagram can help break down communication into its component parts, allowing us to separate the parts and study the role each plays in the total process. The following model diagrams a simple two-way communication.

speaker — message — listener

This is an example of a "simple model." It diagrams communication as it seems to most people. Most people know exactly what they want to say, when they say it, and they believe they are expressing themselves clearly and are being understood. However, the information we wish to convey and receive is many times distorted by factors in ourselves, in the environment, and in other people. Since a good part of the operators job is communication, it is imperative for the operator to understand what happens in the process.

VERBAL COMMUNICATION

To understand the complexity of the communication process let's review the steps involved when a person wants to send a message. First, a person must have an emotion, idea, or thought he wishes to express. How he expresses it will be governed by such factors as age, status, sex, education, background, cultural heritage, mental and physical health, environment, attitudes, and many other variables in his field, experience, or frame of reference, and day by day these variables change. He must express himself with words — the choice of which is also determined by another set of variables such as vocabulary, knowledge, situation, emotional state, person receiving the communication, and so on. These factors also vary from time to time.

He must then decide how the message is to be transmitted. When his message is oral other factors are brought into play: voice tone, inflection, and body language, which often say more than words (non-verbal communication). If it is written, he must realize that his message does not have the advantage of immediate feedback and non-verbal cues to clarify the message.

The *channel* of communication may be altered by interference of various kinds such as sound, external noise, etc. What the receiver hears, reads, or sees could be considerably different from the message that was intended. Everything that is done by a sender and receiver is interrelated and the resulting interaction creates the *process* of communication. The receiver also has a strong impact on the message because he edits according to the variables generated by his own field of experience or frame of reference. When there is an overlap in the fields of experience of the two communicants, and the variables for both the sender and receiver are reduced, the communications process is improved. Communication must be a two-way process, open at both ends.

Effective communication is the proper coding and decoding of a message. To better understand the process by which the communication process functions, and to help us visualize the complexity of the communication process, a human communication skills flow chart is presented.

At this point, you are aware that communication is a process that centers on people, and that there are five elements basic to all human communication. Therefore, our "simple model" of communication that we began with has had some changes. We could now diagram it in this way:

COMMUNICATION SKILL FLOW CHART

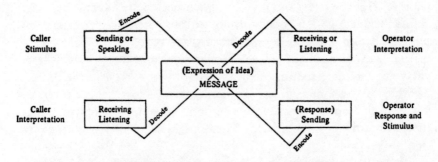

Referring to this flow chart, the five elements basic to all human communication can be identified as:

1. A person originates a thought or idea and the words or mannerisms one selects to convey the idea (encode).
2. The idea itself is expressed (message).
3. A medium or channel is used to express the idea (verbal, nonverbal, written).
4. A person receives and interprets the idea (decode).
5. There is a context or setting in which the transmission of the

idea, attitude, thought, or emotion occurs.

Utilizing the five phases of communication we have established one-way communication. The sender, or speaker, forwards a message intended to reach a receiver, or listener. To be effective, however, communication must be two way. There must a response in some manner to insure the sender that the message was received and that the required action will be taken.

Communication is not always conducted through the use of words alone. Many times the real meaning of what one is thinking is conveyed through facial expressions, tone of voice, gestures, eye movements, or even silence. These are examples of communicating through the use of non-verbal cues.

NON-VERBAL COMMUNICATION

Another aspect of communication of which we often lose sight of is the communication that takes place outside the language. We also communicate meanfully in many non-verbal ways. Consider, for instance, how silence itself is a way of communication. When someone says "Good morning" and we fail to respond, we are communicating something. When someone asks us a question and we fail to answer, this is also communicating. The silence that occurs with a group of people, when the subject of their prior conversation enters the room, may tell that person a great deal about what kind of things were being said about him in his absence.

It is surprising to discover that research in communication by Ray Birdwhistell (1952) resulted in his estimating that in a normal, two-way conversation the verbal band carries less that 35 percent of the social meaning of the situation; more that 65 percent is transmitted by non-verbal bands. Apparently, a great deal of non-verbal communication goes around us. Many of the meanings that are given to human encounters are given because of glances, touch, vocal tones, gestures, or facial expressions and with or without the addition of words. From the moment of greeting until the moment of separation, people observe each other with all of their senses, hearing pauses, and tones in the voice; observing the way the other person dresses and carries himself, observing glances and facial tensions, as well as observing the works spoken.

In his book, *Sense Relaxation*, Bernard Gunther (1968) describes non-verbal communication as follows:

Shaking Hands	How Close You Stand to Others
Your Appearance	The Way You Stand
Your Posture	The Way You Move
Voice Tone	How You Touch Other People
Your Smile	Your Confidence
Your Clothes	Your Breathing
Hair Style	How You Listen
Facial Expressions	The Expression in Your Eyes

Although the spoken word is the main device through which people communicate, non-verbal cues often tell more. The shrug of resignation, or doubt, the bowed head of despair of defeat, or the frown of anger sometimes are even more expressive than words. However, this non-verbal part of communication is not seen over the telephone and its absence presents one of the barriers of effective telephone communication that will be discussed next.

BARRIERS TO EFFECTIVE TELEPHONE COMMUNICATION

Barriers to effective communication can enter the picture at any stage of the communication process. Barriers can occur in the encoding phase when the speaker does not give sufficient attention to the words selected or fails to organize them into a logical pattern; that is if the speaker does not speak clearly, or uses words that the listener cannot understand, or fails to give complete information in the process.

The most frequent communication breakdown occurs in the *encoding* (selecting and speaking the words) and *decoding* the listener interprets what was said) phases because of the assumption that words have the same meaning to everyone. A word in itself is merely a symbol; the meaning is conditioned by past experiences, usage, and understanding.

A prejudiced operator, although not actually reflecting his attitude in words, often conveys a prejudice in his tone of voice. Attitude is an extremely important part of verbal communication. Voice inflection and personal demeanor contribute as much to conversation as the words spoken, and when coupled with words, an improper attitude can be devastating. Accepted words, used arrogantly or sarcastically, create the impression that the words don't really mean anything.

Poor listening habits is another barrier to communication. The art of listening is an important communication factor that requires effort and constant practice to achieve proficiency. These are just a few of the many barriers to effective communicating that the operator should be aware of. Following are some of the many others that are inherent in the communication process.

The Effect of the Loss of Non-Verbal Cues

Telephones have become so omnipresent that they are almost a bodily extension that puts people no farther away than a live dial tone. Yet, though we all take advantage of this accouterment of modern life many times in one day, how often do we stop to take into account that talking over the phone is entirely different from talking to someone in person?

Phone conversations are, after all, blind. Both beauty and body language are useless over a telepone. You must carry on without the other party ever seeing your eyes, your smile, or your head nod sympathetically. What's left to convey an impression is merely a combination of voice and words — a limitation some people do well within and some do not.

How will the operator overcome the 65 percent of communication that is transmitted by non-verbal bands and lost through the use of the telephone? Aside from the normal energies used to complete effective communication the operator must now make an additional 65 percent effort in order to come back up to effective communication that is present under normal conditions. This extra effort takes away energy that was being used to stabilize the operator's communicating abilities. Therefore, it is now no longer there because it is being redirected in order to compensate for non-verbal communication. The operator begins with a loss of 65 percent of his efforts because he must overcome this loss of communication through non-verbal bands.

The strain that occurs because of the operator's efforts in attempting to overcome the loss of the 65 percent causes the operator to become more vulnerable to the *contagiousness of crisis*. The operator becomes hooked in the contagiousness of crisis because he must place extra effort in understanding what the caller is saying. The operator may become accusatory, abusive, and reduced to anger because of the strain that this extra effort causes. His tolerance is lowered, as the ability to communication effectively is lowered, to a state of becoming critical. The operator may become critical easily because the energy used to stabilize tolerance is not being used to overcome the loss of 65 percent of the communication process. Therefore, criticism is released easily and more quickly.

There is enough difficulty inherent in most emergency and crisis telephone conversations that it is unfortunate that there is an additional burden placed on the call. That is, the operator does not have non-verbal communication to assist in effective message taking. In addition to causing strain and lowered tolerance on the part of the operator, this loss of non-verbal cues can also cause misunderstanding and insensitivity to the emotional state of the caller in crisis. After all, if the operator cannot see the caller's eyes, facial expressions, and body movements, how will he be able to understand exactly what the caller is trying to communicate to him? In this section we will discuss some of the other barriers to effective communication that arise in caller/operator interactions and explain in detail the ways to overcome these barriers.

The Deterioration of the Communication Process

As a result of violations to the principles of proper communication, psychological distance begins to develop. The communication process, as we have seen, is complex and can be difficult at times, even when the sender of a message and the receiver of the message are face to face. The very nature of the *hard communication system* (i.e. communication through air and wire where there is no face-to-face contact), where one cannot see the other smile or frown, generates in many cases psychological distance. In addition, human violations of certain rules of communication further deteriorate the relationship.

The more psychological distance we place between the caller and ourselves, the less emphasis we tend to place on the human side of the contact. The less emphasis placed on the human side, the more energy that will be available to become more efficient with the technological function of the computer. Therefore, the pleas of the victim for emotional support will tend to be ignored and not even heard.

This process disintegrates the bond that is necessary for effective communication, i.e. body language, the human appeal, emotional support, and the effective choice of words. Therefore, the caller and the operator isolate themselves on either end of the electronic channel and attempt to communicate from these isolated positions. They both ultimately begin yelling and screaming at each other in an effort to be really heard, because basic human needs are not being met.

The ill feeling and abrasive reactions that develop do so from not being able to communicate effectively, and both parties experience feelings of inadequacy. This inadequacy is blamed on the persons involved and the inability to communicate instead of where the blame really belongs: on the *regressive dynamics* of a crisis situation. Since both parties are not aware that a crisis does impair human abilities to communicate, the caller blames the listener and the listener blames the caller. These are defensive reactions to being unjustly accused, and unfortunately this behavior carries over in the conversation and becomes accumulative.

If it happens that the caller is a victim of a crime, and the operator doesn't establish human contacts, the victim begins to see traces of the same behavior on the part of the person he called that was displayed by the assailant. These similarities are: (1) that the assailant treated the victim like an object; and (2) by abusing them oftentimes verbally, if not physically, there was a discount of their humanness. There is naturally a psychological distance in assailant/victim interaction, in that the success of the assailant's act is based on the fact that he is able to treat the victim as an object. If the operator doesn't make human contact as the assailant didn't, the person that the victim is calling for assistance begins to display the same kind of behavior used by the assailant by being impersonal and inattentive.

The Regressive Dynamics of a Crisis Situation

One of the characteristics of a crisis is the inability for the person in crisis to exercise control; therefore, in an effort to gain control and to restablize their surroundings, the person will tend to behave differently, which tends to be viewed as abrasive. Instead of placing the blame for this abrasiveness on either the operator or the caller, the blame should be placed on the regressive process of human behavior in a crisis situation. The regressive process is psychological in nature. A crisis impairs one's ability to make decisions; it impairs and dissipates one's frame of reference. The person's vocabulary also becomes limited, because this frame of reference has become impaired.

In addition, sensitivity to harsh words is even more amplified because of the loss of this frame of reference, the ability to reason has been impaired. These impairments all appear and can operate in subtle ways, as well as in an acute, obvious way. A person's behavior regresses to a point that he displays behavior he feels best with or most comfortable with, therefore, the degree to which different people regress in a crisis may vary.

Instead of blaming the listener or blaming the caller, the blame for the display of abrasiveness should be placed on the crisis situation and the ensuing regressive dynamics of the crisis. In Chapter 4, we will further describe the effects of a crisis on human behavior and how the operator can assist the caller in crisis.

Attitudes

Attitudes develop as a result of this regressive kind of behavior or this negative interaction. Everyone has feelings, beliefs, opinions, or views which determine how they behave towards other people. The way people feel about things determines to a great extent what they do about them. It is common knowledge that everyone develops attitudes and that their behavior is influenced by them. Attitudes are definitely an important factor in the relationship between a caller needing assistance and the operator providing that help. Your personal attitudes and those of the people you come into contact with in your daily activities are important to the performance of duties. The inferences that are made about the attitudes of people with whom one comes into contact helps to determine how one will react to him.

Conversely, the way a caller judges the attitude of the operator determines how the call will progress. If it appears to the operator that he is dealing with a person who resents the police department and who regards him and his job with disgust, his reactions to him would be quite different than it would be if he seems to be reasonable and respectful. On the other hand, the caller is also reacting to the operator according to his judgment of the operator's attitude toward him.

What is an attitude, how are attitudes formed, and how do they affect your behavior? It is important for a well-prepared emergency operator to know the answers to these questions because clashing attitudes are the cause of much conflict.

An attitude is a combination of a person's knowledge and feelings about someone or something that influences him to behave in a certain way in regard to that person or thing. Attitudes are learned and develop as a result of experience. What has happened to us as we go through life determines what we will have as attitudes. Our attitudes are formed during the process of learning or acquiring information about the world around us.

Through repeated contacts we gradually learn what certain objects, people, and situations mean to us. We also associate certain feelings to these objects, people, and situations, so that when these contacts arise again the same feelings are repeated. Some of our attitudes are developed independently on the basis of our own experience and judgments, while others are adopted from the meaningful people in our lives while we were young.

Attitudes can vary in strength, in that some are very strong and others are very mild. In general, you can say that the greater the importance of something to you, the stronger your attitude about it is likely to be. Something that is not important to you, about which you feel indifferent, is not likely to have any strong attitudes associated with it. As the importance varies, so will your attitude about it.

Attitudes begin to develop in relation to the performance of your duties on your job, and they affect you and the calls that are handled daily. The operator develops attitudes, for example, about people and the difficulty some of the callers have in articulating their needs. The operator may begin to stereotype callers because of their accents or their manner of speaking and this affects the way the operator responds to the caller. If this is not realized and dealt with, a void will develop between the operator and the caller.

Mechanical Conflicts

Mechanical conflicts arise because of the dichotomy between human needs and mechanical needs. The demand for human needs and the demand for mechanical needs can cause conflict within the operator. The operator can become mechanical-like in nature in response to this inner conflict and lose the human side of the situation he is involved in. The operator then becomes insensitive and mechanical when he loses the human side and is more likely to use disrespectful modes of address and sterotyping at these times.

There are numerous telephone and television commercials emphasizing the human touch of telephoning friends and relatives across the nation, and yet there is a tendency for those in the helping professions, who use the telephone as a means to their day's work, to violate all the principles that are necessary for the human touch.

The telephone offers a dilemma in particular for modern law enforcement. The most common form of police discourtesy is encountered in telephone conversations between the public and the police. It can be quite shocking for someone to telephone the police for assistance concerning a matter that is important to him to receive a disinterested, annoyed greeting such as "Yeah?" in response to his need.

If the operator can develop skills for dealing effectively with people under difficult circumstances, he can make his job easier and more pleasant. The circumstances of many of the telephone contacts are not entirely under the operator's control, yet there are certain things that the operator can do that will help. In his own self-interest, the operator should make a study of these matters and carefully analyze his own behavior in order to eliminate ineffective or troublebreeding contact techniques, adopt new and better methods, and polish the rough edges which everyone has. There are some problems that every human being has to face, and in some ways the operator's aims and purposes are no different from anyone else's who works with people. Because of the nature of the operator's official responsibilities, however, and the often highly charged emotional climate in which he works, it is essential for the operator to be skilled in the art of dealing with people.

The police emergency operators are the focal points around which most services to the public revolve. Operators have a vital responsibility: the prompt receipt and processing of emergency and routine messages. Police officers and the public must rely upon the alertness and initiative of the operator, especially with which the operator handles a problem may prevent the situation from becoming a major emergency.

In many of the operator's contacts with the public, the person calling is experiencing his first contact with the police. The initial response he receives from the operator will leave a lasting impression on him. Every effort must be made to insure that daily telephone contacts with the public reflect a genuine desire to give help and that information is processed with speed and efficiency and in a courteous manner.

There are some human relations techniques that an operator can cultivate with good effect, and there are people who have developed excellent human relations skills. These people seem to be able to relate to other people better than most. They have a knack of dealing effectively with almost everyone. Why is this? Is it in part because they are able to present themselves in a non-threatening way? Is it because they have found ways of minimizing the threat with which their identity as a representative of the police department endows them. Is it in part because they have learned how to handle threats and challenges hurled at them?

There are some techniques that the police emergency operator ought to cultivate for strengthening their human relations skills. Learning how to be an effective person is essentially a matter of developing skill in relating to others. When you think about it, does it not seem logical that if a person believes that you are going to give him a hard time, that he will try to avoid you or, failing that, that he will be unreceptive or perhaps even hostile?

Don't you find yourself tensing up when you think someone is going to make trouble for you? An unpleasant and difficult situation will surely result if by your approach you give a caller reason to believe so. The unfortunate fact is that many times a difficult situation can and does develop even though there was no intention of giving the caller a difficult time because: (1) the caller expects it; and (2) the operator does nothing to offset this expectation.

The Police Image

Effectiveness in contacts with the public is important from another point of view, as the operator is not the only one affected. Every contact produces some kind of result beyond the present situation in that every contact has some impact on the image of your particular department or organization. The person who calls for whatever reason carries away with him an impression of the operator not as a person, but as a representative of an organization. The caller integrates his impression of the operator with the notions he already holds concerning the police department.

The operator's influence on the other person's views and beliefs about the police can be helpful or harmful. If what the operator does and the way he does it makes a good impression, not only is that specific incident made easier for him, but it has also helped to make it easier for anyone who has to deal with that particular person in the future. Direct contact or confrontations with the callers who are in crisis or in times of stress situations are the most important kinds of contacts because they leave the strongest impressions.

Every operator should be aware that the police department is symbolically threatening to many people. The police are regarded as disciplinarians, wielders of power and authority, and someone to be feared in many situations. The presence of the police constitutes a threat to many people even when they are not doing anything deserving police intervention. Most people will slow down, for example, while driving when they see a patrol car, even though they are not exceeding the speed limit. Undoubtedly, many people immediately take a behavioral inventory (Am I doing anything wrong?) and become wary when they see a police officer approaching. This wariness, uneasiness, or apprehension is part of the aura of threat with which the police are surrounded. The officer is thus often seen as a person to be avoided.

This fact that many people see the police department as a threat has some undesirable consequences, and the tendency to avoid contact is one. Another is a lack of cooperation by some people because they are reluctant to contact the police.

What can be done about problems growing out of human relations in which threats or challenges are significant issues?

As we have already explained, such strained relationships are inherent in widely held concepts of the police role. Some people expect the relationship to be an adversary one. This means that the operator must take special measures to relieve the strain. If by your approach in a non-adversary contact the operator can avoid appearing to be threatening, he will have overcome a major obstacle to an effective contact. Moreover, if he avoids downgrading the caller and avoids giving the impression that he regards the caller as a threat, he will have removed some more obstacles.

The very nature of police work and other bureaucratic-type agencies leads to both private and public resentment, though a certain amount of resentment is natural and must be expected. As representatives of the police department, emergency operators must be realistic and realize that the people they may be serving will not universally like or respect them. In order to promote and maintain a good operator image, it is of paramount importance that the operator understand this. The operator must be tolerant under all conditions, even in the face of intense provocation, to offset a negative psychological effect on an already impaired psychological state. Bearing this in mind, the problem becomes one of creating the most favorable image possible; that is, being the most courteous and effective and most humanistic police emergency operator possible.

HUMAN STYLES OF COMMUNICATING

People who need to use the telephone as their means of communicating tend to select styles of communicating that is most protective of their emotional stability as opposed to styles of communicating that promote effective communication. Therefore, most communicating begins and proceeds either through practice or procedure, without the benefit of any concern for the human element of the interaction. That is, most conversations over the telephone become too mechanical, very much like the machine being used. Therefore, the individual who communicates over mechanical devices has to be even more sensitive and direct their attentions to hearing what is being said between the lines instead of just listening.

There are *human styles* of communicating that further place us in conflict when attempting to attain effective communication. Personality types may have a tendency to select particular human types of communication, for example: one-way (authoritarian) or two-way (democratic).

One-Way (Authoritarian)

Organizations such as police agencies tend to use this style of communicating. The language of the police department usually is of an authoritarian nature. In one-way communication, the listener does not have the opportunity to reply or ask questions. Their style is one of order-giving or of just complete inattention and lack of response. The nature of police work often demands an interrogative or an investigative style of communication. This style unfortunately tends to carry over even in the area of "service," where the function is not of an investigative nature.

There are times, for certain, when the one-way style of communicating is effective. This would be during emergencies, where there is no time for feedback and the caller *needs* to be directed, for example: a child caller who needs help, or an elderly victim of a crime who has been so traumatized that they have no control over their behavior and has lost confidence in their own decision-making abilities.

This style of communicating reinforces the police image of itself as an organization of authority and, therefore, more effective styles of communicating are disregarded as being too soft. The one-way style of communicating may then be chosen as opposed to two-way communication, which allows for a mutual exchange as in the interview situation.

Two-Way (Democratic)

This style of communicating allows for input and exchange of information. Two-way style of communicating is very much like an interview situation, in that there is an active dialogue between the parties and both are able to speak and to question. It has proven to be more effective during calls where there is adequate time for mutual exchange. Two-way is more time consuming, but more effective because it allows for feedback and corrections in misunderstandings. This is opposed to one-way, where mistakes and misunderstandings go unchallenged and unquestioned, because the speaker allows no feedback. Therefore, even in emergencies, the operator may choose to employ the two-way style of communicating in order to extract correct information and clear up any doubts or misunderstandings.

An analysis of these two styles and their effect on the communication system can be made. One-way, if employed all the time, tends to have a negative effect and further deteriorates the communication process and is less satisfying to the person who is unable to participate. It suppresses the need on the part of one party to express themselves and suppresses any anxieties that could be exhausted through catharsis. On the other hand, two-way promotes harmony and understanding and puts both communicators on equal footing. When a person feels that he is equal, it builds confidence and improves communication effectiveness.

THE "FIVE WS" AND ROLE AMPLIFICATION

Ordinarily the communication process and the gathering of information seeks to satisfy the following conditions: who, when, why, what, where, and how. You can identify the details of any situation by just asking good fact-finding, open-ended questions that start with the "five Ws."

"Who" means all persons concerned with the call. "Who" includes the suspect, victim, witness, reporting party, or anyone else connected with the caller's problem or situation. "Who" includes name, age, color, residence, business address, telephone number, and any and all other identifying data.

A complete and correct name is required. The wrong name may result in failure to provide needed assistance. The spelling of names also can be a particular problem. Some names are spelled differently than what they sound like, for example, it could be Wilson or Willson, Wallace or Wallis, Francis or Frances.

"What" demands an answer to what took place or what happened. It tells about the occurrence. It is a description of the event. What has happened to cause the call to be made in the first place? The amount of detail, of course, depends upon the nature and purpose of the report. If an offense has been committed, the description should identify the offense. If property is missing, the description should indicate what specifically was taken.

"When" asks when did the incident occur? When was it discovered? When was the offense committed? When was it brought to the attention of the police? This is essentially the fixing of time, and there is more than one time involved in every report. Time in this instance includes day, date, time, month, and year.

"Where" asks the location of the occurrence. Also to be included is the location of the object to which the caller wishes to call to the attention of the operator. The operator will want to note the address, floor, apartment number, part of the room involved, direction of the street, and perhaps the nearest intersections.

The type of premises is necessary supplemental information for the address. This could range from a vacant lot to a tall building. Usually, premises can be classified by a general name, such as garage, warehouse, hotel, or apartment.

"How" means simply, in the case of a crime, the *modus operandi*. What was the method of operation? How did the incident occur? This question covers the general manner in which the event took place. How was the offense committed? How was the property or person attacked? The how can be the *modus operandi* of the person committing an offense, i.e. the method used.

"Why" is answered, in the case of a crime, in terms of a motive. Why did the incident occur? Was it murder for revenge, or assault as a result of a drinking bout, an auto accident as a result of an engineering defect or excess speed, or whatever?

Under this heading is listed the object or desire that motivated the offense. For example, in crimes against the person, the object of the attack might be revenge, ransom, or a rape. In crimes for gain, the reason why is to acquire money or property.

The use of the "five W's" will help the operator identify the details involved in the situation requiring the calling for assistance. However, all of the "five W's" are useful and important to the police emergency operator except for the asking of the question "why." In the gathering of information, the asking of the question "why" serves no purpose except to place blame. There is a blaming element inherent in the asking of "why." For example, one operator was overheard asking the caller, "So, why did you let him back into the house?"

"Why" is inherently part of the police style. We tend to have less sensitivity to the asking of the question "why" when our role has been amplified to a greater level of authority. The police agency and it's investigative attitude is a classic example of communicating in a prying kind of way, however, the attitude permeates other social agencies and private industry as long as the organization is bureaucratic in nature. This also occurs whenever and especially if the agency has a chain of command where titles are emphasized.

Role Amplification .

Once the operator begins to ask the question "why," this is the beginning of the problem of role amplification. It is at this time that the operator develops an inflation and a negative expansion of their role. What purpose does the asking of the question "why" serve during the process of gathering information? As we have stated previously, the asking of the question "why" satisfies the need for a motive, for example in a crime. The asking of this particular question has an air of interrogation about it. Is is really necessary for the police emergency operator to ask "why?"

To illustrate this point, an actual dialogue between an emergency operator and a caller is presented. A male caller states that there is a young lady in his house and is threatening to set it on fire. Observing the interaction, one could label role amplification on the part of the operator and the unnecessary prying nature of his questioning:

Operator: How did she get in?
  Caller: I let her in.
Operator: Then you must know her.
  Caller: Yes, I know her, but don't you understand, she is about to set my house on fire.
Operator: Is she a friend of yours? How old is she?
  Caller: Yes, she is a friend of mine. She is sixteen years old.
Operator: Is this your house?
  Caller: Yes, this is my house.

At this point the operator begins to compute the age of the female and the age of the property owner and decides that there must be a wide disparity between them because the man obviously must be much older since he is a property owner. The operator then focuses on his own dislike for the relationship of the sixteen-year-old and a man that must be much older because he owns a house.

Operator: Oh yeah! You used her and then abused her and now you want to have her locked up, huh?
  Caller: No sir. Please send a radio car. She is going to set my house on fire.
Operator: I don't have any cars to send to you, just because you

want to throw her out to solve your own personal problems. We have more important things to do.

Caller: Please send a car. This girl is about to set my house on fire.

Operator: Okay. I'm going to send you a car. When they get there, I personally am going to lock you up for messing around with a minor.

This call is a classic example of two important points about role amplification. First of all, there is the asking of the question "why" to satisfy the personal needs of the operator. Secondly, there is the asking of the question "why" in an emergency inappropriately. Instead of gathering the location, and other information needed to prevent possible criminal activity, the operator focused on his own biases and began making moral judgments about the caller's situation.

As one very bright and intuitive student in a training class of 911 operators so aptly said it, "I guess once we begin to work for the police department, we all tend to behave like detectives!"

CONFLICT BETWEEN PROCEDURAL AND EMOTIONAL NEEDS

Most police emergency operators will agree that they often have difficulty in their contacts with many of their callers. As we have already noted, there are several reasons for this difficulty. In the first place, emergency operators frequently have to intercept in situations where some kind of conflict is going on. These situations are usually emotionally charged and produce excited behavior on the part of the callers. Secondly, some contacts because of their crisis nature, produce such unusual behavior that neither the caller or the operator can truly understand what is happening. This puts the operator in the position of sometimes acting cold and abrupt and sometimes hostile in response to this behavior.

Thirdly, the operator is often unavoidably in the position of being mistakenly victimized by the caller's behavior. Even relatively minor contacts, such as those required in ordinary complaint calls, produce a strong resentment because of the caller's negative image of the police department.

Finally, the operator sometimes has to ask questions and detain a caller for questioning at times when they don't really want to be questioned. Many persons when questioned at these times resent the procedure and react with hostility and occasionally verbal abuse. Built into this type of contact is conflict, which, of course, can make the operator's job more difficult and unpleasant.

For exampe, the *operator's* primary concern when the phone rings is "where" the emergency is happening. In fact, the recommended response police emergency operators give is, "Police emergency operator No. _____, where is the emergency?" This response initiates immediately the need for establishing the location of the incident by the operator. On the other hand, the *caller's* primary concern is "what" is happening. The caller has the need to immediately relate to the operator what has happened to them; that there is this need to call for assistance. This is definitely another source of conflict.

Operator	C	Caller
	O	
	N	
	F	
	L	
	I	
	C	
Where is it	T	What is
happening?		happening?

This is a source of conflict because the mechanics of asking "where" the incident is happening does not give a natural lead in for the victim caller to say what is happening, which is their emotional need at this time. It also suppresses the effort on the part of the caller to state what is happening. The very first phrase from the operator demonstrates coldness and insensitivity.

The operator should be aware of the effect procedures have on the communication system. Although it is necessary to gather information, the operator should realize that it is necessary immediately after the required identification is gathered to start to fuse that quality that tells the caller that he is concerned and sensitive to their emotional needs. If the operator is ready to give of himself, especially in crisis calls, the caller will recognize the operator as a sensitive person who is already to listen to the problems of the caller.

OTHER BARRIERS TO
EFFECTIVE TELEPHONE COMMUNICATION

Communication requires at least two people, and no two human beings see the world alike. The way in which we see the world depends on what sociologists call our *frame of reference*. We all have individual personalities, separate backgrounds, and different motives for our behavior. We each interpret what we see and hear from our perspective. If it weren't for such human differences, communicating would be easy. Whatever we said would mean to the listener exactly what we had in mind. Whatever we did would be interpreted the way we meant it to be. Therefore, there are many barriers to communicating effectively with others. Some of the barriers we will now discuss are:

Misunderstanding	Cultural differences
Halo effect	Psychological barriers
Distortion	Physical conditions
Stereotyping	Explosive words and phrases
Testimonials	Disrespectful modes
	of address
Thoughtless jests	

Misunderstanding

In any communication process there are three general sources of misunderstanding: first, the person communicating may not clearly communicate what the intended message is; second, the person receiving may not clearly understand the message; and, third, the message itself may be ambiguous (because of conflict between the channels of communication or because of confusion within one channel), so that neither communicator nor receptor is certain about what is being said. Of course, these could interact with each other to produce even more confusing situations. Making the atmosphere better for the listener so that he or she will be more likely to hear what you are trying to communicate without becoming defensive is one way of assuring good communication. There are therefore three mechanical conflicts or points of misunderstanding in a communication system: 1. what the speaker thinks he said; 2. what the listener thought he said; and 3. what the speaker actually said. All three can be different and, consequently, generates an environment of conflict or misunderstanding; this initiates the blaming process. People become defensive and begin blaming in their communication when they perceive a threat or a possible threat towards them. When one is defensively aroused, it is difficult to pay accurate attention to the messages that are being sent. It is at times such as these when one is likely to misinterpret what the other person is saying or to distort what is being heard. There are certain paired characteristics that describe defensive communication within interpersonal interactions. These characteristics are:

Defensive	*Supportive*
1. Evaluate	Descriptive
2. Control Oriented	Problem Oriented
3. Strategically Planned	Spontaneous
4. Emotional Neutrality	Emotional Empathy
5. Superior Attitude or Status Inequality	Peer Attitude or Status Equality
6. Dogmatism	Openness

Let us take a closer look at each of these paired characteristics.

Evaluative/Descriptive

Although you should feel that others can evaluate what you are saying, when you know that others are evaluating you, there is a tendency to become defensive. Discussions flow more freely when neither person in communicating is placing labels such as "good" or "bad" or "right" or "wrong" upon the situation being discussed. Value judgments and moral labelling increase defensive communication.

Control Oriented/Problem Oriented

Much communication revolves around the need for some people to control others. Many people communicate in order to change attitudes, shape opinions, or influence perceptions. Insofar as control is involved in the communication process, there will be resistance on the part of the person being controlled to resist the communication. When communication is involved with solving problems, the listener will be more receptive.

Strategically Planned/Spontaneous

People react strongly when they think that they are being manipulated or if they think that there is a hidden strategy in the communication, and this leads to resistance. On the other hand, if the person feels that the interaction is spontaneous, the listener will be receptive to the message being given.

Emotional Neutrality/Emotional Empathy

When it is suggested to the emergency operator that they be non-evaluative, this does not mean to be unemotional. The caller must feel that the operator is concerned about them, about what they are saying, and their problem. If the operator comes across the telephone as detached and disinterested, the caller will sense the rejection. To be empathetic doesn't mean that we are suggesting that the operator be artificial or phony. What we mean to say is that the operator should express understanding and the desire to offer assistance to the caller and their situation.

Superior Attitude/Peer Attitude

Whenever there is the attitude on the part of one individual that he is superior to the operator, or when actual status differences exist, the communication between them will not be quite free. This attitude will cause the listener to react emotionally and not rationally to the message being given. When both participants in a conversation are peers or equals, communication will be easier. The individuals involved will feel more able to share their problems with equals rather than with those who act or feel superior.

Dogmatism/Openness

The more dogmatic (certain without any question) one is, or expresses himself to be, the less likely people will listen to that person. People who are dogmatic also tend not to listen to others; they are less likely to accept feedback from other people. Dogmatic people believe that they know the answer already and that anyone who disagrees with them is wrong or misinformed. When someone shows that they are open to new ideas or thoughts, he increases the ease with which the person they are conversing with will be willing to communicate with them.

If the operator will think about some of their recent interactions with others and include in their future conversations the above-mentioned supportive characteristics, defensiveness in their communication will be reduced and the operator can then more easily solve the problems that face them in communicating with others.

Cultural Differences

All families in a given culture share certain common beliefs, customs, and values. While growing up, the child learns to behave in ways expected by the culture. However, people from different cultures have different outlooks on life. They see and interpret things differently and attach different meanings and values to them. Rarely do people of different cultures think exactly alike, although through awareness and education the gap can become closed.

A culture as complex as that of the United States contains numerous subcultures, each with its own views about such things as moral values, standards of cleanliness, style of dress, and definitions of success.

It is important to understand these cultural differences and its impact on communication, because if we are unaware of them we may misinterpret what others mean. Since norms differ from society to society, the cultural meaning of the same act can have large differences from place to place. These cultural differences can lead to serious misinterpretation that can interfere with effective communication. Therefore, listening, and trying sincerely to get the caller's interpretations and ideas, and acting on the basis of what they think, not what we think or what we wish they would think, are absolutely essential to realistic communication.

Halo Effect

The operator should also be aware of what communication experts call the *halo effect*. It simply means bias. We all have our personal likes, dislikes, and beliefs, which have grown out of our individual experiences with people, such as redheads are hot-tempered, blondes tend to be dumb, fat people are happy, ruddy complexions reveal dishonest tendencies, short people think they're Napoleons (i.e. domineering), people with close-set eyes are unintelligent. We tend to think that all are "good" beliefs because they are ours, but all are usually completely unsupported in fact. We are biased in favor of some people but against others because in our own personal experience we have had pleasant or unpleasant experiences with people who look, act, speak, dress, write, laugh, or lisp in a manner similar to the person we are dealing with at the moment.

Distortion

People sometimes unconsciously distort the meaning of what they hear or see. When do such distortions occur? Quite frequently this occurs when we like or dislike someone intensely. When we like someone, we are likely to hear things that make a favorable impression. On the other hand, if we dislike a person, we tend to hear other things that make an unfavorable impression.

Nearly everyone has played the communication game in which an individual whispers a statement that is passed from person to person. By the time the message gets back to the originator, the context is usually distorted and sometimes totally different from the original. Each person in this communication chain has acted as a resister or booster, emphasizing certain aspects of the message while de-emphasizing others. In interpersonal communication, each of us receives, makes judgments about, and modifies messages before we pass them along. Each of us acts as a checkpoint in the communication process — we refuse to transmit some messages, overemphasize others, and play down still more.

PSYCHOLOGICAL BARRIERS

We structure our perception of the world in terms that are meaningful to us and according to our frames of reference. Applied to communication, this suggests that people tend to communicate in ways that are consistent with their self-concepts. Put another way, people try to live up to the labels they give themselves and that are given to them by others. In consequence, people express themselves in words and behaviors that reveal how they feel about themselves, how they are accepted, and what kinds of identity they hold.

Identity

A clear and acceptable identity is important to the development of a positive self-concept. A sense of identity evolves from what a person believes and what a person decides to do in life. People usually arrive at some acceptable balance between a *personal identity* — how a person has come to view himself or herself — and a *social identity* — what perception tells him or her about what others expect and how they judge. A third type of identity often reveals and reinforces personal and social identities: it is called a *paper identity*. If you open your wallet or purse and take out all of your identification cards and papers, you will find such things as your driver's license, student body card, Social Security card, credit cards, membership cards in organizations, and other official documents. Together these papers constitute your paper identity. They distinguish you from all others. They tell others that you are who you claim to be.

Self-Concept

Closely related to the idea of identity is *self-concept*. If you have a membership card to an athletic club, for example, and you are also chosen as a member of the track team, you have evidence of your identity as an athlete. You may begin to believe that you have athletic prowess, and that belief then becomes an aspect of your self-concept. All of the beliefs and feelings you have about what you can do constitutes your self-concept.

Physical Conditions

Our perceptions are altered by both *internal* and *external* physical conditions, which help heighten, diminish, accept, or reject messages. Internal physical conditions refer to the well-being or health of the individual audience member. When physically ill, a person filters messages differently from the way he does when he is in good health. A migraine headache, a bleeding ulcer, or an abscessed tooth can radically alter message filtering. The pain of a smashed thumb affects the sense of touch so intensely that sight or sound is impaired. In some, physical discomfort may heighten the communication experience. For example, Pepto-Bismal® commercials are reacted to differently when we have upset stomachs from the way they are when we are feeling well. A beer commercial is reacted to in one way by a man who is hot and thirsty but in another way by a man suffering from a "morning after." Also, inattention of physical impairments, such as partial deafness and fatigue, affects understanding, and the listener may interpret the message erroneously, attaching a different meaning to the speaker's words when he decodes what was said.

External physical conditions refers to the environment or surroundings in which we receive messages. If the room in which you are reading is too hot, too cold, too dark, or too noisy, it will affect your senses and the way you understand what you are reading or hearing. Background noises and other distractions can also distort the message. Physical noise contributes a possible error factor to the message received by the listener. A wailing siren or a loud vehicular engine may blank out a word or phrase resulting in a message that either makes no sense or takes on an entirely different meaning.

Explosive Words and Phrases

A primary agent of communication is the spoken word, a powerful instrument in personal interaction. A person who hears the pleasing ring of words of praise about his efforts and a dejected individual who listens to consoling words of sympathy may not be able to describe it, but they certainly know something of the power of the spoken word. They, along with the victim of a severe tongue-lashing or one who witnesses a demagogue turn a peaceful, orderly crowd into a hostile, frenzied mob, might even liken the tongue to the atom. Both, in their own way, have enormous potential power that can be released as creative, constructive energy or unleashed as a diabolic, destructive force. Many psychologists agree that certain words have an emotional impact on people. Some words, almost automatically, have a strong emotional appeal no matter how they're used. Communication experts have tried to identify these power-laden words, and their research has proved valuable to those professionals who deal with people.

The meaning of words is a reflection of personal experience. Many words and expressions accepted as proper and inoffensive within one group may have a degrading connotation when spoken in the presence of someone from a different group. Dictionary definitions of many words do not have "bad" connotations, but, when directed at certain persons or groups, the words have a special significance. Only the context in which a word is used determines its meaning.

Some words may have two kinds of meanings: *denotated* and *connotated*. The denotated meaning of a word is its socially agreed upon "impersonal" meaning. As an illustration, the denotation of "pig" is " . . . domesticated mammalian quadruped of the kind generally raised by farmers to be made into pork, bacon, ham, lard. . . ." The connotations of the same word are in the aura of personal feelings it arouses as, for example, "Ugh!" Dirty, evil-smelling creatures wallowing in filthy sties, and so on. The existence of feelings such as this permits a speaker to use a word solely for its connotation. When some people call a law enforcement officer a "pig," they most certainly are using the connotation of the word.

The operator must be careful to select expressions and words that the receiver will not only understand but also not be offended by. What might be appropriate for a close associate or someone the speaker may know very well might be completely meaningless and offensive to someone else.

Take a simple word like *tough*. The "over 30" crowd would define it in the context of "the meat is not tender" or "tough break" in the sense that the situation was unfortunate, while the younger generation may define tough as great, wonderful, or terrific. It has been said that there are an average of twenty-eight separate meanings for each of the 500 most commonly used words in the English language.

Speech mannerisms and slang terms that mean different things to different people can and do cause serious communications problems. For example, the new operator trying to compliment his experienced partner for his skill in handling a difficult call may say, "Man, that was wild, just wild." This could be misconstrued into meaning that the call was handled carelessly and lacking in caution, when in reality the speaker was saying in modern colloquialism, "You did a terrific job."

Stereotyping

We all tend to have preconceived ideas of what people mean: when we hear something we identify it with, or compare it to, a similar experience. Instead of hearing what is told us, we hear what our minds tell us what has been said. It could be the same or completely different in reality. An extreme form of letting expectations determine communication content is *stereotyping*. We will ignore information that conflicts with what we already "know." Stereotyping, in the assumption that the members of any group are all alike, is damaging and unfair.

Because of our preconceived ideas about various groups (stereotyping), we tend to select a mode of communication reflective of what we think of that group. In a crisis situation, for example, or during a particularly difficult call in which our ability to remain in control is challenged, there may be a tendency to get caught up in the contagiousness of the call and therefore our mode of communication may regress to one of anger and insults. These insults may encompass negative remarks about the ethnic group that the call may represent.

The operator must be aware of the danger of stereotypes. He, as well as any other citizen, can be guilty of selecting certain traits and applying them to every member of a group that calls for assistance.

Stereotyping is not always a negative. It can result in positive characteristics being associated with all members of a given group, such as "our kind" or "people from a 'good' neighborhood." This, too, can be a pitfall in a different way. Nevertheless, it is still stereotyping and should be avoided by the emergency operator.

Barrier Builders

Most public speaking textbooks urge students of oral communication to find a common ground with their audiences. They are told to create feelings of mutual identification between themselves and their listeners with regard to the purposes of their speeches. Some books go one step further and caution students against building barriers that ". . . block potential communication when speaker or listener misconstrues his role and those of others — whether consciously or unconsciously."

The operator should be a serious student of the basic rules of oral communication since it is one of his basic tools. He should constantly bear in mind that status fluctuates, that each individual operates in many social groups and institutions and serves in a variety of changing roles of authority and responsibility. Speakers and listeners often anticipate each other's behavior and even have preconceived notions about one another's personalities. The roles the speakers and listeners play are, by and large, determined by these factors.

The operator can construct a barrier between himself and the people he serves by misconstruing his role or by continually focusing on that which distinguishes him from them. Too often minorities are referred to as "they" as opposed to "we." Likewise, expressions such as "your kind," "you Puerto Ricans," "those people," etc., may seem small and unimportant but they can be highly offensive to others. Statements such as "me and you" and "we and they" should be replaced by "we and us." All of us have much in common. We should attempt to tear down barriers and build bonds by emphasizing these similarities.

Disrespectful Modes of Address

Courtesy is a barrier breaker and a bond builder. The corollary of this is also true. Discourtesy is a bond breaker and a barrier builder. If one remembers this, as well as the old but valid adage, "A first impression is a lasting one," and the golden rule, "Do unto others as you would have them do unto you," he will have very little trouble choosing the proper mode of direct address as he approaches an individual in the community he serves.

Everyone appreciates being addressed in a polite fashion and resents being spoken to in an overly familiar or rude way. No matter what his station in life, every adult, including the young adult, is entitled to be addressed in terms that imply respect. Ladies, gentlemen, madam, miss, and sir are normally the proper titles for one to use. "Hey you, Mack, Jack, or Jim," are insulting appellations. Addressing young adults as kid, boy, or girl should also be avoided because such labels imply that the listener is immature, inferior, and ineligible for personal respect. Similarly, addressing a stranger by his first name is objectionable because he is at a decided disadvantage inasmuch as he is unaware of the speaker's given name. Moreover, one should not address another in such a familiar way even if he is not a stranger unless he expects or even wants him to respond in kind. If one violates this norm, he is almost certain to evoke a hostile response from the addressee.

Referring to a woman with whom one is unacquainted as dear, sweetie, honey, doll, etc., is also invariably a breach of etiquette and an invasion of psychological privacy. These expressions also suggest familiarity and when they are uninvited they become phony and insincere and create barriers to effectively communicating with the caller.

Thoughtless Jests

Professional humorists frequently find material in their own experiences and, consequently, use the racial, religious, national, and ethnic groups to which they belong as the source of their jokes. A significant number of eminently successful Irish, Italian, Jewish, and Black comics have tastefully presented the incongruities they recognize in the mode of living of people. Hence, they brought the gift of laughter to America. In relating their tales, an Irishman may label himself as a mick with mock pride, or a Jew might relate incidents about fellow Jews that would be insulting if they came from the lips of a non-Jew.

Each of us has heard numerous tasteless Irish, Italian, Jewish, Black, Polish, and other such jokes that provoke laughter from some but evoke tears from others and, consequently, are not worthy of the label "humor." They tend to demean a whole group of people unjustifiably.

Conclusion

Thoughtless or malicious words by an operator directed toward someone who has already had a crisis is inconsiderate and a barrier to effectively communicating with callers. The operator's primary communication tool is *speech*. By being aware of the impact of words, an operator may sharpen his communication skills in order to better communicate with callers and to avoid the kind of speech that can be offensive. As we have seen thus far, there are many barriers to effective communication, and for every barrier that we have mentioned, we need to replace that barrier with expert/professional communicative skills. These skills we talk about are not just mechanical but also require a necessary amount of human skills. One must also have the human skill or the ability to integrate his human skills with the mechanics of technology. In the next section, we address the specific issues that explain this integrative process. This integrative process is the one that unites man and machine in order to better serve society.

Have you ever spoken to a stranger on the phone and thought, as you hung up, "He sounded really nice, and he was so helpful — I wish I knew him." Everybody appreciates a nice "telephone presence" when they encounter one. How, then, can you be as charming, gracious, and likable on the phone as you are in person? What follows are some thoughts on how to develop effective telephone skills that will bridge the distance that the use of the telephone generates, and how to further maintain these skills during calls that involve crisis events.

BRIDGES TO EFFECTIVE COMMUNICATION

Effective Listening

Until now we have been emphasizing one side of verbal communication (i.e. talking) and only mentioned listening. Conscientious listening is just as important as speaking in the communication process. People spend far more time listening than reading, writing, or talking, yet few know how to really hear what's being said.

To listen is to do more than hear. *Hearing* is a physiological function and involves receiving a message, while *listening* is a mental function that involves perceiving a message (interpreting and giving meaning). Skill in listening is dependent upon how well the message is translated and understood.

We are dealing then with a mental process. Actually, there are two mental processes to be considered. Listening is part of two-way interaction between the one who originates the message and the one for whom the message is intended. To effect real communication, speaking and listening must work in concert; the two participants in the exchange must mentally engage one another in shaping the message. They cooperatively build thought and determine meaning and significance. If the listener invests nothing in the enterprise, communication will suffer.

Speaking, many times, is obscure or partially developed; therefore, listeners must "fill in" the gaps with their understanding and experience. If the listener is "tuned in" to the speaker's purpose, he can supply the data that is necessary for adequate completion of the thought and fulfill the speaker's purpose: to evoke appropriate responses from the listener.

Although people differ in their ability to listen well, recent research has shown that — barring organic disfunction — listening ability can be improved through properly guided practice. In addition, any particular act of listening can be made productive if the listener will bring to it a correct physical adjustment and a proper mental attitude.

Good listening requires an active effort to derive meaning from all aspects of the communication situation: from the speaker's tone of voice, movements, gestures, and facial expression, as well as from the words he utters. In addition, it includes interpretation and appraisal: a constant and critical consideration of the ideas presented, the materials by which these ideas are supported and explained, the purposes which motivate them, and the language in which they are expressed. In short, good listening is comprehensive but even more important, it is creative. Only the listener can provide the feedback necessary to enable the speaker to determine the degree to which his message is being received or rejected and, consequently, the extent to which it must be modified or redirected.

We hear, but we don't really listen. Individuals spend 80 percent of their waking hours communicating in one way or another; of that time, about 45 percent is spent listening. But the focus in our educational programs is unside down. We spend the greatest amount of time teaching people to do what they spend the least time doing: writing. And we spend the least amount of time teaching them what they do most in life: listening.

It's lamentable because listening is much more complex than reading. What we read is locked on the printed page. If people are distracted, they can put aside their reading and return to it later. If they don't understand the message right off, they have the means to repeat it. But in listening, the message is written on the wind. It's transient. If we don't get the message the first time, there's usually no going back. It has been said that we hear half of what is said, we listen to half of that, we understand half of that, we believe half of that, and we remember half of that.

Keep in mind that listening is a combination of what we hear, what we understand, and what we remember. The efficiency of listening for most people in learning situations is about 20-25 percent.

There are reasons for improving your listening skills. If you are alert and listen you will be better able to perform in the operator role effectively. You will be better equipped to answer questions and improve your self-confidence. You'll be able to relate to and understand the people you come in contact with. When you listen carefully you improve your own vocabulary and language ability. Ideas and concepts can be heard more quickly and clarified easily when one listens intently.

Improving Listening Skills

In a recent study of the abilities telephone operators considered to be most critical for their success, they rated listening as number one — the most important competency to be developed. But, again, as most operators have not been taught how to listen well, they don't necessarily perform well.

Like others, operators often do not hear what is being said. They're either busy, preoccupied, distracted, or misunderstand, due to their expectations, preconceived notions, experiences, or special perspectives, or they misevaluate or fail to respond to the messages of others.

Of course, these listening problems are not limited to operators, but they are of special concern to operators due to the nature of their task.

More important, thousands of operators are recognizing this critical need and are working at improving their listening skills.

When you seek to improve a skill, such as listening, it is well to identify the problems to begin with. They may appear at any time but they are particularly evident in long conversation or lectures.

Some problems are:

1. Viewing a topic as uninteresting or being bored and disinterested in what is being said by the speaker.
2. Criticizing a speaker's delivery or appearance, instead of his message. Too often we get hung up on a voice, mannerisms, ethnicity, use of slang, foreign accent, or other external factors that have nothing to do with the worth of what he has to say. It is foolish and self-defeating because the message is important, not the wrappings.
3. Getting overstimulated to the extent that we are more concerned with our own response than in what is being said. We become so eager to express ourselves that we don't even hear what is said.
4. Listening only for facts. Many people, especially in classes, spend so much time making notes of names, dates, and other details that they miss the main points which give the facts significance. Facts have no meaning by themselves, they must relate to an idea, concept, or principle.
5. Another problem is tolerating, creating, or failing to adjust to distractions. Relax and try to position yourself to see and hear the speaker and avoid creating noises and movements that are disruptive of good listening.
6. How many times have each of us been guilty of faking attention? Frequently we get caught by being asked a direct question and are not aware of what was said. This is self-deceptive.
7. Another bad listening habit is paying attention only to what is easy to understand. If it is superficial or relaxing like a TV series or a variety show then it is easy to follow but hardly prepares anyone to grasp more difficult concepts or ideas.
8. The next problem is letting emotion-laden words interfere with listening. I'm sure you've gotten uptight when certain words are used — "trigger" words like "pig," "radical," "puke," "system," and others. When we hear these words, the rest of what a speaker says is often blocked out.
9. Deep-seated opinions or convictions impair comprehension. Whenever your ego involvement is strong in a situation and there appears to be a threat to deeply held opinions, little real listening takes place.

The Necessity of Feedback

The single, most important method of improving communications and avoiding misunderstanding is *feedback*. False perceptions and small errors magnify into major distortion if the recipient does not have the opportunity to respond.

We are in a much better position to evaluate the effectiveness of our communications with others when we are aware of the complexity of the process and how easy it is to be misunderstood. The process of feedback is a way to reduce misunderstanding. The receiver can *paraphrase* the message as he understands it and ask the speaker whether he received the message the speaker intended. The paraphrasing technique should be used when you want to enhance clarity and understanding between yourself and another person. It would seem most important when you give or receive directions to teach or try to pass on data. However, it works whenever you attempt to better understand someone else. It allows you to know what the other person means and assures the other person that you understand.

Paraphrasing consists of restating in your own words what the other person's statements mean to you. With this sort of restatement, the other person can determine whether the message getting through to you is the one intended. The paraphrase technique is based on the premise that when an individual expresses an idea, and that idea is restated in another way by the listener, the initiator of the statement will clarify, expand upon, or further explore the ideas and feelings embodied in the statement. For example:

> Caller: Operator, I was robbed. I came home and all my valuables are gone.
>
> Operator: Do you mean to say that someone came into your house when you were out and stole your valuables?
>
> Caller: Yes, operator, that is correct.
>
> Operator: I see. Then your house was burglarized.

This technique is valuable, in that it prevents communication breakdown between operator and the caller and clarifies the message being communicated.

State your paraphrase for the other person according to these guidelines:

1. Restate the other person's expressed ideas and feelings in your own words.
2. Preface your paraphrase with a tentative introductory phrase such as:
   "Are you saying . . .?"
   "You mean that . . .?"
   "You feel that . . .?
   "You think that . . .?"
   "It seems to you that . . .?"
   "It appears to you that . . .?"
3. Avoid any indication of disapproval or approval:
   refrain from blaming, expressing rejection or strong support; avoid giving advice or persuading.
4. Wait for the other person's response.
5. Where necessary, paraphrase the other's response in order to secure the most accurate understanding possible.

To increase the effectiveness of listener feedback consider the following guidelines:

1. Send feedback that is appropriate to the speaker, the message, and the situation.
2. Be certain the speaker understands the feedback. If there is any question, send it again to insure proper understanding.
3. Make certain the feedback is clear.
4. Send the feedback quickly. Delayed response or silence may be misinterpreted as ambiguous or negative feedback.
5. Beware of sending too much feedback in too short a time. Don't overload the system. Time your responses at appropriate intervals.
6. Delay performing any activity that might create an effect you did not intend.
7. Keep your emotional or personal feelings out of any feedback to the caller.
8. Use neutral, non-critical feedback.
9. Be sure that you understand the message before you respond.
10. Realize that initial attempts at giving more effective feedback may seem difficult at first. However, with practice, it will become easier.

The Aural Picture — How to Look Good on the Telephone

Anytime your get into a conversation on the telephone, you project some picture of yourself to the other person at the other end. This "aural picture" can only be conveyed in two ways: by what you say and by how you say it. So powerful are the sensory impressions that you're sending out over the wires that before you have even finished saying "Emergency operator. Where is the emergency?" the person on the other end will be able to tell whether you're sad, happy, interested in assisting him, or just plain bored and disinterested in him and his problem.

Your concern, then, is to make sure the "aural picture" you're sending out is a friendly, positive, and helpful one. To begin with, the operator should have a smile on his face. This may seem ridiculous at first, to smile into a telephone, but would you feel foolish greeting someone with a smile on a face-to-face basis? A smile can be heard 3,000 miles away when you are on the telephone. So put that smile on your face and the person at the other end will hear it in your voice.

Preparation

Good work habits are essential to an operator's effectiveness. Before you start to receive calls, get all the necessary material together that you will be needing. This includes such things as pencils, forms, paper, reference books, and other necessary information. If you have everything you might need available during your receiving of calls, you will assure the caller of your competence and interest when you are able to repeat details back to the caller for affirmation. Be mentally and physically prepared to listen.

Techniques for Answering the Phone

Build a favorable impression — answer calls promptly. Most calls require quick action on the part of the emergency operator, therefore, every call should be treated as an emergency. In any event, whether the call is an emergency or not, a prompt response has a positive psychological effect on the caller and helps you build a reputation of efficiency and courtesy. Since the caller cannot understand the reason for delays, waiting time seems longer than it actually is when a caller is waiting.

YOUR VOCAL PORTRAIT

The most basic rule of phone etiquette is that the operator should identify himself immediately. This simply means that the caller is entitled to know that the right number was dialed and the identity of the person answering the phone. For example, police emergency operators may identify themselves by saying, "Police emergency operator No. 000. Where is the emergency?" When telling the caller who you are, speak slowly and distinctly. Do not slur or run words together. The caller may need to know who you are for later reference. In addition, when names or numbers are unintelligible, the caller may receive the mistaken impression that you are trying to hide your identity.

Proper identification at the beginning of the call gets the confidence of the caller. It indicates that the person answering is a responsible individual. It further sets the limit on psychological distance. From this point forward, the operator, aside from the gathering of information, should be trying to pull that person closer psychologically. The closer that person feels during the interaction, the more satisfied he will be with it's outcome. This is true whether the operator helps the person or not. If the person feels the sense of human contact, there is a greater chance for satisfaction. Closing or limiting the psychological gap, from the onset, is ever so important because, in the absence of this closeness, the interaction will tend to be abrasive and negative and keep sliding in that direction unless curbed.

Language

Build a pleasant image. Use simple, straightforward language. Avoid repetition of mechanical words or phrases, particularly technical terms and police jargon. Proper English must always be employed without the use of slang. Complete sentences should be used. In selecting words and phrasing, choose those that are distinct in sound and that will convey a definite and unambiguous meaning, subject to only one meaning or interpretation.

Speak directly and distinctly into the phone. Answer warmly, speak clearly and at a normal level, neither too loudly or softly. Some people say "hello" and make it sound expectant and happy; others give the impression that they.would like to punch you for disturbing them. Don't bark into the telephone. Never convey the attitude of being annoyed at having to take the call. A well-modulated voice carries best over the telephone. Use a normal tone of voice and talk at a moderate rate. Vary your tone of voice and inflection. It will bring out the meaning of sentences and add vitality to what you say. A monotone that does not vary can be equated with lack of interest.

Perhaps the most effective way to project a welcoming mood is to put a lilt in your voice by inflecting frequently. Voices that naturally rise on a question, fall slightly for an answer, and, overall, charge up and down the scale of expressiveness, convey more charm and appeal than those that drone on in a "ho hum" monotone.

Still another way to insure that your "vocal portrait" is an attractive one is to pay some attention to the quality of the sound you're emitting. Introducing any kind of electronic equipment between speaker and listener alters the sound of a voice.

., A radio announcer will come across differently in person than he will over the airwaves; an individual, hearing herself for the first time on a tape recorder, is apt to think (and hope) she's hearing someone else. Telephones distort sound as well. A phone magnifies a voice in order to carry it long distances and raises pitch slightly so that voices sound higher than they would face to face. In other words, a strong voice that sounds nice and soft in person can swell to the size of a sonic boom over the phone.

Nobody wants to communicate a vocal portrait entitled "screamer." If you're one of those who yell into phones, instinctively considering the inanimate phone receiver to be deaf, make a note to cut your volume in half. Before long, the softer voice will become habit, an appealing habit.

Of course, equally grating to the listener is someone who is too shrill, which is easy to be, since telephones tend to raise pitch. Anger, fatigue, and even excitement will also cause voices to rise an octave or two, and talking on the phone when you're furious virtually guarantees you've alienated the caller on the other end.

Never chew gum, drink beverages, or eat food while on the

phone. Sounds such as these are magnified over a telephone; the sound of jaws grinding can be deafening. In addition, all are indicative of not being attentive and, therefore, are counterproductive to closing the psychological gap. Remember, that many callers may be under severe emotional strain caused by pain, fear, panic, anxiety, or injury. Emergency callers often exhibit incoherence and are speaking without giving a great deal of thought to what they are saying. In fact, if it is a crisis situation, their thinking process has been impaired, which is part of the effect of the crisis itself. Communicating with the operator is a strain for the caller and it is anxiety-producing itself. It is the operator's job to elicit needed information from the caller without showing confusion, annoyance, or disinterest. Further, the operator must always remain calm, unemotional and demonstrate competence to callers.

Avoid Excessive Humor

Police emergency communication is serious business and not the time and place to be humorous or for comedy routines. Occasionally, a caller may be rude or argumentative, at which time the tact and effectiveness of the police operator is put to the test. Although humor can be helpful in particularly stressful times, crisis situations are not the time for humor.

Using Caller's Name

It is important to use the caller's name when asking questions or when speaking in general to the caller. It is another way of getting the caller's attention and, more importantly, it personalizes the contact between the operator and the caller. However, it is important to note that the operator should never jump to a first-name basis, unless the caller indicates that this should be so. Once the psychological gap is closed, and the caller has given the operator permission to use their first name, the use of the first name helps to stabilize the closeness of the call and prevents the gap from widening again. Otherwise, using the first names can be considered an invasion of privacy and a violation of personal space. Use appropriate modes of address such as Miss, Mrs., Mr., or Sir, and last names only in such cases.

Repeat in Digital Form

Repeat numbers back to the caller in digital form. That is, if the caller states that the address is, "One ninety-seven East three hundred and twentieth Street," the operator should repeat the address back to the caller saying, "Is that address One, Nine, Seven, East, Three, Two, Zero Street?" Do not repeat numbers verbatim as the caller stated them, as this tends to sustain any mistakes the caller may have made. Do not ask, "You mean . . .?" This statement preceding an address tends to be leading and suggestive and is incorrect English. Furthermore, this type of questioning tends to reinforce any error in address that may have been made by the caller in his confusion. Numbers should be repeated in digital form, because digital form tends to correct possible mistakes in addresses.

Attention

Give your undivided attention to the caller. If the operator is distracted or disinterested, this will be detected in their voice by the caller. Give the impression that you are wide awake, alert, and interested in the person calling. If you give the caller your undivided attention, and you are prepared properly, chances are the caller will give you all the information you need immediately by ventilating. The process of active listening closes the psychological gap. Once you've listened and taken notes, the operator need only ask minor questions, as all of the information needed is already gathered.

Avoid Interruptions

Unless the operator hears the complete story, it is easy to jump to the wrong conclusion. Unnecessary questions are eliminated when the caller is allowed to finish his story without interruption. Remember, that a caller's terminology or way of speaking may be different than yours. Listen and evaluate the content of the message, instead of judging the speaker's delivery, accent, ethnicity, or the details of the incident he may be calling about.

Lack of attention is a frequent complaint of people calling for assistance. A caller is almost sure to detect a lack of attention when they are frequently interrupted. Also, when they are asked to repeat themselves or when they are subjected to numerous mechanical "uh huhs." Although you cannot see the caller, you nevertheless can learn a great deal about the caller by training yourself to "listen between the lines" and note changes in voice tone and inflection. Good listening is an art that can be mastered. It requires concentration and practice, but the result in increased telephone effectiveness is well worth the effort.

Explanations

When an explanation, instructions, or directions are necessary, give them when logical to do so and make them reasonable, clear, concise, and easy for the caller to understand. Use words that will convey your intent to the caller. If necessary, rephrase your information in different words, if the caller indicates that he does not understand. If you cannot assist the caller, explain the reason why you cannot do what the caller asks. For example: "I'm sorry, Mr. Rodgers, this number is only for emergencies. You will be better served if you call the Sanitation Department. May I give you their number?" Show a real concern when you cannot do what the caller asks. Suggest an alternative to help them.

Empathy

Place yourself in the callers position. Attempt to see their problem as they see it. Give the kind of service you would hope to receive if you were the caller.

Giving proper interest and assistance means giving each caller individual attention, being sincerely interested in their problem, displaying a real desire to help, and taking all the action necessary to help the caller. It is the sum total of *what* you say, *how* you say it, and what you *do* for the caller. Interest and assistance cannot be an on-again, off-again approach. It must be an expression and reflection of genuine concern for people's requests and problems and a recognition of the importance of the caller and their situations.

On Hold

If you must place someone on hold, a friendly voice, a few words of apology, and a word of encouragement every now and then to whoever is waiting would be good phone courtesy. If it is necessary at all to put the caller on hold, explain the reason. Explain to the caller why it is necessary to leave the line. Never say "hold on," or "just a minute," or "wait a second." Short phrases such as these sound abrupt and may be misunderstood by the caller. A better statement would be to say, "Will you please wait while I check?" Tell the caller what must be done and how long it will take.

Careless handling of the hold situation may result in the caller overhearing information or remarks between you and some other person, which was not meant to be for his consumption or interpretation. Never repeat on an open line any mechanical difficulties or lack of information that should be available to you. For example, "This information doesn't go into the machine," or "I can't get this information." Avoid casual conversation with another person while the caller's line is open. Be cautious of uttering obscenities that may surface because of the confusion surrounding crisis calls. This would indicate that the operator has been caught up in the events of the crisis and causes a loss of the caller's confidence in you. Avoid, if it is at all necessary, placing crisis callers on hold. This is not a favorable practice. Being placed on hold, depending on the time, can generate a negative psychological effect and cause greater psychological distance.

Give Progress Reports

A progress report is information given to the caller waiting at the other end of the line to advise him what progress is being made regarding his call. Since the person cannot see what is going on, the only way he has of knowing his call is getting attention is through a progress report. Time seems like eternity when waiting on the telephone. A minute of waiting can seem like two, or even three. Time, distance, and space is amplified on the telephone when one is waiting. Therefore, every thirty or sixty seconds, let the caller know that you are giving his call attention and advise him on what progress is being made. If the time off the line was more than a minute, apologize for the delay. For example, "Thank you for waiting, Mr. Dalton," or "I'm sorry to have kept you waiting so long," as opposed to "OK, Bill, I'm back." During crisis calls, progress reports must be integrated with the exchange of information during the call itself.

Crisis calls may be a one time contact, where information is given very quickly and excitedly. The satisfaction that a progress report gives must be given during the initial interaction, many times, in order just to hold the caller on the phone.

Anonymous Callers

If a caller is reluctant to give his name or telephone number, process the call immediately and try to obtain the information after assistance has been dispatched. This may occur in situations when information is being given very quickly for later investigations and where the caller may not wish to be identified. In either event, the operator should be cautious not to take the caller's lack of cooperation as a personal affront to him.

Terminating the Call

Calls should be concluded politely as soon as all necessary information has been obtained. Close in a friendly, unhurried way so that the caller will get the impression that you were glad to have had the opportunity to be of service. Maintain a friendly manner. Just as you can make a call or take a call politely, you can hang up gracefully or in such a nasty fashion that the other's feelings are hurt. Some insensitive people think nothing of interjecting a brisk, "OK, we'll take care of it, bye" into the midst of the caller's ventilating, then hanging up with a clunk. This will appear as complete rudeness to the caller. The unfortunate part is that the operator may not mean to be rude. In an effort to be efficient and process the information as quickly as possible, at some point after gathering all the information needed, a mental alarm goes off in their heads and that's it. They simply don't realize that a brusque farewell can seem like a slap in the face. All goodwill built up during the call can be destroyed if it is terminated improperly. Avoid trite closings such as: "Bye-bye," "Okey dokey," "S'long," "OK Hon," etc. Say pleasantly, adding the person's name, "Mrs. Walker, thank you for calling." In a crisis situation, where the operator may need to be supportive, you may want to say, "You did the right thing by calling us," or "I'm sorry that this happened to you." We will refer to this again later on in Chapter 4 in section entitled, "Psychological First Aid."

Always let the caller hang up first. It is courteous to pause before hanging up to allow the caller time to say "good-bye," express an afterthought, ask a question. This will also allow time to summarize the arrangements made, eliminate possible errors, and insure complete understanding between the caller and the operator.

Conclusion

It is essential that each operator be made aware of the important role that he as an individual plays in the successful operation of their organization he represents. The newest technological advances are not only important but necessary, and yet these advances do not embrace the human needs that is conveyed by dedicated personnel. Everytime you receive a call, you are the representative of your organization to the person at the other end of the line. The organization that you work for is judged by the voice that speaks for it over the telephone by what is said and how it is said. If your voice is warm and friendly, if you are courteous and tactful, people will enjoy dealing with you and your organization.

Remember callers are people just like you. We sometimes tend to regard the caller as a "number" or a "voice" instead of thinking of them as a person with feelings. A good telephone personality will win friends for yourself and your organization. Telephone contacts warrant special considerations since the person calling can't see you, your smile, or your facial expression. He can only draw his impression from your voice and manner.

Our efforts are aimed in the right direction when we go out of our way to give that "little extra" service. When we apply common sense to our work, show enthusiasm and tact in our work, when we prove to callers that our service is continually in their interest, and when we make an honest effort to be helpful, understanding, and efficient, we are letting the caller know that we are sincerely interested.

Finally, even if you are seething with rage about your job or against your boss or some other personal problem, don't take your distress out on innocent callers. They don't know what is going on with you, but you have the advantage in knowing that they have a problem and need your help.

To further understand the communication process, we need to

understand what motivates various styles of communicating. The following chapter on "Transactional Analysis" will explain why we tend to use certain words, certain facial expressions, and certain body mannerisms in order to express ideas. The process by which one person may select various attitudes and the mode of communication that follows is discussed. It will further explain and give how to analyze the communication process from various modes and predict the likelihood of conflict and/or communication barriers. Included is helpful suggestions on which mode of communication and/or expressive attitude is most productive is a given situation.

Points to Remember

LIMIT YOUR OWN TALKING. You can't talk and listen at the same time.

THINK LIKE THE CALLER. His problem and needs are important, and you'll understand and retain them better if you keep this point of view.

ASK QUESTIONS. If you don't understand something, or feel you may have missed a point, clear it up.

DON'T INTERRUPT. A pause, even a long pause, doesn't always mean he is finished saying everything he wants to say.

CONCENTRATE. Focus your mind on what he's saying. Practice shutting out outside distractions.

TAKE NOTES. This will help you remember important points.

LISTEN FOR IDEAS, NOT JUST WORDS. You want to get the whole picture, not just isolated bits and pieces.

INTERJECTION. An occasional, "Yes," and "I see," shows the caller you're still with him, but don't overdo it or use a meaningless comment.

TURN OFF YOUR OWN PERSONAL CONCERNS. This isn't always easy, but personal fears, worries, and problems not connected with the call can alienate the caller.

REACT TO IDEAS, NOT THE PERSON. Don't allow irritation at things he may say or at his manner to distract you.

DON'T JUMP TO CONCLUSIONS. Avoid making unwarranted

assumptions about what the caller is going to say or mentally trying to complete his sentence for him.

LISTEN FOR THE OVERTONES. You can learn a great deal about the caller from the way he says things and the way he reacts to things you say.

Chapter 2

TRANSACTIONAL ANALYSIS

THE primary function of an emergency operator is to interact with people who call in for assistance. Whether the caller is a member of the police department or the general public, we often find that there is a strain in the interaction. In fact, most of the time this interaction is a difficult one.

Many people who have jobs dealing with the public on a daily basis often claim that most of the individuals they deal with are rude, demanding, impolite, and difficult to interact with. One of the reasons for this strain is that the operator deals with people when they are most threatening and most vulnerable. Police emergency operators in particular deal with people under extremely stressful crisis conditions. They deal with the young and old, rich and poor when they are angry, frightened, drunk, violent, desperate, and ashamed.

Emergency operators get involved in the most intimate, personal way with people who call for help. Callers seek police assistance when these conditions are in existence. The operator needs to interact with these people in the most effective way in order to render the proper service. Therefore, the right words and attitudes on the part of emergency operators need to be such that it influences the overall outcome of the situation in the best interest of all concerned.

Why are some operators able to calm a hostile, abusive caller or an excited caller, while others tend to bring more stress to the situation? Transactional analysis is one way we may develop the skills necessary to analyze each interaction the operator encounters, evaluate the situation, and respond appropriately.

Using transactional analysis (T.A.), people can be better understood, and situations can be more easily brought under control. Its one realistic advantage lies in its ability to cover a wide range of human behavior in a consistent and understandable manner.

The first step towards changing yourself and your interactions is understanding. T.A. provides an approach to understanding yourself and your interactions with others. This kind of emphasis on interpersonal relationships lies at the heart of law enforcement and other service-oriented agencies, public or private, and suggests that interactions between people can be understood and, more importantly, modified and controlled to mutual advantage.

This is accomplished through the recognition of meaningful patterns. Through this recognition, we can change our patterns of interactions in a rational and appropriate manner. T.A. offers a unique way of looking at human interactions, increasing the opportunity to understand oneself and others, in order to reduce conflict and cope with crisis. Using T.A. you will find that you will be able to calm a person down quickly, get the information you require, and avoid a lot of useless shouting and misunderstanding without creating hard feelings.

Considering the amount of communication the operator is engaged in on a day-to-day basis, T.A. will prove extremely useful.

The concepts of T.A. and the language used to express them are simple and easy to understand. Therein lies its effectiveness as a human relations tool. The result of using T.A. techniques and concepts will be a clear understanding of yourself and others and a method of control over your behavior at work and that of others. With the insight of T.A. you can:

1. Discover good and not so good attitudes about yourself and others.
2. Achieve an understanding of self and others so as to enhance self-control necessary to handle other people under stressful conditions.
3. Select the appropriate response for difficult situations.
4. Understand the importance of giving and receiving positive recognition.
5. Improve communication on the job.
6. Examine the transactions you have with others and develop more effective ways of interaction.
7. Avoid getting "hooked" into behaving like the crisis caller.
8. Prevent minor disagreements from becoming an obstacle to effective communication.

It is realistic in that it is simple to understand and its vocabulary is devoid of the technical jargon of some other complex communication theories. The language of transactional analysis consists of words that can be used by everyone at any level and easily identified. This simplistic language is also beneficial in dealing with other crisis victims. The crisis victim, because of the psychological impairment, interprets in a very literal sense (childlike), and the more simple the language the least likely it will be for a message to have alternative implications. Simple language tends to be more exhaustive in its meaning.

Development of T.A.

T.A. was developed by Dr. Eric Berne, a clinical psychiatrist, best know for his book, *Games People Play*. During the period that Eric Berne was developing his theory of T.A. he observed that, as he watched his patients, he could actually see them changing. There were simultaneous changes in facial expression, vocabulary, gestures, tones of voice, and posture. He observed three distinct and separate states emerging, which he called *ego states*. These states, he noted, exist in all people and are apparent in their manner, appearance, words, and gestures. It was as if in each person there still existed the same little person he was when he was three years old. Berne called this the *Child state*. Also, within him are his own parents; Berne called this the *Parent Ego state*. Besides these two states, he observed a third that he called the *Adult state*.

According to T.A., everyone's personality is composed of these three parts, which are ego states. *An ego state is a system of feelings and expressions related to a pattern of behavior.* Individual behaviors during transactions with another person are determined by the particular ego state in action at that particular time. The ego state that is activated depends on many factors, including early life's experiences, the circumstances of the transaction, and the other person's ego state.

In T.A. language, the three terms utilized, Parent, Adult, and Child, have special meanings and are captialized when used. The ego states are diagrammed in Figure 2-1.

In T.A. language, Parent is not the same as Mother and Father, Adult means something quite different from a grown-up, and Child is *not* the same as a little person. The following chapter describes

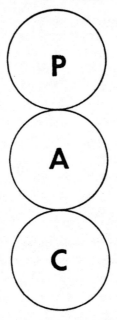

Figure 2-1. The ego states as diagrammed.

what they are in T.A.

There are two major elements to transactional analysis: (1) types of ego states; and (2) types of transactions.

A *transaction* is defined as *a basic unit of communication composed of a stimulus and a response*. Each time two or more persons meet, sooner or later one of them will speak or give some indication of acknowledging the presence of the others. This is called the *stimulus*. The other person will then say or do something that is in some way related to the stimulus, which is called the *response*. *A transaction is a stimulus followed by a response*. When you say something to another individual, he receives what was said, interprets what he thinks you meant, and responds. His interpretation includes a consideration of your gestures, posture, dress, voice tone, etc., and reflects his perception of the situation, not yours. His perception and ways of reacting usually are determined from past experiences and were learned during his formative years.

The T.A. model presents each individual as a human system divided into three basic behavioral ego states: Parent, Adult, and Child. Each ego state contains characteristics that make it unique.

The interplay between the ego states of two individuals serves to identify the nature of the transaction occurring between them.

With T.A. you will learn how to recognize, identify, and describe the Parent, Adult, and the Child as each appears in our transactions with others. You will be able to identify where people are "coming from" and develop analytical skills to identify problem stimulus, which might require special handling. By classifying human behavior and characteristics, you will be able to respond in a manner that will prevent the transaction from becoming inflammatory. Ego states are easy to identify if you know what to look for. Analyze posture, gestures, facial expressions, and tone of voice as well as behavior, as all are important clues to the particular ego state in action.

The ego state of each of us develops differently depending on our life experiences. However, even though we are each unique, we share common characteristics that we develop through socialization. What follows in the next chapter is a discussion of the identification, general description, and similarities that exist among all of our ego states and the differences that define each ego state within us.

THE EGO STATES

The Parent

The characteristics contained in the Parent ego state are referred to as *taught concepts* of life. They are included under the term "Parent" because most individuals are socialized by their parents and are taught many of their values and beliefs by parents or other authority figures. The characteristics include the directions, instructions, and the imperatives such as do's, don'ts, shoulds, shouldn'ts, always, and never that we learned or were taught throughout our younger years. It is a huge collection of recordings of unquestioned or imposed external events seen the first five years of life. It is a recording of the individual's perception of what significant figures in his life have done.

When people feel and act as their parents and other authority figures once did, they are said to be in their Parent ego state. Each person has learned unique attitudes, opinions, biases, and prejudices from parent figures. As children, we observed, listened, and drew conclusions about what we saw. We internalize these parental values and norms and they become a part of us. The situation of the little child, his dependency, and his inability to construct meanings with words made it impossible for him to modify, correct, or explain what was occurring around him. These impressions were unconsciously filed away in our memory bank, along with our feelings about the situations. Although we may not consciously remember many of these events, the impressions of them are still with us and influence the way we behave today. Our responses to events in our present day interactions are influenced by these past recordings and impressions. Therefore, each person will also be different when acting from his or her Parent ego state.

The Parent is the conscience and provides us with a sense of security by establishing rigid rules for our behavior. All admonitions, rules, laws, and proverbs that were heard from parents or authority figures are also in the Parent. What is important is that all this information is recorded as valid and extremely important, considering it is information from someone the little child is anxious to please and obey. The data becomes established as a permanent recording and gets replayed in current situations whenever we need to come on as Parent.

The Parent ego state can be viewed as having two parts, one containing those characteristics that are critical of self and others, called the *Critical Parent*, and one containing those that are nurturing and supportive of self and others, called the *Nurturant Parent*.

The Critical Parent is the judgmental part of us. The following are typical behaviors associated with the Critical Parent: furrowed brow, talking with arms folded, wringing hands, pointing a finger at someone, demanding looks, disapproving looks, pursed lips, and staring. Typical tones of voice used by the Critical Parent are stern, critical, condescending, scolding, and superior. When one moralizes, lectures, and scolds, that person is in the Critical Parent state.

The Nurturant Parent is the supportive part of us, the part that you use when you take care of someone. Typical behaviors associated with the Nurturant Parent are patting someone on the back, a comforting supportive touch, or an empathetic look. Typical tones of voice used by the Nurturant Parent are comforting, soft, protective, and sympathetic. When one is supportive, caring, concerned, and compassionate it is said that that person is in the Nurturant Parent state. Thus any of our current behaviors that show caring, consideration, concern, protectiveness, helping, or love, or which show condescension, authority, rigidity, punishment, evaluation, or ridicule are expressions of a Parent ego state.

The Child

The Child ego state is that part of the personality that recorded all the *internal* events *felt* in childhood. While external events were being recorded as data we now know as Parent, the feelings or the responses that accompanied these external events were simultaneously being recorded in the Child. The infant communicates through feelings. The ways the Child communicates through feelings are by crying, laughing, showing excitement, anger, and moodiness. These are all strong, spontaneous emotions. The Child responds emotionally to stimuli it encounters. All of our emotions (hunger, fear, joy, sexual drives, pain, etc.) arise out of our Child. *The Child is our emotional self.*

The characteristics associated with the Child ego states are referred to as *felt concepts*, because they represent how one feels about and reacts emotionally to what one sees and hears and to what one receives while growing up in the form of critical or nurturing and supportive stimuli from parents.

These reactions and emotions may either be natural and unsocialized or adaptive because of socialization. Therefore, the Child ego state has two parts, the *Natural Child* and the *Adapted Child*. The Natural Child enjoys life, needs affection, is curious and spontaneous, is free, warm, friendly, carefree, fun-loving, and accepting. Playful, joking activity comes from the Natural Child, as well as the capacity to love and be loved based upon intimacy and openness. The Natural Child expresses himself spontaneously without concern for the reactions of others. On the other hand, the Adapted Child is that part that makes adjustments in our behavior in order to be accepted by those around us. These adjustments stem from our need to conform, to be obedient, and to please others. The Adapted Child acts compliant, withdrawn, conforming, and manipulative. The manipulator in the Child is powerful and intuitive and knows just how to get its way with others. It is astute and knows just how far to go to test other people's endurance and tolerance. A master strategist, the Child state can trick or con people into getting them to do what it wants.

Typical behaviors associated with the Natural Child are: excitedly jumping up and down, smiling, skipping, hugging, and joy. Typical tones of voice associated with the Natural Child are cheerful, teasing, excited, laughing, happy, and cheery. When one is playful, spontaneous, and carefree it is said that person is in his Natural Child ego state.

Typical behaviors associated with the Adapted Child are forlorn appearance, pouting, quivering lips, withdrawing, pursed lips, downcast eyes, and drooping shoulders. Typical tones of voice associated with the Adapted Child are appealing, complaining, nagging, highpitched whining, protesting, and grumbling. When one is sullen, dejected, sulky, and scowling it is said that person is in his Adapted Child ego state. The Child is also characterized by non-logical, immediate actions that result in immediate satisfaction. Child inputs into behavior are loaded with feelings and emotions.

In the Child resides creativity, curiosity, the desire to explore and know, as well as destructiveness and danger to others. When these elements predominate a person's communication, the person is in the Child ego state.

As in the case of the Parent and the Adult, the Child is a state into which a person may be transferred at any time in current transactions. There are many things or events that happen to us today that can recreate the helpless situation of childhood and bring on the same feelings we felt then. Frequently, we find ourselves in situations where we are faced with impossible alternatives; we find ourselves in a corner, either realistically or the way we are perceiving things. These "hook the child" feelings can cause replay of the original feelings of helplessness, frustration, rejection, or abandonment that we felt then. When a person is in the grip of these feelings, we say the Child has taken over, which at that time, his anger dominates his reason. We say his Child is in command when he is acting unreasonable.

The Adult

The Adult ego state serves as the data processing center and contains the *thought concepts* of life as differentiated from the "taught concepts" of life in the Parent and the "felt concepts" of life in the Child. The Adult develops a thought concept of life based on data gathering and data processing. It objectively appraises reality. It is reality oriented and deals with factual data accumulated from the external environment, which it analyzes and evaluates and responds to in an objective and rational manner.

The Adult is that part of the personality that is the problem solver. Rational, logical, and objective, it provides clear thinking and analysis. It asks who, what, why, when, where, and how. The Adult works like a computer. It stores and collects information about everything. When you need to solve problems, you push the Adult button. It's the part of you that asks "Does it work?", and "*it*" means anything you need to make a decision about. It separates facts from opinions or inference, analyzes them, computes the alternatives, and selects the best one. When you are thinking, gathering facts, estimating probabilities and evaluating results, you are in your Adult state.

The Adult processes inputs from the Parent and Child ego states, validates this information against current reality, and integrates the influence of the three in order to balance the system.

The Adult is the seat of rational thinking, is computer-like in gathering and validating data, carries the non-emotional aspects of decision making and probability estimating, and works to impose and/or carry out the mandates of law and legal authority.

The Adult in you is not emotional, it does not get angry, and makes decisions based on information. Whatever the decision, while you are deciding you don't laugh, you don't cry, and you don't get angry. You put your feelings aside while thinking.

The Adult is the rational, logical part of us. It is governed by thought, it helps us objectively decide between alternative courses of action, and it makes realistic choices based on the facts presented. In this way it is different from both the Child and the Parent. *The Adult is always calm and reasonable.*

Typical behaviors associated with the Adult are: a calm, collected, straight, relaxed stance, regular eye contact, and a confident appearance. Typical tones of voice are: relaxed, self-assured, reasonable, assertive, objective, and calm. When one is realistic, rational, and reasonable it is said that person is in his Adult ego state.

You are all three persons. All three are important. No ego state is better than any other. The situation and the Adult determine what is appropriate. It is desirable to have your Adult functioning all the time to be aware of the Parent, Child, and the situation so that the Adult can help with the decisions. The Adult can turn off the Child or the Parent or both. You do have some control over your emotions. This is not the same as suppression or repression. It involves the changing of ego states. Choice and decision are the key words — freedom to be ourselves. To choose how we will feel, think, and behave in a given situation, to be aware of our choices and the decision we have made, and to be aware of many other options and alternatives is a fulfilling life-style available to those who attain this freedom.

The least anxiety-causing ego state is, of course, the Adult. In its rational, reasonable approach to confrontations it gives us the ability to make objective decisions. The Adult appears to be an advantage for police personnel, for while we are in it we can think, speak, and act clearly; we can control the situation. A person is usually less sarcastic and abusive to others while in the Adult and generally less reactionary over minor abuses aimed at the person. It would benefit each of us if we could maintain our Adult, but it is very difficult to do without making an extra effort at it.

The big problem with the Adult is that it is fragile and is easily "knocked out" by commands from the Parent and the feelings of the Child. Since the Parent and Child are learned first, and require no conscious effort on the part of the person, they become habits of the mind. Without thinking about it, many people automatically use the Parent and Child in different situations. Most of the time we are correct in our use. However, sometimes the Parent and Child may be unproductive.

Which ego state we come from depends on our awareness of the situation and our degree of control over our own behavior. When we respond to someone else's behavior without thinking about the alternatives, that person is controlling our behavior. It is only when we respond out of thinking that we are truly in control. It is the Adult that should make the decision on whether the appropriate response is from the Adult, Parent, or Child. Any response may be appropriate in the given situation; it is only when we assess which is best and use it to achieve our goal that we are using T.A. to its full advantage.

SWITCHING EGO STATES

If the operator is observant he will see changes in the people he deals with daily.

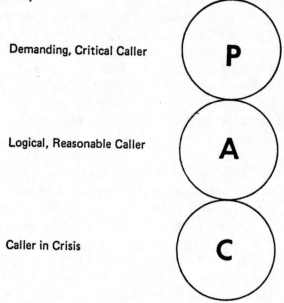

Demanding, Critical Caller

Logical, Reasonable Caller

Caller in Crisis

Continual observation has supported the assumption that these three states exist in all people.

Changes from one state to another are apparent in manner, appearance, words, and gestures. For example, a reasonable Adult turns into an angry, demanding Parent or scared Child when faced with the possibility of a situation threatening to his ability to exercise control over his own life.

A common mistake is to believe that some people are in one ego state all the time. Unless a person has rigid ego state boundaries, which would then be a problem, we all flow through all three ego states. One of the goals of T.A. is to be able to shift energy from one ego state to another at will. You may observe some people's behavior coming most frequently from the same ego state, which is why we often see typical recurrent patterns of behavior. Well-adjusted people function from all three, with none overlapping another.

It is also not intended for any of the ego states to be viewed as inherently good, bad, right or wrong. Rather, they all are natural and equally necessary to maintain the whole system in balance. We need values and beliefs to survive as an individual and as a society. Also, as operators, there are times when one needs to make judgments and to take control or impose authority. There are times when we must be rational and objective. There are times when Child behavior (not to be confused with childish) is desirable. For example, although the intellectual, reasonable approach is necessary for some situations, when calls are in regard to a death in the family, that caller may need a Nurturing Parental sympathy from the operator, not a cool, unemotional lecture.

With awareness, each of us can develop a good integration of the three states. When we use them in a way appropriate to the reality of the situation, we are functioning most successfully. In fact, one of the goals of T.A. is to get all three parts of you working well together.

EGO STATE CONFLICT

At one time or another most people exhibit all three ego state behaviors. Often the three disagree with one another, and you feel that one part of you wants something and another part of you wants another. Usually the best way to solve a problem like that is to have your Adult decide. The three ego states are like voices in you. The Parent may say things like, "You Must," your Child may say, "I Want," and the Adult may say, "This is how this works."

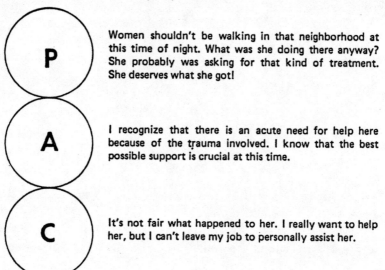

P — Women shouldn't be walking in that neighborhood at this time of night. What was she doing there anyway? She probably was asking for that kind of treatment. She deserves what she got!

A — I recognize that there is an acute need for help here because of the trauma involved. I know that the best possible support is crucial at this time.

C — It's not fair what happened to her. I really want to help her, but I can't leave my job to personally assist her.

Consider the conflict of an operator receiving a call from a rape victim at 4:00 AM.

You can also hear these words in other people's statements. For example, a young man, caught while trying to break into a private home, said to the arresting officer, "I *knew* exactly what I was doing, I *shouldn't* have done it, but I *felt* like doing it anyhow." If you analyze this statement you will be able to determine which thought probably came from which ego state. Another example is a police officer making an arrest who said, "It's not that I *want* to do this, I *have* to do it." Who do you think was doing the talking? The police officer's Parent, Adult, or Child?

Unless a person has rigid ego state boundaries, energy flows between the different ego states.

When was the last time you felt the *Parent* "in control"?

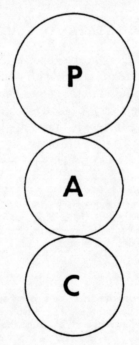

Remember! The goal of T.A. is to be able to shift energy from one ego state to another at will.

Well-adjusted people function from all three. When we use them in a way appropriate to the reality of the situation, we are function-

When was the last time you felt the *Adult* "in control"?

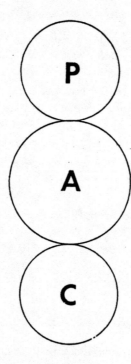

When was the last time you felt the *Child* "in control"?

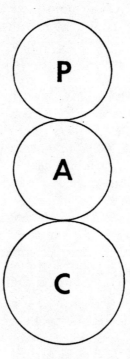

ing most successfully. Think! Your goal is to think at the proper time so that you have . . . . *control over any situation.* In using T.A. you call on your Adult for choosing values and feelings that will make your life happier. What part of you makes the decisions for you? Is it your Parent, Adult, or Child? You control them. You may shift your loyalty from your Parent to your Adult so that you can make better decisions about your life. You will be able to examine the transactions you have with others. You can learn what you try to do with people and what other people try to do to you.

Which part of you is in control? What ego state are you in most of the time? What ego state is most satisfying for you? Why? Which ego state seems to create a cooperative atmosphere with others? Which ego state seems to create an atmosphere of tension? Which one do you use when you want to be sarcastic? Which one do you use when you want to make love?

WHICH EGO STATE IS IN CONTROL?

There are ways of checking which part of you is in control:

1. CHECK YOUR BEHAVIOR. It includes the way you stand, sit, or walk, your voice, and the words you use. Listen for the following words: cute, marvelous, awful, and filthy (usually Parent words); suitable, practical, and correct (usually Adult words); and gee, wow, won't, and can't (common Child words).

2. CHECK ON HOW YOU GET ALONG WITH PEOPLE. If the Parent in you is bossy, or thinks he knows it all, he will often upset the Child in others. If the Child in you is fun-loving and happy, the Child in others will enjoy being around you and have fun with you. When you behave as Adult, there is a good chance that others around you will act as Adult towards you.

3. CHECK YOUR CHILDHOOD MEMORIES. You may remember how you spoke when you were little and how your parents spoke to you. Sometimes you may notice that you are talking exactly as you did as a child. Then you will know you are coming from your Child. Sometimes you will hear yourself say things exactly the way your mother or father did. You are then coming on as the Parent ego state.

The following test was developed to give you an opportunity to discover what ego state seems to characterize at least some of your everyday transactions. Complete the test and score it. Compare your responses on the test with the way in which you usually interact.

Ego State Self-Analysis

From the following statements, check the statements that you think is most appropriate for you. There are no correct or incorrect answers. Whatever you select is correct for you. The scoring guide follows.

1. _____ In doing my job, I stick to all the rules and regulations of the department.
2. _____ I can have a lot of fun doing telephone work.
3. _____ My greatest satisfaction on this job comes from helping people in need.
4. _____ I enjoy making decisions for others.
5. _____ It's never appropriate to break the law.
6. _____ It's my duty and responsibility to support the department in every way I can.
7. _____ Most people are able to make their own decisions.
8. _____ I usually comfort others when they cry.
9. _____ Most politicans can't be trusted.
10. _____ I enjoy being with little children.
11. _____ I seem to be more observant than many of the operators I've worked with.
12. _____ An operator who works hard is conscientious and foolish.
13. _____ I think children can sometimes be loud.
14. _____ I laugh infrequently.
15. _____ Every chance I get I goof off on the job.
16. _____ I tend more so than many of the other operators I know, to keep my "cool" when being baited by callers.
17. _____ I'm always laughing.
18. _____ I'm able to maintain a sense of alert detachment when other operators become emotional.
19. _____ When I don't win, I think about the next time.
20. _____ I'm afraid of being involved with politics.
21. _____ I enjoy helping people with their problems.

22. _____ Everyone should be able to take care of their own problems without calling the police.
23. _____. Military service can be a lot of fun for kids.
24. _____ I want to find someone to solve my problems.
25. _____ Most of these juvenile delinquents would benefit from a tour of duty in the military service.
26. _____ I think young people can decide for themselves whether or not they'd benefit from the military service.

Use the following guide to determine the number of Parent, Adult and Child statements you've selected. Total each "P," (C.P. and N.P.), "A." and "C" (A.C. and N.C. combined) score.

1. A.C.	14. A
2. N.C.	15. N.C.
3. N.P.	16. A.
4. N.P.	17. N.C.
5. C.P.	18. A.
6. A.C.	19. A
7. A.	20. A.C.
8. N.P.	21. N.P.
9. C.P.	22. C.P.
10. N.C.	23. N.C.
11. A.	24. A.C.
12. C.P.	25. C.P.
13. A.	26. A.

This test is somewhat predictive of the ego state that you might use predominately.

"P" score (number of "P" (C.P. and N.P.) statements selected) = _____Parent

"A" score (number of "A" statements selected) = _____Adult

"C" score (number of "C" (A.C. and N.C. combined) statements selected) = _____Child

Draw an ego state diagram of yourself using circles of different sizes to represent the totals of each ego state.

RECOGNIZING EGO STATES — 1

	POSTURE	*VOCABULARY*
Critical Parent	Arms folded Pointing an accusing finger Looking down over rim of glasses Toe tapping Hands on hips Demanding look Head leaning forward	You should always, You should never, You ought to, You must, Why don't you, Don't tell me, You always, Everyone knows that, Ridiculous
Nurturing Parent	Patting on back Comforting Touch Supportive Hug Empathetic look Open arms	Cute, Nice, Poor thing I'll protect you Don't worry it'll be all right I love you.
Adult	Calm, Collected A straight, relaxed stance Regular eye contact Confident appearance Thinking Active listening Alert	I see your point Who, Where, What, When, Why, How I recognize How do you feel about. . . Offer of alternatives and options Manageable, Predictable Practical, Workable
Adapted Child	Forlorn appearance Sulky, Scowling Withdrawing Drooping shoulders Pursed lips	Try, Please, It's not my fault If only — I wish One of these days It's not fair

POSTURE	VOCABULARY
Dejected	Oh boy
	How did I do?
	Did I do OK?

Natural *Child*	Skipping	Joyful
	Hugging	Great!
	Twinkle in eyes	Wow!
	Smiling	I can
	Playful	I will
	Loose	I want
	Spontaneous	Gee
	Uninhibited	I enjoy
		Hi!

RECOGNIZING EGO STATES — 2

PATTERNS	TONE OF VOICE
Moralizes	Stern
Lectures	Scolding
Scolds	Harsh
Critical Values	Judgmental
Parent Habits	Indignant
Judgments	Demanding
Laws	Commanding
Blames	Critical
	Condescending
	Disgusted

PATTERNS	TONE OF VOICE
Supportive	Comforting
Empathetic	Compassionate
Nurturing Nurtures	Sympathetic
Parent Protective	Caring, Loving
Concerned	Soft
Encourages	Soothing

PATTERNS		VOCABULARY
	Organizes	Relaxed
	Examines Facts	Assertive
	Rational	Self-assured
Adult	Realistic, Plans	Reasonable
	Decision Making	Calm
	Solves Problems	Unemotional
	Objective	Even
	Logical	
	Process Information	

	Reacts:	Appealing
	Angrily	Pleading
Adapted	Moodily	Nagging
Child	Sullen	Complaining
	Compliant	Protesting
	Conforming	Grumbling
		Whiny

	Reacts:	Happy
	Playful	Cheerful
Natural	Joyful	Excited
Child	Friendly	Joyful
	Affectionate	Spontaneous
	Trusting	

STROKING

In T.A. language, a stroke is a special form of stimulation one person gives another; it is a recognition by fellow human beings of one's existence. Exchanging strokes is one of the most important activities in which people engage. Strokes are necessary for physical and mental health; therefore, throughout life we all need and seek stroking. As infants and children, most of us received positive strokes in the form of hugs, caresses, and kisses that made us feel good. Sometimes we received negative strokes in the form of physical punishment of scolding; as bad as they may have made us feel, they were preferable to no strokes at all. As we get older we may not need as much cuddling, but we continue to seek strokes, symbolically, in word strokes, as a substitute for the physical. This may take the form of a greeting, compliments on our apearance, or praise for performance. We become willing to take word stroking, instead of physical stroking we had when we were little, because words are more socially acceptable. We still need and want physical stroking but often have to settle for word (symbolic) stroking.

Types of Strokes

Strokes can be verbal or non-verbal, positive or negative, or conditional or unconditional. A wave or gesture, such as a handshake, a warm smile, and pats on the back, are positive nonverbal strokes. Greeting a person and using his or her name, "Hi Anne," or "Good Morning Herman," and giving honest compliments are positive verbal strokes. A positive stroke is one that carries a "you're OK" message and usually evokes good feelings in people. Expressions of loving, caring, respecting, knowing, and responding to a need are positive strokes.

On the other hand, a negative stroke is one which carries a "you're not OK" message and may result in unpleasant feelings. They are painful forms of recognition we get and give when we do something irritating to another, are criticized, or put down. Shouting or greeting someone sarcastically with "Well, at last you've arrived" are negative verbal strokes. Disregarding a person, showing contempt, or talking down to a person are also negative strokes. Example: "What's the matter, can't you do anything right?" or "Get away from me, I can't stand you." Expressed hating is a negative stroke. Or the same message may be implied non-verbally by frowning, sneering, or pounding on the desk. A kick in the shins is also a non-verbal negative stroke. This stroking pattern carries a message of "I'm OK, you'll never be OK unless you do things my way."

Whether someone listens to you, pats you on the back, or says you're a pain in the butt, it's still stroking.

All people need strokes; they need to get and give some kind of stroking, pleasant or unpleasant. If they can't get positive strokes then they will take negatiave ones. To many people, negative strokes are better than no strokes at all.

Unconditional and Conditional Strokes

Strokes can also be unconditional or conditional. An unconditional stroke is a stroke for being, whereas a conditional stroke is a stroke for doing. Unconditional strokes are words or behavior that convey a message: "I like you for what you are, not for what you achieve." When a stroke is given to you for what you are, rather than for what you do, as when someone says to you, "I love you because you are you," or "I like to be near you," that stroke is unconditional. It has no strings attached. It is a stroke given to you for being you. Everyone seems to need much unconditional stroking. You probably prefer to be told that you are OK for what you are, rather than only for what you do.

A stroke given for what you do rather than for what you are is a conditional stroke. Examples: "John, if you take off your shoes, momma will like you," or if a parent says to a child, "I like you when you do as you're told," a stroke is given on the condition that something is received in return; he is not stroking the child for what he is. Whenever you hear an *if* in a transaction, you can almost be sure there is some conditional stroking coming your way. The following are some examples of conditional stroking:

"I love you if . . . . "
"If you're good . . . . "
"If you make lots of money . . . . "
"If you don't bother me . . . . "

It is possible, therefore, to think of strokes in four categories:

POSITIVE UNCONDITIONAL: "I like you."
POSITIVE CONDITIONAL: "Thank you for rubbing my back."
NEGATIVE CONDITIONAL: "I don't appreciate your sarcasm."
NEGATIVE UNCONDITIONAL: "You're no good and never will be."

In the hands of a competent emergency operator, stroking can be a powerful tool. A pleasant, positive stroking operator can gain more cooperation than a negative operator, and he can do much to gain cooperation and goodwill and establish good relations with the community. The effective use of stroking in crisis situations will be further explained on the following pages.

Quiz

Stroke Scale

Think about the past twenty-four hours. Evaluate the strokes you gave and accepted.

- Whom did you stroke? How did you stroke them? Positive or negative? Conditional or unconditional?
- Did you avoid stroking someone? Why?
- Who stroked you? How did they stroke you? Positively or negatively? Conditional or unconditional?
- Did you avoid letting someone stroke you? Why?
- Evaluate your need for stroking one the scale below.

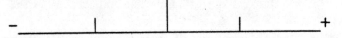

- Evaluate your ability to give strokes to others.

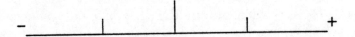

- Are you satisfied with your placement on the scales?
- Think about the strokes you gave and received. What changes would you like to make?

A good question to ask yourself is "What kind of strokes do I make sure I get?" and "How do I make sure I get them?" Remember, one of the best ways to get positive strokes is to give them!

CONTAMINATION

Although we show the three ego states as being separate and distinct, in reality it is not quite that simple. None of our behaviors are pure Parent, Adult, or Child. Generally, we are unable to keep our ego states entirely separate. In conditions where the Parent overlaps the Adult, we speak of the Adult contaminated by the Parent. In this state our previously learned values, ideas, and beliefs decrease our ability to objectively examine reality. Our perception is distorted and we act out of bias and prejudice.

In the healthy adult personality, the three parts remain separate and the individual is able to cathect the ego state of his choice. He chooses the ego state that appears to be most functional for the situation he is involved in. For example, the Parent for nurturing someone, the Adult for solving a problem, and the Child for having fun. The Adult ego state is available for each of us, which contains accurate data upon which to estimate probabilities in order for us to make appropriate decisions and carry them out in an interaction. Parent prejudices and Child fears do not masquerade as Adult information in a healthy individual.

Psychopathology is present when the Adult boundaries break down and become contaminated by the Parent and/or the Child and the Adult does not correct or check out this information (*see* Figure 2-2).

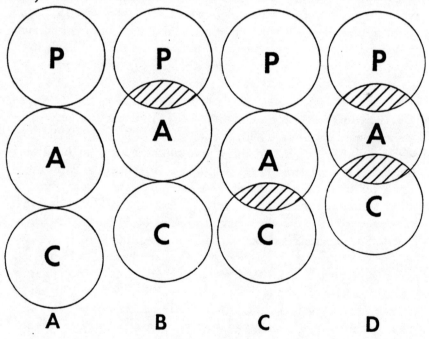

Figure 2-2. (*A*) The Uncontaminated Adult; (*B*) A Parent-Contaminated Adult; (*C*) A Child-Contaminated Adult; (*D*) The Adult contaminated by both Parent and Child.

In the Uncontaminated Adult, a healthy Adult is uncontaminated by neither Parent recordings or Child fears, and a Parent-Contaminated Adult results in prejudices and biases (*see* 2-2*A*, *B*). In some situations you may think you are using your Adult, but if you are prejudiced, the Parent in you is doing the talking. For example, if your mother thought people of another race were not good, the Parent in you may talk the same way she did. Your Adult may then be contaminated by your Parent ego state. That is, your Adult may take what your mother said as fact without really checking it out.

Whenever feelings, opinions, attitudes, and prejudices are expressed by us automatically without previous thought, contamination has occurred. These opinions, attitudes, and prejudices seem to be the result of our own thinking, but when they are not thought out thoroughly, they are just playbacks of old recordings — Parent recordings. Everyone has some degree of contamination in some areas of their lives. It most often occurs when conversations center around sex, politics, childbearing, or other topics that arouse strong childhood feelings and parental opinions that are not based on fact. If these opinions are not thought out thoroughly, they are likely to be expressed as prejudices. Prejudices are strongly held opinions that have not been examined on the basis of objective data.

A Child-Contaminated Adult results in phobias and delusions (e.g. elevators are scary *see* Figure 2-2*C*). Your Adult can also be contaminated by your Child. In some cases, it is the Child that overlaps the Adult. When the Child contaminates the Adult our perception is distorted differently from that in which the Parent contaminates the Adult. Paranoia and hallucinations result from the Child contamination of the Adult. For example, if you think that people are against you when they really are not, it may be the scared little kid in you that is contaminating your Adult thinking.

The Adult can be contaminated by both the Parent and Child ego states (*see* Figure 2-2*D*). (A person may hear words from his Parent and expresses fears about them from his Child.) Stressful situations heighten the danger of contamination. The fears of the Child in a person at the site of a burning house, for example, may immobilize his Adult and keep him from taking appropriate action. Contaminated thinking usually leads to the wrong decision. Rooted as they are in the past, contaminated thinking and behavior are often inappropriate guides to current action.

Operators must be particularly careful to recognize contamination in others and to avoid contamination in themselves, because they are in a position to make decisions that can affect the lives of others. They must then make every effort to remain fair and impartial. You may allow one of your three ego states to stay in control too much of the time. Then you are a *Constant Parent, Constant Adult,* or *Constant Child* at the expense of being a whole human being. This problem is called *exclusion*, in which you shut off or exclude two of your ego states.

Exclusion of an Ego State

Another variation in the relationship of among ego states concerns the exclusion or blocking of the functioning of a particular ego state. If the Parent was excluded, the person would not have a conscience. The person would not have an ethical foundation for his behavior and would violate the norms of society (*see* Figure 2-3*A*).

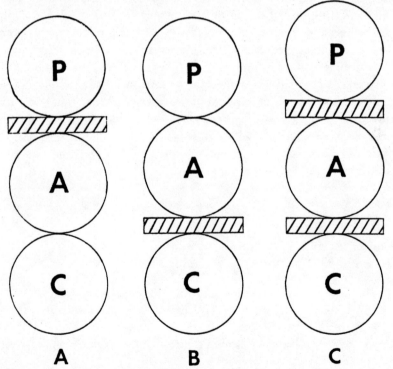

Figure 2-3. (*A*) Exclusion of the Parent; (*B*) Exclusion of the Child; (*C*) Exclusion of the Adult.

The exclusion of the Child (*see* Figure 2-3*B*) would result in a lack of emotion. The person may devote full time to work and not enjoy leisure. This type of person would not be able to empathize with other people's emotional problems.

The exclusion of the Adult ego state would result in an abnormal personality, a "psycho." The person's behavior would shift between Parent and Child, without the rational influence of the Adult (*see* Figure 2-3*C*).

In summary, the Parent ego state represents a set of behaviors and attitudes that seem to be derived from a parental model. The Adult ego state expresses accurate analyses of reality and provides for the continued well-being of the individual personality. The Child ego state consists of a pattern of behaving that comes from the feelings and attitudes of childhood. The Child in all of us helps to give free expression to pent-up feelings that result in self-expression and impulsive reactions. From the point of view of transactional analysis, the behavior of any individual at any moment can be identified as fitting one of the three ego states: Parent, Adult, or Child.

The second major aspect of the technique of transactional analysis involves recognizing the consequences of people interacting from similar and different ego states. A complete set of interactions between two people is called a *transaction*. Thus, transactional analysis involves recognizing the types of transactions that occur and understanding the consequences of different kinds of interactions on the people involved. As with ego states, all transactions are of three types: complementary, crossed, or ulterior. These three types are discussed in the following chapter.

Quiz

Analyze the Following Statements and
Determine the Ego State Being Expressed

1. I'm sorry sir, but we only handle emergency calls.
2. What's going on at 911? I called over an hour ago and the police aren't here yet!
3. May I have the telephone number from where you are calling?
4. For goodness sake, I already gave you my address two times

already. What's the matter with you?

5. Please operator, please help me. My daughter is sitting on the window ledge threatening to jump.

6. What is the address of the building where the incident occurred?

7. I'm sorry miss, but we don't give medical information over the telephone. I will send you an ambulance.

8. Who the hell do you think you're talking to?

9. You poor thing, you're so upset. Don't worry, I'll send help immediately!

10. "Wow!" I feel great. I just got a great evaluation from the supervisor.

11. Who the hell do you think you're talking to, lady. You think you're the only person who has been mugged today. I have a lot of other people to take care of.

12. I feel terrific. I feel like hugging everyone in this room.

13. Haven't you got any calls to take? If I ever catch you goofing off on the job again, I'll have you fired immediately.

14. I care about what happens to you. I'll help you.

15. Mister, you always call us for help with the same problem. Isn't it about time you made some changes.

16. Oh operator. Thank you for your empathy and concern. Thank you for caring.

17. I'll have an ambulance there as soon as possible. Don't worry. It'll be alright.

18. Boy, what luck. This new assignment to Communications Division is exactly what I wanted.

19. I try and try, but no matter how hard I try, I can never get these codes correct.

20. I realize you're upset; that was a terrible accident. Please calm down. You're not injured. I'll help you.

1. A.		11. C.P.	
2. C.P.		12. N.C.	
3. A.		13. C.P.	
4. C.P.		14. N.P.	
5. A.C.		15. C.P.	
6. A.		16. A.C.	

7. A.	17. N.P
8. C.P.	18. N.C.
9. N.P.	19. A.C.
10. N.C.	20. N.P.

TRANSACTIONS

The essential unit of T.A. is the transaction. A transaction is defined as *a basic unit of communication consisting of a stimulus and a response.* You say something to another individual, he receives what was said, interprets what he thinks you meant, and responds. His interpretation includes a consideration of your gestures, posture, dress, voice tone, etc., and reflects his perception of the situation, not yours. His perceptions and ways of reacting usually are determined from past experiences and were learned during his formative years.

A transaction is some sort of exchange between two people. It can be any sort of exchange: a friendly word, angry blows, presents, or bullets. When you say hello to someone and he says hello back, that's a transaction. The Parent, Adult, or Child in you will be answering the Parent, Adult, or Child in the other person. All conversation is a series of transactions, one exchange after another. These can be Adult to Adult, Adult to Child, Adult to Parent (*see* Figure 2-4). It can also be Parent to Parent, Parent to Adult, Parent to Child (*see* Figure 2-5) or Child to Parent, Child to Adult, or Child to Child (*see* Figure 2-6).

Whenever any two people get together and talk as Parent to Parent, Adult to Adult, or Child to Child, they are communicating by coming from the same ego state, and it is a good transaction. There is no rule saying that these transactions are the best kind, however. All combinations are possible. Be in any ego state you wish to communicate with any ego state in the other person. Communication may originate from any of the three ego states in one individual and be responded to by him from any of the three ego states. Two or more people talking to one another can switch from one ego state to another easily with no break in the communication and with all lines of communication remaining uncrossed.

Analyzing transactions is the function of T.A. Each time two or more persons meet, sooner or later one of them will speak or

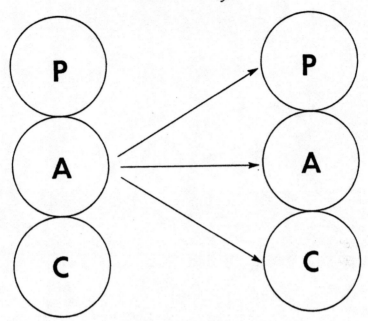

Figure 2-4. Adult transactions.

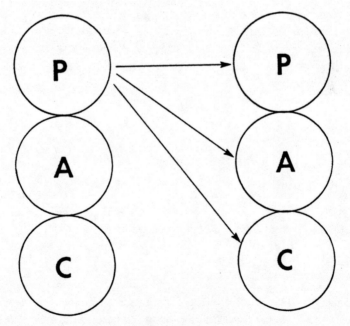

Figure 2-5. Child Transactions.

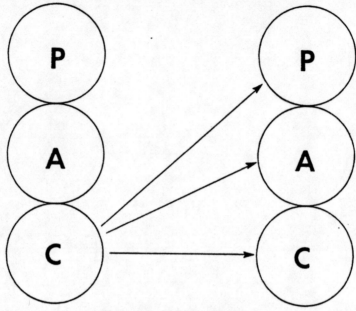

Figure 2-6. Child Transactions.

give some indication of acknowledging the presence of the other person. This, as previously mentioned, is called the *stimulus*. Another person will then say or do something that is in some way related to the stimulus, which is the *response*. A transaction is a stimulus followed by a response.

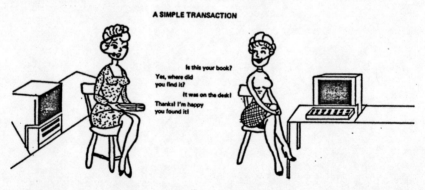

Transactions do not exist in isolation. Each transaction may serve as an initiator for following transactions. Thus, the response to the initial transaction may serve as the stimulus for the second transaction. The response to the stimulus does not have to be in words. It may be a gesture, such as a wave. Almost anything can serve as a stimulus for further transactions.

In analyzing a transaction, three factors must be considered: (1) what was said, (2) what was meant or implied, and (3) how was that received and responded to. Therefore, we do more than listen to the words: we examine the tone of voice, the mannerisms and the patterns of interaction. All of these variables taken together constitute the person's behavior. We also examine the thoughts and feelings that are behind that which was expressed in the behavior.

People communicate with each other, not only to exchange information, but also to reinforce their feelings about themselves and each other. In a transaction, each person gains something from the exchange. What they give and what they get depends upon which ego state in each person is most active at the time and the kinds of transaction that go on between them.

ANALYZING TRANSACTIONS

Now that you can identify statements and behavior as Parent, Adult, or Child, how can this be used to your advantage? The purpose of analyzing transactions is to determine which part of each person (Parent, Adult, or Child) is originating each stimulus and response. In order to control a transaction it is necessary to analyze it to determine what is happening between the parties involved. We have to be able to identify our own ego positions as well as those of the persons with whom we are dealing. When we can do this, we can choose the proper stimulus or response to "hook" the person into a desirable behavior. For instance, if we are dealing with someone who is angry and upset, we can hook that person from the Child ego state and into the Adult. Now, let us consider the different types of transactions. Transactions are divided into three types, depending on the characteristics of the transaction: (1) parallel or complementary, (2) crossed, and (3) ulterior.

Parallel Transactions

These types of transactions are generally pleasant and can continue without much stress or discomfort to either party. Stimuli that are directed to one ego state and have a response back from that ego state are *parallel transactions*. It is a transaction in which the stimulus from the sender receives the expected and predicted response from the receiver. When stimulus and response on the P-A-C transactional diagram make parallel lines, the transaction is complementary and can go on indefinitely. It does not matter which way the arrows go — whether it be from Parent-Parent, Adult-Adult, Child-Child, Parent-Child, or Child-Adult — if they are parallel.

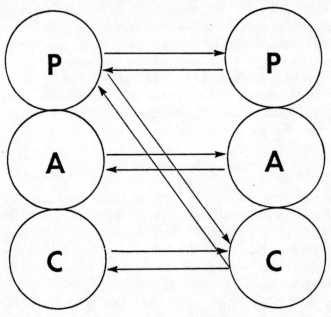

Figure 2-7. Parallel transactions: complementary and pleasant.

A parallel transaction is one in which the reactions seem appropriate and anticipated. For example, if a mother is concerned about an ill child and her husband consoles her, the transactions would be parallel. The interactions making up the transaction complement each other. A parallel transaction can take place between any of the ego states. Two operators may engage in a Parent-Parent complementary transaction when they discuss problems of their calls, in Adult-Adult complementary transactions when working together to solve a mutual problem, and in complementary Child-

Child ego state transactions when they are at a party. As long as the interaction is anticipated and consistent with the ego states involved, the transaction is called *complementary*. As long as the interaction continues to be complementary, the lines of communication are probably still open. The following are some Parent-Parent transactions between two operators:

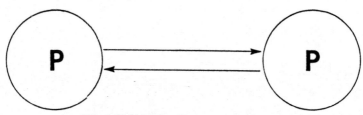

Figure 2-8. Parent-Parent transactions.

First Operator: Looks like another family fight at the Smith house.
Second Operator: Never fails, it's Friday night!

First Operator: This city stinks. Working on this job is getting more and more difficult.
Second Operator: You said it. The public doesn't appreciate us anyway.

First Operator: How could anyone do such a thing to a helpless little child.
Second Operator: Yeah! Poor thing, children deserve a better life than that.

These transactions are Parent-Parent in that they proceed without

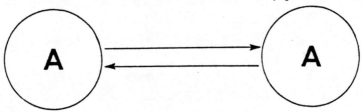

Figure 2-9. Adult-Adult transactions.

the benefit of reality data and are the same kinds of judgmental blaming and fault-finding that is recorded in the Parent. They represent an exchange of value judgment that support each other with firm agreement.

If you asked someone the time and they responded with the correct time, it would be an example of a parallel transaction from Adult to Adult ego states. For example:

First Operator: What time is it?
Second Operator: It's five o'clock.

_____

First Operator: What tour are you doing tomorrow?
Second Operator: I'm doing an 8X4.

_____

Operator: May I have your address, please.
Caller: Sure, my address is . . . .

The above transactions represent an exchange of objective data and are therefore Adult-Adult transactions.

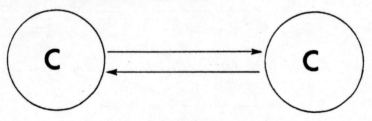

Figure 2-10. Child-Child transactions.

First Operator: Oh my God! What a horrible accident!
Second Operator: Oh wow! I've never heard of anything so horrible. What do we do? What do we do?

_____

First Operator: Wow! Great! I made the new Supervisor's list. Boy, am I happy!
Second Operator: I didn't make the list. I try and try, and never pass any exams.

_____

First Operator: I don't like the Supervisor on my tour. He's always criticizing me and looking over my shoulder. I just want to do my job and leave.

Second Operator: Yeah. It's not fair. No matter how hard we try, he criticizes us anyway!

The previous transactions represent Child-Child transactions because they are expressions of anger, self-centeredness, fear, and excitement. They are complementary because the responses are from the same ego state. As long as the arrows do not cross, complementary or parallel communications can continue indefinitely. However, transactions are not necessarily exchanged between like ego states. They might well be between unlike ego states, such as the following.

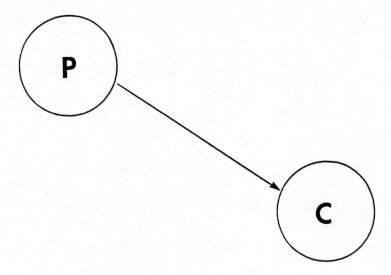

Figure 2-11. Parent-Child transaction.

If the Nurturant Parent in someone says "Let me give you a hug," and the Child in the other person says "Wow! Great!" the lines in the transaction are uncrossed and still parallel (*see* Figure 2-12).

In Figure 2-13, we diagram a complementary, parallel transaction between two operators. The first operator doesn't feel well and wants comforting. His friend realizes he is ill and is willing to give his partner the support he needs. This transaction can go in a satisfactory manner indefinitely, as long as the nurturing partner is willing to stay in that role. If one of the other changes their role, the parallel interactions are disturbed and changes again.

This type of transaction can also be seen in crisis situations,

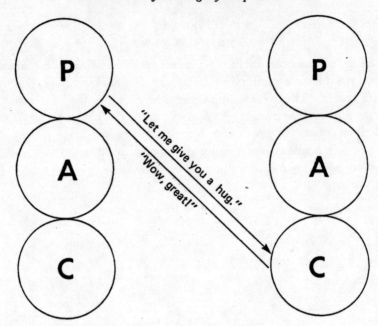

Figure 2-12. Parent-Child transaction.

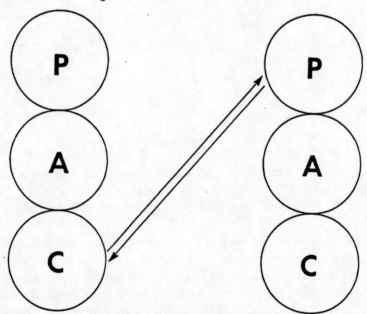

Figure 2-13. Child-Parent transaction.

where the responding operator may temporarily assume a nurturing role to comfort someone.

Crisis Victim: Please, please help me! I don't know what to do, my baby is hurt!

Operator: Don't worry, I'll take care of your call. I'll have your baby rushed to the hospital immediately.

First Operator: I just can't figure it out. Could you help me?

Second Operator: Don't worry about it, it'll be all right. I'll help you.

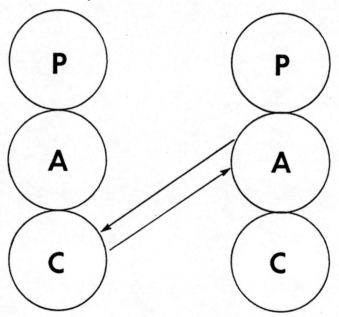

Figure 2-14. Child-Adult transaction

Another type of complementary transaction is one between Child and Adult (*see* Figure 2-14). A person in the grip of not OK feelings may turn to another person for realistic reassurance. For example, an operator may be expressing his own doubts about passing an upcoming promotion examination. Even though he is qualified and can pass any exam easily, his doubts are causing an overload of not OK feelings. He expresses his fears to his friend, who responds with realistic reassurances as to why he can easily pass the exam.

First Operator: Oh, I'm so worried about that promotion exam. I doubt I can pass it. I'm really worried about it. I hear it's really a hard exam; I'll never make it.

Second Operator: I understand you're concerned about taking the test. However, you've passed all the other exams you've taken, and we both know you can easily pass this one also.

Crossed transactions

Sometimes, though, transactions become crossed and there is a breakdown of communication. The kind of transaction that causes trouble is the *crossed transaction*. If, for example, you asked someone the time — which is an Adult stimulus, seeking information — and the person responsed with "Why are you always bothering me?" there would be a breakdown in communication. The transaction is crossed.

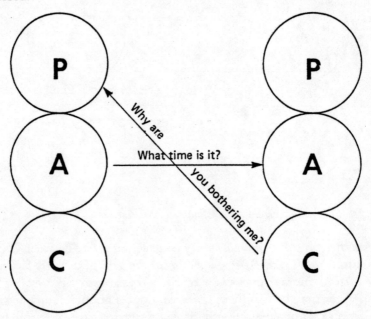

Figure 2-15. Crossed transactions.

A crossed transaction occurs when an unexpected response comes from the other person. It results from reactions that are not expected or not consistent with what was expected. The lines of communication cross and the process is disrupted. For example, if you ask a friend how he feels and the response is "Why don't you mind your own business!" you have a crossed transaction. If you ask your spouse where your socks are and the answer is "Why can't you keep track of your own clothes?" it's a crossed transaction.

Crossed transactions are usually conducted on the brink of a personal confrontation. The decision to cross the transaction remains with us. By our response we can minimize confrontations or increase their probability. It is at the point when we are confronted with the stimulus that we can analyze it, respond accordingly, and keep it under control. These types of transactions are less satisfying, since they do not satisfy the needs of the communication. However, we may sometimes consciously enter into a crossed transaction, as in the situation where we try to get someone who is coming from their Child to Parent to come from their Adult by crossing the transaction with an Adult-Adult communication. Following are some examples of crossed transactions.

First Operator: How could anyone do such a thing to a helpless little child?

Second Operator: Don't be a fool feeling sorry for these kids. These kind of people always treat their kids this way!

First Operator: Do you remember the name of the caller who was an attempted suicide last night?

Second Operator: How can you expect me to remember yesterday's callers? You want me to memorize names when you can't even remember your own?

First Operator: I have to finish this report tonight before I go off duty.

Second Operator: Why must you always leave things until the last minute (*see* Figure 2-16)?

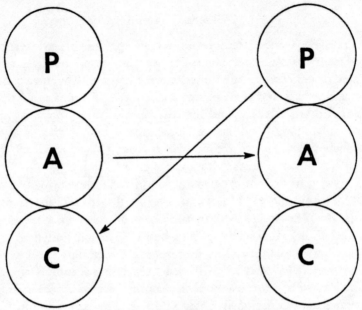

Figure 2-16. Adult-Parent transaction I.

Man: Hello, operator, we locked our car door and left the keys on the front seat. Do you have any suggestions about how we can open the door?

Operator: Who's the bright one who did something so stupid?

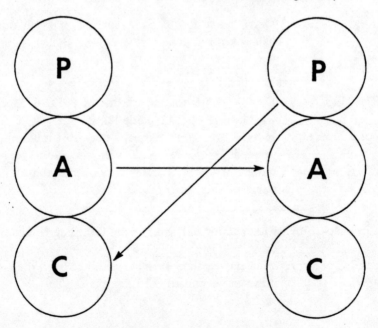

Figure 2-17. Adult-Parent transaction II.

The Adult has a choice as to how it will respond to a stimulus in a complementary or parallel way that will protect both the relationship and the individuals in the relationship. This sometimes takes some very quick and intuitive computing, which can become second nature to you if it is used regularly.

ULTERIOR TRANSACTIONS

The third basic kind of transaction is called *ulterior*. In this kind of transaction there is an apparent message on one level, but there is a hidden message being conveyed (*see* Figure 2-18). It involves hidden messages between ego states that are different from the surface or apparent ones. For example, a salesman is talking to a customer saying, "This is our best model, but there are only two left." He may be telling the truth, but his Adult is talking not only to the Adult of the customer, he is also sending a secret message to the Child in the customer. That message is "You'd better grab it! You might miss out!" The Adult of the salesman politely directed himself to the Adult of the customer, but he hooked the Child by sending a secret

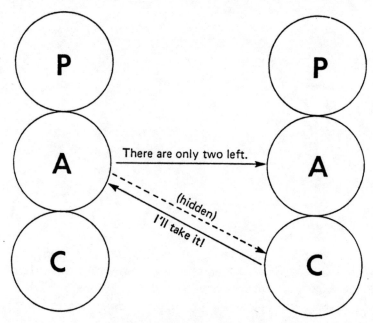

Figure 2-18. Ulterior transaction.

message so that he could quickly close the sale. The customer's Child answered to himself, "Gee, I might miss out," and aloud says to the salesman, "I'll take it!"

An ulterior transaction is dual in nature. It contains an implied message (the ulterior motive) at one level, disguised by a socially acceptable message sent at another level. Sarcasm and game playing are examples of this type of transaction. Another example of an ulterior transaction would be:

John: You really know what you're doing. This is an excellent report. I have to write one myself. I would like you to do it for me.

Mary: Here, let me help you with it. It's not that hard.

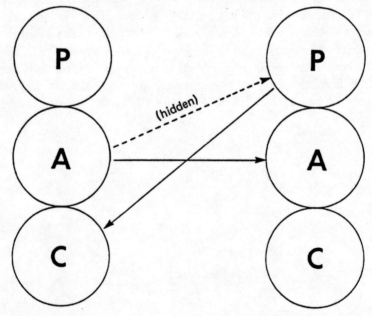

Figure 2-19.

Transactional analysis allows you to classify behaviors into simple categories so that interaction with others can be studied for desirable and undesirable patterns. Transactional analysis allows you to review and evaluate how well you and those with whom you interact are getting along. It provides a simple way of identifying differences in styles of communicating that might be sources of misunderstandings. Using the categories of behaviors associated with ego states, you may be able to make changes in how you communicate to increase the number of complementary transactions and reduce the number of crossed transactions. You will also be able to, with the analytical framework provided, be able to observe the behavior of others so that you might help them understand and change any behavior they may find undesirable.

In the following chapters we will discuss how to utilize what you have learned thus far in order to identify the many ways of expressing the behavior of the different ego states. Those persons who are not satisfied with their style of communicating may also learn how to change their current way of performing their job.

Think about some of the transactions you were involved in recently.

1. Were there any parallel transactions?
   How did you feel — OK or not OK?
2. Were there any crossed transactions?
   How did you feel — OK or not OK?
3. Were there any ulterior transactions?
   How did you feel — OK or not OK?

IDENTIFYING TRANSACTIONS

Analyze the following transactions. Which ego state is each coming from? What type of transaction is in progress?

Diagram these transactions by drawing an arrow from the correct ego state of the first person to an ego state of the second person. Then, draw a second arrow to indicate the response. Identify the type of transaction on the line provided. Note the following sample shown in Figure 2-20:

1. Potential Suicide: I want to die, leave me alone. Nobody understands me. Life's not fair. There's no hope.

   Operator: I understand, I care. Don't worry, I'll help you. We'll work this out together.

2. Burglary Victim: Could you please advise me on how to prevent this from happening again?

   Operator: Here is the telephone number of the crime prevention unit at the precinct. They will

Supervisor: What is your tour of duty for tomorrow?

Operator: I'm doing an 8 x 4 tomorrow.

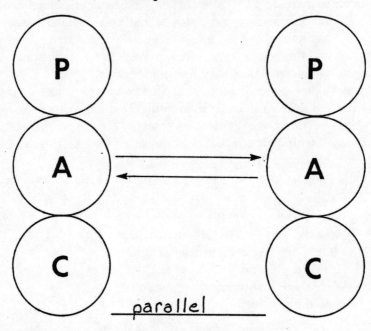

parallel

Figure 2-20.

advise you about security.

3. Operator: This is a safe neighborhood, but I'd be careful if I lived here.

Lady: Oh! That's interesting. (I'm afraid, maybe I'd better not move here.)

4. Operator: If you two don't stop arguing, I'm hanging up. Do you think I've got nothing to do better than to listen to you two argue?

Disputing Wife: So hang up, who cares? We don't need help anyway.

5. Woman: There's a man in my apartment; he has a gun, and he's threatening to kill my daughter. Please, help me. I'm scared.

Operator: Don't worry, I'll help you. Please calm down.

6. Tourist: Excuse me operator. Could you direct me to Second Avenue from where I am now?

Operator: You fool! This is not a tourist service. We handle only emergency calls!

7. Operator: If you don't stop acting that way I'm going to have you arrested for disorderly conduct.

Angry Caller: You can't tell me what to do! I'm a citizen, and I have my rights!

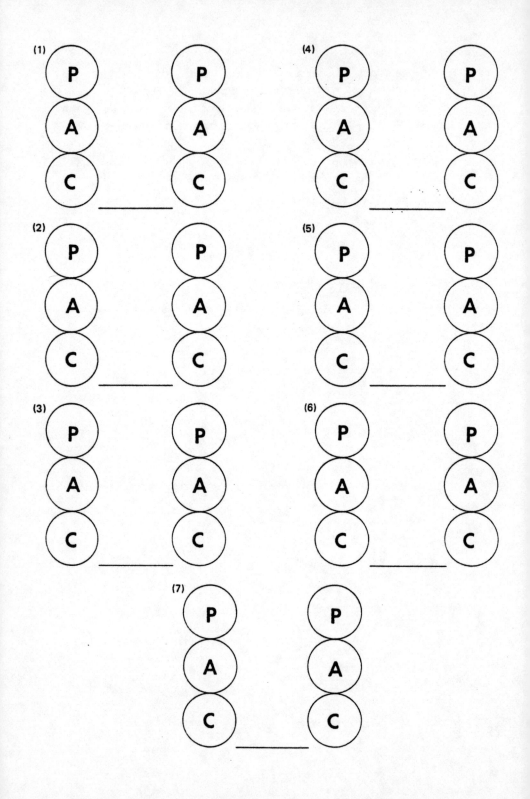

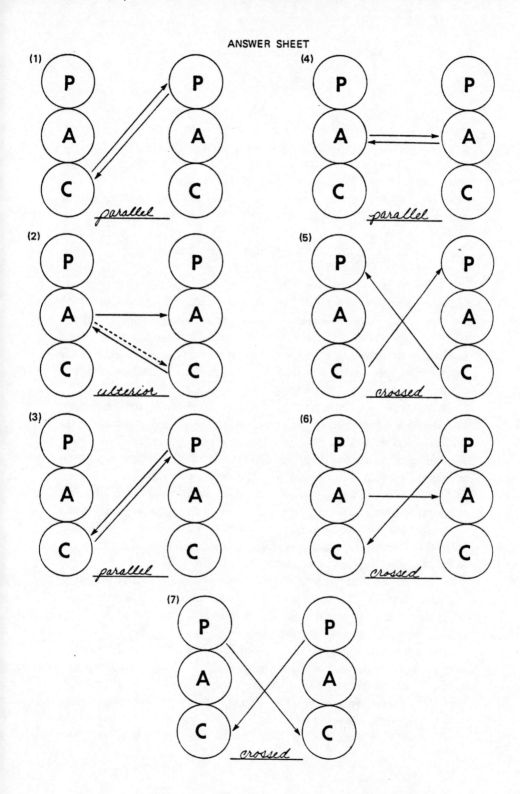

HOOKING

When a person speaks, that person is sending out a stimulus in order to hook a particular ego state in another person. When they get a response, they may or may not get the response that they initially set out to get. Depending on which ego state a person responds from, that transaction may be a smooth, complementary transaction or an aggravated, crossed transaction. Very simply, by using verbal statements (stimuli), a person can get us to react (respond) from any ego state that they desire, if we are unaware. By realizing this, we can stay in our *Adult* ego state and avoid unnecessary problems.

By the same token, we can use our Adult to hook the person, whom we are interacting with, from either their Parent or Child into the Adult ego state. Therefore, we might consider hooking to be a two fold operation: (1) how to hook, and (2) how to avoid being hooked. Consider the following: When you are confronted with a demanding, disagreeable caller, do you respond as a complaining Child, a stern, scolding Parent, or a calm, alert Adult?

When you need information quickly in an emergency situation and the individual with the information is in a scared Child state, do you respond as a demanding Critical Parent, an angry Child, or a Nurturing Parent who comforts the individual allowing him to ventilate and therefore hook him into the Adult ego state?

T.A. can help us to not become emotionally upset or hooked by an antagonist if at the onset we understand the psychological aspects of a transaction. Remember, the purpose of T.A. is to help you smoothly complete potentially difficult human transactions through swift identification and control of the situation.

You can see that the utilizing T.A. you have options in responding to a stimulus. While others around us are responding emotionally to stimulus and often without provocation, you can select to remain unemotional and in control.

Thus far, you have learned to identify where the stimulus is coming from and how to respond wisely. Making a wise response can cool off potentially dangerous or highly emotional human interactions. The question you must resolve is: Which is the best ego state to remain in and for what situation? Is there one best ego state to use in your work? How often do we want to come at someone from our

Parent and Child ego states? Is it more effective for us to act from our Parent? If we come from our Parent ego state what ego state are we trying to hook in the other person? If we choose to act in order to hook the other persons Child ego state, we must first ask ourselves, "Why is this the best way to deal with this situation?" Generally, what is the best ego state for us to be in as operators?

It is in this process of analyzing, identifying, and separating the three sets of data that we begin to make sense out of our behavior and feelings. Once separated, the three bodies of data and behavior can be examined by the Adult ego state to see what is valid or useful and what is not useful. The goal is not to do away with the Parent and Child ego states but to be able to free the Adult to examine these data. We cannot erase the Parent and Child recordings that are an integral part of us. We must be sensitive to them, but we can change from the Parent and Child ego states if we want to. We can choose to turn them off when they are inappropriate to the situation in which we are involved. By analyzing your own actions and responses, and by recognizing your own Parent and Child, you can switch into your Adult at will. The Adult can also recognize the Child responses and can choose not to respond in the same way. For example, when faced with a stimulus that would normally trigger your Critical Parent response, if you recognize your own tendency to respond that way, you have the option to change and respond as an Adult. Analyzing one's own ego state and switching to the Adult for more satisfactory problem solving is a professional approach to human relations.

By now you have probably realized, in thinking about your relations with the public, that *most* operator/caller contacts involve either the Child or Parent ego states. Because your job is basically involved with dealing with other human beings, and because of the complexities of each individual's personality, it would probably be best in most situations to stay in the Adult ego state. We would be able to then analyze the situations in which we are involved, select the appropriate ego state for the situation, and, when responding to problem stimuli, respond swiftly and wisely. As professional human relations specialists, one of our responsibilities is to keep our own intellect and emotions in good order, so that we may handle other people's problems. By maintaining our Adult ego state we can do it.

As operators, then, in the majority of situations in which we are involved, the Adult appears to be an advantage for us. While you are in your Adult you can think, speak, and act clearly; without emotion, you can control the situation. In addition, you are less sarcastic and abusive to others because of the lack of emotion in the Adult and, generally, less reactionary over minor abuses aimed at you. By staying in your Adult you will be able to observe the situation, not react according to other people's expectations, and remain calm, cool, and *in control*. You will be able to avoid being hooked and controlled by any and all antagonists. The least anxiety-causing ego state, of course, is our Adult. In it's rational, reasonable approach to confrontation, it gives you the ability to make objective decisions.

It is important to note that in staying in our Adult ego state we will be able to hook the Adult in others. In interviewing a complainant, or just getting information, you can understand how important it is to hook the computer in others.

On the following pages you will learn the ways that some people deal with operators intentionally in an antagonistic way and how they plan their strategy in order to control an operator by hooking him into behaving the way they want him to. We will discuss how to recognize when you are being hooked, how to avoid being hooked, how to hook the Adult in others, and situations in which it would be advisable to hook the Adult in others.

How Do You Know You're Being Hooked

Since the Parent and Child ego states develop first, and since they are the emotional states, they are very easy to hook. Aroused feelings are a clue that the Child or Parent has been hooked. The Child and Parent act immediately and impulsively to stimuli. They want immediate results. It is a reflective response, the "gut reaction" you feel when your feelings have been aroused.

The Adult in us can understand that patience, and time will take care of everything, but unfortunately the Child and Parent doesn't understand this. Therefore, these ego states jump to conclusions and want to act immediately. This makes them easy to hook in interactions with others. It is important to remember: (1) when the Parent in others is critical of *you*, they're trying to hook your Child; and (2) when the Parent in others is critical of *things*, they're trying to hook your Parent.

"What are you, stupid or something? I gave you that address already!"

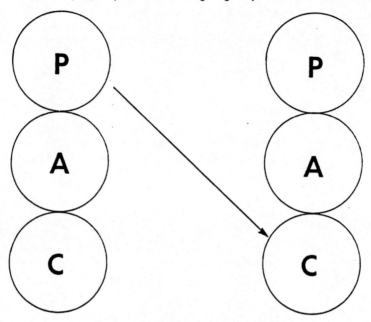

Figure 2-21. Hooking the Child.

"Why don't all of these people stop bothering us. Don't they know that there is nothing gained by complaining to us?"

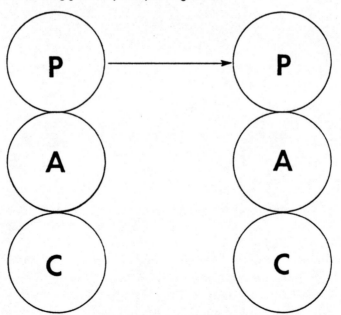

Figure 2-22. Hooking the Parent

Consider these remarks directed towards you from angry and abusive callers.

Analyzing the kind of transaction you are involved in, the ego states involved, and the presence or absence of aroused feelings in you will help you realize the kind of response to make. For example, a person coming on to you from an Adapted Child position saying, "I'm helpless," is looking to hook your Parent, either Controlling or Nurturing, and to elicit responses from these states (*see* Figure 2-23).

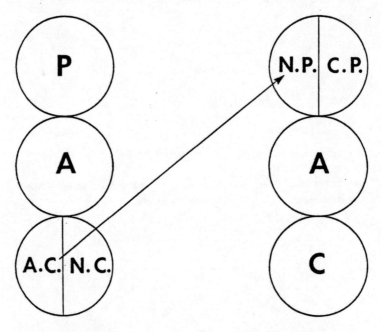

Figure 2-23. Adapted Child-Nurturant Parent hook.

How you respond to other people also provides clues to help identify ego states. For example:

1. If you are aware that you want to have fun with someone, he is probably in his Natural Child ego state and is hooking your Natural Child.
2. If you are inclined to respond from your own Adapted Child, the other person is probably in his Parent ego state and is hooking your Adapted Child.
3. If you respond to another person with fact and information,

that person is most likely in his Adult ego state and has hooked your Adult. Considering some common operator/caller encounters will help make this clearer. First, lets consider the hostile, abusive caller.

HOW TO AVOID BEING HOOKED

The Hostile, Abusive Caller

The emergency operator often finds himself as the unenviable middleman caught between the caller and the particular service agency being represented. This is a difficult position for the operator to be in. Conflicts between opposing views, demands, and attitudes of those seeking help, and the agency offering help, cause widened psychological distance and heightened emotions. The behavior that results from the excitement, and the specific emotions accompanying it, spreads quickly and is often directed at the operator.

Some callers, because of the fact that they are anonymous, may take advantage of the increased sense of power and anonymity to do things they wouldn't ordinarily do in other circumstances. A caller may (by taunts, obscenities, challenges and degradation) attempt to hook the operator into overreacting and, therefore, displaying unprofessional behavior. The hope is that the operator will become angry and that he will follow an unprofessional course of action. In attempting to hook operator into his Critical Parent ego state, the caller hopes that the operator will retaliate with the use of excessive anger and criticism.

The following is a list of some problem stimuli the operator is likely to encounter from hostile callers, which is designed to evoke a response from the operator. Analyze each statement, and determine which ego state each statement is coming from. Where would you come from in response?

1. You jerk, I called fifteen minutes ago! You must be a real incompetent fool!
2. You operators can't be too bright, otherwise you wouldn't be working as operators!
3. Boy! That's what I call typical dumb operator mentality! You don't even answer me when I talk to you!
4. I gave you that name three times already! What the hell's the matter with you?

5. You damn operators! You sit on your butt and take two calls a day and even that you can't handle!

If these statements were directed at you, how would you feel? If you felt angry about the statements and felt a reaction to them, where did that reaction come from? Were they automatic, immediate responses from the Child or Parent, or were they from an objective evaluation of the situation? How would you respond to these statements?

In each meeting with another person there is a constant adaptation to the moves of the other person. Each person reacts to the other person's stimulus. The person who knows what is happening and has analyzed the situation and the interaction has a decided advantage. He is in the position to control how he acts.

Antagonists plan their tactics in order to control an operator by hooking him into behaving the way they want him to behave. By getting an operator to act the way they want him to, they are relying on knowing how people react in certain situations. The professional operator always plans to stay in control. He wants to stay calm, cool, collected, and able to stick to his objective of gathering information and rendering service. *He plans to avoid being hooked and controlled by an antagonist.*

Reflexive responses from the Child or Parent can get an operator needlessly involved in conflicting situations. These responses are not based on an objective Adult analysis of the situation. They are not good habits. The emotions tied to them may cause a response that may interfere with your objectives. Every situation we are involved in is unique. We have to rely on past experiences to some degree, but don't forget that responses used in the past may be inappropriate for the present situation. Remaining calm in the face of provocation is difficult, but the ability to make reasonable objective decisions requires that the Adult ego state be utilized.

MAINTAINING YOUR ADULT

In order to maintain your Adult it is necessary to use your Adult to think so that you might plan a wise response. When you discover a crossed transaction occurring, use your Adult ego state to resist reacting from your Child or Parent, therefore avoiding attempts to respond in ways with the expectations of the other person.

Since the Adult develops later than the Parent and Child ego states, our tendency is to respond from the more emotional Parent and Child, rather than the thought-out, reasonable Adult. As has been noted already, aroused feelings are a clue that the Parent or Child ego states have been hooked. Therefore, in order to be able to stay in one's Adult, it would be absolutely necessary to be aware of your own Parent and Child responses. What is the signal that your body gives you at the instant your emotions are aroused? Clue into them. It could be one of many responses. It could be a sinking sensation in the pit of your stomach, sweaty palms, gritting your teeth, a notable increase in your heart rate, a feeling of anger, a flash of heat rising in your body, or clenched fists. These are only some of the many responses that the body has when emotions are hooked. How does your body respond?

This is the first requirement for Adult data processing — to be aware of what is happening within your own body. This awareness of what is happening in your body will keep you from externalizing these feelings into action.

By taking time to process this information quickly, and by analyzing what is happening in the transaction, you will gain control of yourself and the situation and maintain control of the transaction.

The following is the most effective way of dealing with a situation when you realize your emotions have been aroused:

1. *Take a moment to survey the situation.* What is going on? Why are your emotions aroused? Ask yourself, "What did someone just do or say to hook me?"

2. *Hold back on any instantaneous responses until you have analyzed the situation.* The operator has an official status that demands a certain kind of conduct. In restraining the automatic, archaic responses of the Parent and Child, you will give the Adult enough time to compute an appropriate response. In order for this to occur, though, there must be a data bank of planned Adult responses in the computer to draw upon. It would be helpful, therefore, if you program into your Adult computer some responses that would be appropriate to call upon in the event that your Parent or Child is hooked. In this way the Adult will work faster and more effectively.

3. *Some of the questions you might ask yourself are: Is this true? Does it apply? Is it appropriate? Where did I get that idea? What is the evidence? What is important here?* The more familiar you become

with your own Parent and Child responses, the easier it will be for you to recognize when these ego states are hooked. The Adult is prepared to take over transactions with a question, such as "What is important here?", if only it is given an opportunity.

One way to practice identifying the Parent and Child is to monitor your internal dialogue. When you are feeling blue, disappointed, sad, happy, or demanding you can ask yourself, "Why am I feeling this way?" and "What ego state am I in now?" As you get in touch with your own various responses you will be able to recognize your own Parent and Child ego states. You will be doing this with your own Adult, because, by the very process of questioning, you have switched into the Adult. One is able to feel immediate relief in a stressful situation simply by asking, "Who's coming on?"

The Adult can then establish new options to situations based on a more thorough examination of *what is going on*. The Adult can consciously commit itself to the position that Child and Parent responses would not be suitable to some situations and can, in fact, escalate some situations beyond what is necessary.

In summary, a strong Adult is built in the following ways:

1. Clue into the emotional responses of your body. How are your emotions felt and expressed?
2. Get in touch with your Child and Parent. Learn to recognize your Child, its vulnerabilities, its fears, and its principal ways of expressing these feelings.
3. Learn to recognize your Parent, its admonitions, its fixed positions, and principal ways of expressing these admonitions and positions.
4. Give your Adult time to process the data coming into the computer and to sort out Parent and Child from reality. Learn to make "computer time" for your Adult. Give your Adult a chance to operate.

HOOKING A CALLER'S ADULT

In most operator/caller interactions, the transaction is usually initiated by someone who is seeking intervention of some sort. Interviewing a complaintant, investigating a complaint, or speaking to the caller, the operator's main objective is to gather information so that their response will be realistically aligned to the caller's needs. The transaction usually opens with an Adult stimulus from the operator, because the operator needs to assess the complaint while in the Adult ego state. The Adult ego state is of an objective nature.

In previous examples we have used, we have been analyzing which ego state others were coming from in order that you might plan a wise response. We will now analyze situations in which the operator will come from his Adult in initiating interactions with others. This will be the Adult stimulus instead of the Adult response. The stimulus should be of such a nature that it will tend to call upon the other person to come from his Adult in response to you.

Generally, Adult statements are intended for the receiver's Adult. By hooking the other person's Adult, you will get the information you need. You want to hook the Adult instead of the Parent or Child, which can only cause trouble and stress because of the emotion involved. However, if Adult stimulus is received by the Parent or Child, an unexpected and inappropriate response results in a crossed transaction, and effective communication is not possible. Therefore, it is essential to hook the Adult and maintain the Adult in this type of transaction.

INTERVIEWING WITH T.A.

During the interview situation, for example, the operator must be particularly sensitive to the respondent's existing ego state. As we have already stated, victims of crisis may exhibit any type of behavior. They may be composed, matter-of-fact, and totally cooperative, while others may be distraught, disorganized, or even hysterical. The operator will be required to employ a variety of interview techniques depending on the ego state being demonstrated by the victim. The ego state being demonstrated could be either Critical Parent or Adapted Child depending upon the impact of the crime upon the individual victim. This may present a barrier to communication for the operator who is not aware of the ego states, crisis behavior, and victimology.

What the operator needs to be cognizant of is *how to interview a caller under conditions in which the caller's emotional, physical, and psychological abilities have been impaired*. One of the quickest ways to assess these conditions and arrive at a working knowledge of how to respond would be to visualize the following four behavioral categories. These behavioral categories are observable both visually and auditory. These four categories are: verbal expression, decision-making abilities, physical movement, and display of confidence. Chapter 3 has a detailed explanation of the behavior displayed in these categories, and suggested, appropriate responses are offered that incorporate the concept of transactional analysis in a more behavior-oriented manner.

Chapter 3

COMMUNICATING WITH THE VICTIM

VICTIMOLOGY

VICTIMOLOGY is an area of crisis behavior and intervention that takes a closer look at the victim. Actually, *victimology is the study of the victim*. Literature on violent crime in the past has generally focused on the criminal or the criminal act. It has only been in recent years that the third element in violent crime (i.e. the victim) has attracted professional interest. However, even these studies have dealt solely from the perspective of the study of victim behavior, which they have called victimology, but which has examined victim-stimulated or victim-precipitated crimes.

Unfortunately, this tendency of crime investigators to assign responsibility for criminal acts to the victim has merely reinforced previously held and assumed similar beliefs and rationalizations held by most criminals themselves, i.e. "They asked for it." The purpose of this section is to share an understanding of the innocent or accidential nature of the victim's involvement in violent crimes perpetrated against them.

Early in the research of the study of victims of violent crimes it became apparent that society had some strange attitudes towards victims. There seemed to be a marked reluctance to accept the innocence or accidental nature of the victim's behavior previous to the crime being committed against them and after the crime was committed against them. This reluctance was demonstrated by the community responses, police behavior, family reactions to the victim and, surprisingly, by the victims themselves. This reluctance or resistance to accept or believe in the total innocence of the victims of violent crime is shown by the early responses of others to the victim after the initial shock responses of the non-victim observer was dissipated.

The last decade has produced major improvements in our systems for protecting the rights of the accused, providing humane

111

treatment to the convicted, and delivering services to the ex-offender. But what about the victim of crime? While the plight of rape victims and battered wives has received increased attention, what is often forgotten is the suffering that every crime victim endures as a result of the crime, whether it be a purse snatching or an assault. Proponents of victim services point to the disproportionate amounts that are expended on offenders to provide them with transportation, room and board, medical services, legal counsel, and treatment programs ranging from mental health counseling to job placement. Victims, however, must foot the bills for any similar services they might require as a result of their victimization. Moreover, it is the young and the elderly, who are often poor and uneducated, who are most frequently victimized yet least able to cope with the consequences, financially and emotionally.

If the offender is apprehended, the victim as a witness becomes vulnerable to further inconveniences and distress. Victims tend to perceive themselves as "pieces of evidence" within the criminal justice system. If they choose to prosecute they must be questioned, often repeatedly, and must sacrifice work days and secure transportation or child care for seemingly endless court appearances, many of which may be postponed or cancelled with no advance notice. Decisions are made with little or no explanation. Their recovered stolen property needed as evidence may remain lost to them.

The non-victim listener of the victim's story, whether it be police, friends, or family, is in most cases entirely unaware of the psychological trauma that is being experienced by the victim. This psychological trauma may include the loss of power, the loss of dignity, and the loss of security. To the individual in his *normal* routine, these three characteristics function in such a way that they give the individual the ability to communicate verbally, the competence to make decisions properly, and the ability to move about with a sense of confidence and safety. However, to the victim of a crime, the loss of these characteristics impairs their behavior to such a great extent that they are unable to function in their usual way.

The operator should be aware that the impairment of these characteristics greatly affects the victim's ability to communicate when they call for assistance. For example, the victim may have different psychological needs depending on the stage of the victimology that he may be in at the time of the call. The operator then can adjust his mode of communication accordingly in such a way so as to employ the appropriate language that serves as a stabilizing factor for the regressing victim.

The suddenness and shock of becoming a victim interrupts normal daily functions, and it impairs those human qualities that permit a person to function normally. Therefore, one might say that person is experiencing a crisis. To differentiate further, victimology is the study of the regressive mental process that the victim goes through; crisis behavior is the behavior that results from regression. There is an unconscious response that attempts to overcome the effects of the crisis, and this unconscious response usually expresses itself with unique forms of behavior in order to restabilize or prevent a continuing regression.

This chapter, therefore, will focus on the emotional and psychological profile of the stages that the victim will pass through. Chapter 4 on "Crisis Behavior and Intervention" will focus on that behavior displayed by the victim during each of the stages of a crisis event.

The following flow chart depicts the effects of a crisis event and the process by which the victim is assisted back to normal behavior by the person intervening.

DYNAMICS OF VICTIMIZATION

The preceding description of the psychological responses of the victim to a sudden and unexpected loss is easily recognizable as the same phases seen in depression. This concept is of clinical value in the psychological treatment of victims. What has the victim of a crime lost? It is more than just the loss of money and the loss of physical functioning. They have lost the feeling of individual invulnerability. They have lost their trust in society on which they have depended on to protect them from harm. Many of the victims have lost their self-respect and feel shameful when they think about their need for compliant behavior with the criminal. Many of the victims also feel anger at having gained the unenviable status of suddenly becoming a victim.

STAGES OF VICTIMOLOGY

Victims tend to go through four major stages in reaction to their

VICTIMOLOGY FLOW CHART

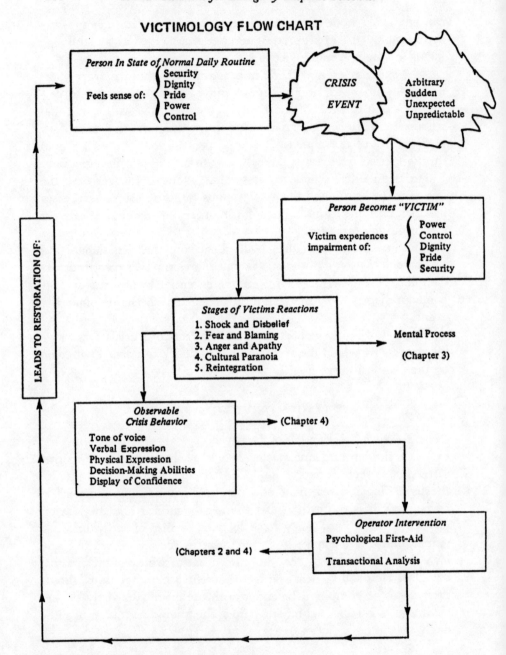

victimization. These four stages are:

1. Shock, disbelief and denial
2. Fright and blaming

3. Anger and apathy
4. Resignation, resolution, and integration

Continuing research with victims of criminal violence supports the notion that the general reactions of victims are similar to the psychological responses of individuals who have experienced sudden and unexpected losses. Loss of any kind, particularly of sudden and unexpected, produces this sequence of response in all individuals.

The first phase of the victim's reactive behavior is shock, disbelief and denial. When the victim's attempts at denial fail, he then becomes frightened and seeks to place blame for what has happened to him. This stage of fright usually is accompanied by clinging behavior. Very frequently the individual finds himself compulsively talking and obsessively ruminating about the event. This stage is followed by anger or apathy, with periods of recrimination and inner-directed rage. There are occasional outbursts of outer-directed resentment and anger to individuals associated to the event or not associated to the crime. The next stage of cultural paranoia finds the victim making adjustments in his environment in order to reassure himself that the crime will not happen again to them. Finally, the stages of resignation, resolution, and integration will occur with either replacement or restoration of the lost object and/or acceptance of the crime perpetrated against the victim. Now, let us consider the stages of victimology as the victim reacts to the crime, during the crime, and after the crime has occurred.

VICTIM'S REACTIONS

Victim's Behavior During the Crime

It is important to note at this point that the victim can move through the five stages during the crime as well as after the crime is committed against them. Whenever one is subject to a sudden, unexpected attack of violence there is the initial response of shock, numbness, and disbelief. When this initial response subsides, depending upon the individual involved, there will follow either fright or anger. For example, in a street crime, where the victim is thrown to the ground, a purse or wallet is taken, and with the criminal running away, the response of fright or anger will ensue without the criminal being present and will follow through with the other stages of victimology after the event. However, in many street crimes the psychological response of fright or anger arises in the victim with the criminal still present and threatening the victim with bodily harm if the victim doesn't comply. These types of crimes usually involve rape, sexual crimes, kidnapping, hostage taking as well as robbery. It is in this type of crime, in which the criminal is still present, that psychological repercussions long after the criminal act is committed are more likely to result.

In these types of crimes the response of victims is usually a frozen, frightened reaction. The reaction of fear is so profound and overwhelming that the victim feels hopeless about getting away. All hope of survival is dependent on appeasing the criminal. Though this behavior is deeply rooted in profound fright, it is confusing both to the victim and the criminal. After the crime, while the victim is reviewing his behavior under more peaceful conditions, the victim will underplay the ingratiating aspect of the way he behaved under stress, because he is ashamed of it. This shame is the basis of his feelings of guilt that will affect the victim. The appeasing, ingratiating complaint behavior of a victim of violence during the phase of frozen fright often leads others to the false conclusion that the victim produced or participated in the criminal act.

On the other hand, there are some individuals whose response to sudden, unexpected criminal violence is not frozen fright but anger directed at the criminal. Even though their behavior was rooted in profound fright, the victims will recall only being extremely angry at what was happening to them. They recall saying to the criminal, "Get the hell out of here!" "What do you think you're doing?" "Leave me alone or I'll call the police."

Some victims have even attacked the criminal with their hands or thrown things at them. The results of this behavior depended on the circumstances and the mental stability of the criminal. While some criminals have backed down and even run away, more often than not the criminal will feel frustrated and angry, which will result in a violent attack on the victim in an attempt to beat them into submission and compliancy. One woman said to a criminal with a revolver, who was robbing her store, "I'll never forget your face." He then shot her in the head, which caused her to go blind.

Victim responses to sudden, unexpected, and violent aggression, then, may range from frozen, frightened responses to action-oriented, fighting-back behavior. In any case, in the post-acute phase, the dramatic events of the crime are continually replayed by the victim. Those victims who fought back and were not hurt seem to have a minimum amount of psychological trauma. They felt exhilarated and potent. Those who fought back and were hurt still felt supported by society and easily found sympathetic responses. However, some had felt annoyed by the reactions of the police. They felt the police were defensive, and their comments took the approach of "You didn't let me do the job" or "Next time, you'll let the police protect you."

In general, victims who fought back seem to have greater social acceptance than the victims who have followed society's rules and have complied with the criminal. This double-bind attitude of society is strikingly evident towards victims of rape, in particular.

Victim's Behavior After the Crime

Stage 1: Shock, Disbelief, and Denial

As we have stated previously, whenever one is subject to a sudden, unexpected attack of violence there is the initial response of shock, numbness, disbelief, and then denial. The victim will freeze up, judgment and thinking may be suspended, and motor ability may be impaired. The victim may say, "I don't believe this!" "I don't know what happened," "I feel so numb." Or the victim may not be able to even articulate what has just happened to them.

Denial is a psychological defense mechanism. It is an involuntary process by which the mind tries to blot out the pain of a reality with which the individual cannot cope. In layman's language it means refusing to face facts. When people are first confronted with a crime committed to them they often refuse to believe that it has occurred. The victim of an auto theft may walk all over a parking lot looking for his car, thinking that he has somehow misplaced or forgotten where he parked his car, before he is ready to admit that it has been stolen. Victims of a burglary coming home to a home in disarray will sometimes firmly believe that someone is playing a joke on them. Victims of rape will report afterwards that during the crime they repeated said, "This can't be happening," and other victims of any type of crime will often say, "I still can't believe that this has happened." This statement is more than just a comment in passing. The victims literally cannot comprehend what has happened to them.

A variation on the defense of denial is *intellectualization.* In this type of response, the victim admits what has happened to them but does not allow an emotional reaction to occur. Such victims will be matter of fact and controlled in their discussion of the crime committed against them. They behave as if the experience has made no impression on them. This involuntary process is a way of coping with the event by dealing with it only at the intellectual level. They are denying the emotional impact that they have experienced and are attempting to control the situation by being rational and self-controlled while talking about it.

Victims of rape and other highly emotionally charged crimes may at times be strongly intellectual in their reactions. They usually take time to "get themselves under control" before calling the police and then describe the details in a flat, emotionless, and well-organized fashion. These defenses are often fragile and easily permeated by a kind word or expressions of sympathy, which will often initiate an emotional breakdown and release of emotions by the victim.

Stage 2: Fright and Blaming

For some individuals, in particular, conforming and dependent people, there may be a prolonging of one or more stages of the victims reactions. For example, some victims remain for months in the stage of fright, with clinging behavior as a result. Extra locks, extra precautions, and excessive suspiciousness are substituted for judgment. The victim will cling to their families and obsessively ruminate about what has happened to them. Compulsive talking may be one of the expressions of this stage. The victim's family will begin to feel after a while that this compulsive talking is not a good idea and will therefore encourage the victim to be silent and not relive the scene over and again. This mistaken concept of protective silence, however, may prolong the depressive reaction of victims.

In this stage of fright some victims report persistent, recurrent fantasies or dreams that have a similar theme. The most frequent theme is that the crimminal will come back and either kill them or injure them more seriously. At other times, the victim may have a fleeting but recurrent thought of killing the criminal, but this thought is completely submerged by a counterthought of "What if I fail, or I succeed and kill him? His family or his friends will try to get revenge in return."

Blaming means more than assigning responsibility when something goes wrong: it implies punishing the responsible party. We learn in our society, however, to equate the two, so that to be responsible means to be blamed. We frequently believe that we will be punished after harm befalls us, if even partial responsibility can be placed upon us. To avoid punishment or scolding, many people will place complete responsibility on others when something goes wrong. The blaming process will be demonstrated in statements such as, "What did you do to deserve it?" A victim of a burglary may be told, "You should have taken better care of your belongings!"

Crime victims reflect this fear of being blamed by going out of their way to blame someone else and to deny that they were anything but completely innocent victims. This desire to avoid blame and to place it somewhere leads to some predictable results. Blame is sometimes focused on particular people who are disliked by the victim or whom the victim fears. "Those people down the street," "Some guy who was hanging around here," and "Those new people who moved in" often become the target of accusations.

The police and the police emergency operator may often become the target for the blame and are often blamed for the crime being committed against the victim. "This is what I pay you to prevent," "Where were you when I needed you?" "You damned cops! I was just robbed down the block, and you guys are standing here talking" are all statements and accusations that have been expressed towards the police. This behavior is simply an example of the old maxim that the best defense is a good offense. The victim tries to avoid blame by placing it on the guardian who failed.

Stage 3: Anger or Apathy

Anger follows from blame. Once the guilty party has been identified, it is legitimate to direct anger at him. However, there are many barriers to doing this. Helping the victim direct anger appropriately and to overcome these barriers is a valuable part of "psychological first aid," which we will cover in Chapter 4, and also often helps increase the victim's cooperation.

What are these barriers? One is that the selection of targets is limited and none are without repercussions, at least from the victim's helpless perspective. One obvious target, as discussed above, is the *self*. Anger turned against the self is manifested as depression. The self-berating and self-accusing victim has turned the anger against the self and is punishing the self.

Another target is the *criminal*. Yet, to the victim, the criminal is a dangerous person toward whom to display anger. The criminal has placed the victim in great danger and has exhibited the power to destroy the victim. To display anger against him is to invite even more punishment. Consequently, victims are often hesitant to voice their anger directly against the criminal. This is especially true when there has been a personal contact, as in armed robbery or rape. Rape victims are often remarkably "understanding" and protective of the rapist and hesitate to prosecute because, "He is a sick man and shouldn't be punished because he is sick." Such a statement may be taken as an index of the fear that the victim has experienced.

Because of these barriers, the victim often expresses generalized anger or focuses on a vaguely defined group or the responding police operator or officer, as discussed above. Police officers and emergency operators, who understand the forces that push the victim to express anger in this fashion, can be very helpful by letting the victim ventilate and by then helping the victim direct it at the criminal. This can be very difficult to do, but serves as a good service to the victim. The operator must certainly avoid becoming defensive and engaging the victim in an argument to prove that it was not his fault at all.

Some victims have a prolonged period of apathy with inner- and outer-directed rage. The victim may become angry at the criminal justice system (police, courts, etc.), the assailant, society, and at himself. After these feelings of anger, the victim starts to feel that nobody cares or can do anything about their predicament. The loss of feelings of invulnerability — the disillusionment in society's ability to protect the individual from harm — quite often intensifies his feelings of resentment and anger and will move on to feelings of apathy. Commonly heard expressions in this stage are "The hell with people, who needs them," "You have to look out for yourself," "People are animals," "The world is a jungle," and "No one gives a damn." A female victim expressed her thoughts in the following manner: "What hurt me the most was the complete indifference and lack of consideration for my feelings in my hour of need by people I know and work with. Who cares? Nobody. Nobody is going to do anything about it anyway!"

Stage 4: Resignation, Resolution, and Integration

During the final stage of victimology there is a calm acceptance by the victim of the misfortune that has befallen them. That is, the victim resigns himself to what has happened. There then follows a resolution — the solving of the problem — where the victim slowly begins to reintegrate his life in an attempt to attain his position previous to the criminal act. The victim will, during this period, gather all the parts of his life that have been scattered because of the crisis event and bring them together to make his life whole and solid again.

The emergency operator plays a very important role in helping crime victims begin to recover from the psychological shock that they have experienced. Victims need help to face the facts, to place blame where it belongs, and to direct anger appropriately. They also need the information and psychological support that an emergency operator can supply to help them develop secure expectations about the future. They need help to regain their feelings of self-respect and control over their environment.

Knowledge of these facts do not tell operators what to do with any particular victim. However, they do give them some ideas about what to expect from victims, and they give them a framework within which to develop behavioral goals. Techniques for achieving these goals will be discussed in detail in the latter part of Chapter 4 in the section on "Psychological First Aid." Prior to discussing these techniques, however, further elements affecting the degree of trauma experienced by the victim will be covered such as the type of offense committed against the victim and the community's response to the victim.

ELEMENTS AFFECTING THE DEGREE OF TRAUMA

The following examples of crimes are incidents that intiate crisis behavior on the part of the victim. Because of the varying degree of stress precipitated by the different types of incidents, the intensity of the trauma will vary from incident to incident. However, even though the intensity of the traumatic experience varies from incident to incident, and from person to person, each of these incidents will influence the full range of crisis behavior, thereby affecting the victim's ability to communicate, their ability to make decisions, their motor abilities, and, consequently, in varying degrees, his perception of his own self-confidence.

Different types of offenses perpetrated against a victim precipitate varying degrees of psychological trauma. The degree by which the victim is affected depends on many factors. However, one observable factor is the amount of aggressiveness perpetrated against the victim by the assailant. For example:

BURGLARY: In the crime of burglary, not only is property taken, but an extension of the victim's self is violated.

ROBBERY: In the crime of robbery, an extension of one's self is removed from the person, therefore, a loss of autonomy is experienced by the victim.

ASSAULT AND ROBBERY: In the crimes of assault and robbery, not only is an extension of one's self removed from the victim, causing a loss of autonomy, but also there is injury to the external self.

RAPE AND SEXUAL ASSAULT: In the crimes of rape and sexual assault, an extension of one's self is violated, i.e. removal of clothing or the soiling of clothing, causing a loss of autonomy, plus the injury to one's external self, plus injury to the internal self. Recent research in this area has indicated that this type of crime has little to do with sexual gratification; that in reality the intent here is to hurt or destroy, with intense anger being the motivator.

HOMICIDE: In the crime of homicide, all of the above is destroyed. In this situation, family and friends of the victim are the persons in the crisis state.

Victims of Property Crimes

In order to appreciate the experience of being the victim of a property crime (e.g. a larceny from a dwelling), we must be aware of the importance of the home as a symbol. In an important sense, the home is an extension of the self. Similarly, but to a lesser degree, one might feel that one's car is a symbolic extension of one's self also. When this type of "sanctuary" is invaded by an "evil force" it is not uncommon that the victim will feel emotionally violated himself.

It is not uncommon to find much unnecessary destruction and degradation at the scene of a burglary. The criminals will enter, destroy things, kill pets, and even defecate on the kitchen table, all in an effort to gain power at the expense of the victim. The victim of these acts feels the loss of power and control when they return home to a scene of this kind of devastation. Many people invest feelings of invulnerability in their homes; that is, they feel most secure and safe when they are at home. Therefore, when their security is invaded, there may be overwhelming feelings of vulnerability, loss of power and control, and loss of security and safety in their haven of warmth and safety from the outside world.

Property victims, particularly burglary victims, generally conform to the stages of victimology response pattern. The first reaction is "shock and denial." This reaction is manifested when many of the victims first return home and find a broken window or an open door. Objectively, one might expect someone coming home to such a situation to: (1) call the police; (2) wait for their arrival; and (3) wait until the police secure the dwelling before entering.

However, many burglary victims, in this stage of disbelief, will enter their dwellings immediately and not even bother to call the police first, in order to assure them that the criminal is still not there.

The victim's next response is fright and anger. Expressions of this fear will surface with such behavior as replacing locks with expensive new mechanisms, window gates, guard dogs, alarms, sleeping with the lights on, not sleeping at home, and finally, moving to a new home. In many cases, there is a fear that the intruder will return to harm them further. Although logically, and statistically, this will not happen, the fear is real and should not be scoffed at or treated lightly.

Of course, in most burglaries the criminal is not present when the victim returns, so this fright or anger cannot be directed at the proper target. We can expect that this anger at the criminal will build up and accumulate until it is triggered by someone or something entirely uninvolved with the incident. In an attempt to develop a rational explanation for having been victimized, people will blame others who might have inadvertently "facilitated" the crime. The facilitation could include such things as leaving a window open, not double-locking a door, not leaving a radio or light on, and so on. It is virtually impossible to live in a stressful environment such as a large city and maintain a level of alertness high enough to always remember to take every precautionary step available to prevent burglary. However, an explanation synonymous with blame must be found if one is operating under the traditional victim-precipitator concept of victimology.

It is not uncommon that blame and misplaced anger will be directed at the emergency operator. There may be a very subtle hostility detectable in the voice of the caller. If the operator accepts this as a personal criticism, the interaction will be strained and not at all beneficial for either of the parties involved.

The misconception of professionalism as meaning cold, unemotional, and therefore efficient is provocative to victims. Any ideas or suggestions for initial contact techniques must really center around attitude preparedness. If one can anticipate or predict the feelings and response of the victims, certain techniques will be apparent. These techniques will be discussed in the section on "Psychological First Aid" later on in Chapter 4.

Victims of Personal Property Crimes

One situation in which the emergency operator may have difficulty appreciating the kind of crisis a victim is experiencing occurs when the victims calls in to report financial loss or personal property damage, as opposed to physical injury. Why is this so? What factors could contribute to this lack of concern, understanding, and empathy on the operator's part? What would cause the operator to minimize the plight of the victim, while at the same time the victim is maximizing his plight?

Consider a situation in which a woman calls to report that she returned home after a week of vacation to find that her apartment has been burglarized. What factors are involved in the efforts of the emergency operator to minimize this situation, and how does the victim feel in reality?

From a human relations point of view the thing an operator has to be aware of in dealing with the victim of a property crime is insensitivity. This lack of feeling for the victim's plight is apt to happen for the following reasons. Several points are to be considered in this situation:

1. The emergency operator tends to minimize the loss incurred by the victim and to treat the matter lightly because:
   a. The operator will tend to perceive the monetary value of the property taken. He realizes what it would cost if it had to be bought again.
   b. The operator knows that there is only a very slim chance that the victim will ever get the property returned.
   c. Small property losses tend to pale in significance when compared to other crimes that the operator frequently encounters.
2. The victim on the other hand tends to maximize the loss incurred and, thus, treats the burglary very seriously. This occurs for at least three valid reasons:
   a. The monetary value of the property taken is only one aspect of the victim's plight. The property could be worth very little from the point of view of the cost of the item, but it could be priceless from a personal point of view. An item can have cherished memories for someone that can never be replaced. It could mean and often does mean that the victim will be inconvenienced by its loss, at least temporarily. All of these facts tend to raise an item's value as far as the victim is concerned.
   b. The victim does not know that there is very little chance of ever getting the property back. She expects to get help and expects results and cannot understand why the operator would treat her situation so lightly.
   c. The victim has only an abstract idea of similar crimes happening to others. All the victim can think of is that, "This happened to me, and it is the worst thing that has ever happened to me."

This situation is a perfect example of two individuals seeing the same incident from opposing points of view. The operator cannot understand why the victim is making such an awful fuss about some small items that were taken and would like to tell her about the auto accident that was just called in to her, in which five innocent people lost their lives in a head-on collision. Now, *that* would be something to be concerned about.

The victim, on the other hand, cannot understand why the operator is treating her loss so lightly: "Doesn't he realize that one of the items taken was a precious locket that has been passed down in the family for generations?"

The result of such a misunderstanding harms both the operator and the victim. The operator could become so annoyed by the victim's emotional state that he does very little to calm her or to reassure her other than simply take the required information. The victim could become so angry at the operator for apparently not caring that she may become embittered toward all operators, police, and the police department, in general.

The operator must then realize that if he is going to help this victim he must try to understand the situation as she sees it. He must treat the incident as seriously as the victim does. Although he realizes that there is little chance that the property will be found, he must reassure the victim that everything that could possibly be done will be done on her behalf.

Victims of Assault

The trauma that the assault victim experiences is far more devastating than the trauma experienced by victims of property crimes and, yet, is different from the trauma experienced by the rape victim. People who are most prone to becoming victims of assault are:

1. The young who are physically weaker and inexperienced.
2. Females, who are physically weakest.
3. The elderly. The aging human being is handicapped in many ways, i.e. physically, mentally, etc.
4. The mentally deficient and other mentally disturbed, the feeble-minded, the emotionally disturbed, the drug addict, and the alcoholic all form another large group of potential and actual victims of assault.

The assault victim is often referred to as a primary victim; that is, victims who may be directly assaulted and injured and who may have had property taken from them. The point of importance here is that face-to-face contact with the assailant is far more traumatic than when this contact is not made with the assailant.

The Victim's Face-to-Face Encounter with the Criminal

The face-to-face encounter is the most dreaded aspect from the point of view of most people. The offenses that are contained within this category of crimes are those that cause most people to fear victimization the most. In most instances, having all of one's valuables taken through a burglary may not be nearly as traumatic as having to confront a thief in a face-to-face encounter. The offenses within this category run the gamut from taking a victim's watch to taking his life. These are the crimes that the urban dweller fears most, because they impinge upon his privacy in a most personal way. The individual who walks down a street carries with him his "egocentric territory," and an infringement upon this personal space is analogous to trespassing on his property. The urban environment is at least partially characterized by fear of such infringement. We lock our doors, stay in after dark, and even in daylight we walk only on safe streets. After dark, the prudent man may be seen walking on the part of the sidewalk nearest the street, thus avoiding possible attack from the dark areas and alleys nearer the buildings.

Because face-to-face contact is so important, we have given it detailed attention. There are two considerations to be given to this type of criminal offense.

1. Given the fears of the general public, it is wise for the operator to be able to distinguish between the types of and frequency of actual physical contact. The operator may then be able to grasp more fully the interaction that has taken place between offender and victim.

2. The emergency operator should also be aware that the victim-offender, face-to-face contact depending on the situation is also qualitatively different. For example, a teller in a bank may be robbed in a face-to-face contact, but loses none of his personal belongings. This face-to-face contact would be qualitatively different, however, if the teller were injured during the robbery. In this case the physiological and psychological consequences would be far more devastating.

Victims of Rape

The psychological trauma experienced by the rape victim is

perhaps the most serious of all cases of victimization short of murder. Enough cannot be said about how vulnerable the rape victim feels after having personal space violated to the limit. This trauma may leave the victim in a state of disorientation. Consequently, the behavior displayed by the victim may be counterproductive to overcoming the traumatic experience. Though this may be the case, it is a desperate attempt to overcome the trauma.

The operator should be aware that Stage 1: Shock and Disbelief, in this case, may remain for a couple of days or even more. The shock and disbelief of having been violated to this degree is far more devastating; therefore, it may take the victim a couple of days or longer to become angry enough (next stage) or get enough nerve to report the incident. Or a person raped may remain in the presence of the attacker for a day or two because of the clinging effect, which is part of the next stage.

The dilemma of whether to report a rape is faced by thousands of rape victims. For many the answer is no. Although regrettable, the response is understandable. The rape victim has long been the victim of the popular but false belief that "she asked for it." Police, prosecutors, and medical examiners have been accused by many rape victims of insensitive and unsympathetic behavior. Social service agencies are often ill-equipped to deal with the rape victim's special needs.

And so a pattern has emerged: the lack of support from the community, and the low priority given rape cases by police and prosecutors, alienate victims and discourage many from even reporting assaults. Those victims who persevered to the trial stage have found themselves "put on trial," as defense attorneys grilled them about their own sexual histories. It's not surprising that actual rapes far exceed the number reported to police. Nor is it any wonder that many women who do report later refuse to prosecute.

The irony of the situation is that when rape victims, police, prosecutors, and the general community can't work together effectively, they unwittingly perpetuate the pattern. The result is that rapists remain free to victimize others, again and again.

SOCIETY'S REACTION TO CRIME

Another dynamic of victimization is the community's reaction to crime. There seems to be a need for individual communities to rationalize and explain the criminal behavior that has taken place there.

The experience of being a victim of a violent crime is tragic enough; however, when we add to this experience the paradoxical attitude of society, the situation becomes compounded. The community has a strange attitude that blocks sympathetic responses to the victim's situation. One of the attitudes is the primitive fear of contamination if one associates with the unlucky victim. The result of this primitive response of fear is to isolate or exclude the victim.

This type of exclusion is seen in the community responses toward the rape victim. The victim experiences isolation, exclusion, and notoriety. There are whispering campaigns questioning the innocence of the victim. If she is young and single, she can be subjected to annoying behavior from the men in the community, without the usual protective interference of other individuals. Some rape victims who had experienced this exclusion and notoriety have had to move from the neighborhood.

That the victim feels isolated, helpless, and alone in a world perceived as being hostile produces profound adaptive and defensive patterns, which form the core of the psychological responses of victims. Any measure that the community will employ that will reduce the victim's feelings of isolation, aloneness, and helplessness will also reduce his secondary psychological trauma.

Another response is that of seeming indifference to the victim's plight. This is the most common complaint of victims of violent crimes. A frequent recipient of this type of complaint is the police. This attitude of seeming indifference of the community, as well as of the police, is due to the fact that by the time the victim is seen, the criminal act is in the past and the criminal is gone. There is nothing active that the listener can do, and the victim's expression of her distress is experienced by the listener as an implied demand that something be done. Also implied is criticism that the listener failed to protect her from the tragic experience.

HOSPITALS' REACTIONS TO VICTIMS

This hostile and indifference attitude can be first noted in the hospital emergency rooms when the staff are, in particular, dealing with the rape victim. The nature of the emergency room physical setting is one of a non-private order. The victim is made to endure lengthy, embarrassing waits in sometimes congested emergency room waiting areas. In that setting, the victim continues to feel vulnerable and not protected. Doctors, because they deal with so many patients, have a tendency not to give the kind of personalized attention needed in rape cases, for example, an unsympathetic and thoughtless doctor, shouting out to the nurse, "Bring in the rape case" or asking in a loud voice, "Where is the rape case?" This type of negative attention causes the rape victim to feel as if the whole world is watching and commenting.

There is a need for training for admissions, nursing, and laboratory staff to sensitize them to the unique needs of rape victims and the standard procedures to be followed. The examining physician's role is critical. That is, by attending to the victim's immediate medical needs promptly and respectfully, he helps to reduce anxiety and further trauma.

REACTIONS OF THE VICTIM'S FAMILY

Husbands are reluctant to believe the innocence of their own wives, though they may be physically present, but emotional support is oftentimes lacking. Due to this reluctance and their suspicions, they tend to blame their wives for what has happened and become accusatory and unsympathetic. This suspicion derives from the reluctance to believe the total innocence of the victim, and so, occasionally, the rape victim experiences divorce because of this suspicion and the reluctance to believe the true victimization of the rape victim, and so victimization continues.

When a community can explain the criminal activity that has taken place there, and why a person was victimized, there is a feeling that it won't happen to them. Since the perpetrator of the crime is not around to answer questions, the community assesses the victim's behavior in order to explain why the crime occurred. People will do this to protect them psychologically by trying to distinguish the victim's behavior from their own.

There seems to be a human need inherent in the questioning techniques that tend to perpetuate a continued victimization of the already helpless victim:

- Didn't you know this neighborhood is dangerous to walk

in after dark?
- Didn't you have the door locked?
- Weren't you suspicious of that man in the elevator?
- Why didn't you scream?
- Did you look before you opened the door?

All of the above are examples of victimizing questioning techniques. In general, the theme is an aggressive questioning of the victim, and these questions generally take the form of "Didn't you know?" or "Couldn't you tell?" and "Why, why, why did it happen?" These types of questions imply that the victim's injuries could have been prevented or avoided by being careful.

This first response to victims stems from a basic need for all individuals to find a rational explanation of violent crimes, particularly brutal crimes. Exposure to senseless, irrational, brutal behavior makes everyone feel vulnerable and helpless. It then can happen at any time, any place, and to anyone. It is relieving to find out that the victim did something or neglected something that plausibly contributed to the crime. It makes the other individual feel less helpless, less vulnerable, and safer. These questions to determine the rationality of the crime are directed towards the victim, since the criminal is not available for examination.

RESPONSE OF THE CRIMINAL JUSTICE SYSTEM

The growing awareness that anyone can be vulnerable to crimes of violence may help the community to be more genuinely sympathetic to the victim. However, there is one segment of society that the victim must come in contact with as a result of his misfortune that seem to lag behind in this growing sympathy and empathy for the victim; this is the criminal justice system. Judges, prosecutors, the legal profession, and the police are still somewhat removed from the personal plight of the victim.

In a recent conversation with a judge concerning victimology, his response was, "You know, I never really thought about it. My concern was always the application of the law. I thought of the criminal act and what to do about the criminal, but not the victim." This indifferent attitude towards victims is derived from the legal model, which is based on the adversary principle. It is not the truth, but the better argument, pro or con, that wins the case. The victim's plight is exploited or attacked when the adversary principle of the law is applied.

In courts, where the victim expects psychological restitution, the victim further experiences continued victimization, not from the assailant, but from lawyers, judges, and other court employees. It surfaces from lawyers in that the prosecutor needs to ask insensitive questions to "bring out the truth," cross-examines in an effort to protect his client — the assailant — and brutally wages a continuing character assault on the already devastated victim.

It also surfaces in the judge's decision, which often is reflective of the law, in that his decision is oftentimes in favor of the assailant and not in defense of the victim, i.e. plea bargaining, reduced charges, and cases dropped.

The plight of a crime victim is not a happy one. Victims' dealings with the police and the courts cause the victim to have feelings of futility and resentment. A survey of survivors of homicidal attacks show that many of them think that the courts are too lenient with the perpetrators, even though many of them can ascribe the rationale of "sickness" of the offender.

While the public cannot change the entire legal system, there is one area that they can substantially influence; that is the police department. The police responding to crimes have just about the same reaction as the community has. One explanation for the seeming indifference of the police that the victim may be aware of is due to a common misinterpretation by the police of the concept of professionalism. In their efforts to be neutral, and since it is a crime in the past with the criminal gone, the police may aggressively question the victim as to the details of the crime. This behavior rejects implied expectations of comfort to the victim, as well as rejecting the victim's implied criticism that the police have failed to do their job protecting him from crime.

One recent report from a woman, who was the victim of a mugging, stated that when the radio car responded, the police officers sat in the car, and she had to lean on the car door, reporting the details of her mugging to them through the car window. In addition, the attitude of the police officers was "You aren't the only one who has been mugged. We get plenty of other calls like this." Such behavior or comments are hardly comforting to the victim and can make her feel even further victimized.

Another possible explanation is that the police must also deal with their own frustration associated with feelings of being powerless to apprehend the perpetrator or prevent the crime. With this in mind, the police are probably even more critical of a victim's behavior.

The police are usually the first individuals the victim meets, and, most of the time, the police meet the victim after the crime has been committed, with the criminal gone. Police attitudes can be quite crucial in reducing the acute psychological trauma of the victim and also help prevent the debilitating secondary traumas that most victims undergo.

Enough cannot be said to make known to the operator and others who respond to victim's needs during a crisis about the emotional, psychological, and physical trauma that is initiated by a crisis event. Therefore, the person who picks up the phone first (i.e. the operator) should be ever aware of the changing behavior patterns emitted during the various stages of victimology. The operator should immediately put into use the human radar screen that defines human behavior and feeds back to him the telltale hints indicating the particular stages that the victim may be in when he calls. It is important to note that a victim may contact or reach out for help during any one of the stages of victimology. Therefore, it is important that the operator should understand the stages of victim behavior and be able to make the distinction between the stages, based on the phraseology of the victim. At that time, the operator may adjust his mode of communicating accordingly in such a way so that he may have a stabilizing effect on the victim.

During Stage 1: Shock, Disbelief, and Denial, the victim is preoccupied with convincing himself that this event did not occur. Therefore, he is not receptive to logic and a productive interchange, and so the operator must be patient and wait for the period of preoccupation to pass. During Stage 2: Fright and Blaming, the ex-victim experiences fear and a need for blame, and therefore the operator should be aware that if the victim raises his voice to him, or blames the operator for his condition, the operator should not take a personal affront to this. It is merely an expression of an emotional need. Furthermore, the operator should expect an immediate switch in behavior, because the victim would express some clinging behavior in the form of attempting to keep the operator on the phone. This is not unusual, yet it may appear to the operator as a contradiction in behavior, because the victim is *blaming* the operator and is *clinging* at the same time.

During Stage 3: Anger and Apathy, if the victim calls, it will be while the victim is in the anger phase. This victim should be viewed as a positive reaction to the victimization, because during this phase ventilation occurs. Ventilation is a healthy response, however, if the victim refuses to talk suddenly, it may mean that apathy has taken over and the victim is now holding the emotions in. If apathy continues and dominates the response, more harm will be done because the repression of emotions can only bring on more stress.

Cultural paranoia is a new adaptive coping behavior adapted during the crisis in an effort to restabilize oneself. During Stage 4: Resignation, Resolution, and Integration, the individual resigns himself to the adaptive behavior and that behavior becomes a permanent part of the victim's character. If the intervention was positive, then the victim will have something positive to say about the person intervening. If the intervention was negative, then comments from the victim will be negative; that is, we gain or lose a friend during crisis intervention. Previous negative experience becomes a fixed part (cathexis) of the victim's character and attitude.

Like the medical doctor who needs to examine the patient in order to properly diagnose the physiological state and prescribe medication for safe return to normal body function, so does the responding party to the crisis victim need to analyze behavior for effective intervention, noting the various psychological stages and determining how to interact within each stage, in order to help the victim overcome the crisis.

Chapter 4

CRISIS INTERVENTION

INTRODUCTION

THE ability to communicate effectively, as we have seen in Chapter 1, is a basic but very essential skill for those who are in a profession whose daily contacts are with the public. During operator/caller contacts that are relatively tranquil, operators must work at being effective communicators. They also must learn to overcome the impersonal characteristics that sometimes comes from interaction with the public and the aura of police authority and attitudes on the part of caller and operator alike that at times cause barriers to effective communication.

With all of these factors to contend with, how much extra effort must the operator put forth in the more serious traumatic events such as death, rape, and suicide that are an integral part of their daily tasks? How are emergency operators expected to accomplish their primary duties during incidents that generate, within the people involved, intense psychological stress and disorientation? And, more importantly, what is the complete task of the operator when they're called upon to investigate that which many people experience as traumatic events in their lives, such as crimes committed against them, conflicts, auto accidents, disputes, and death? What should an emergency operator say to people who call for assistance during a serious crisis and how should the operator say it?

Before answering these questions we should reassert some important points that have appeared earlier in this book. The first point is that those professions that are basically involved with communication are inherently people-oriented; therefore, dealing with people is an essential element of their job. The primary function of this people-oriented profession is *service*. The human service system that is the emergency operator's job, however, is unique in that it is inevitably involved in the typical and stressful events (crises) that may profoundly affect people. The principal attributes of the position of the emergency operator, their immediate response capability, and their authority gives them a role-set replete with crisis management potential. Therefore, an understanding of crisis theory and crisis intervention techniques is a prerequisite for this type of work. Acquiring crisis intervention competence creates a greater sense of security in dealing with the public and facilitates the safe, satisfying, and successful fulfillment of this mission.

This chapter addresses specific crisis situations the operator commonly responds to and discusses the insights and techniques the emergency operator must possess in order to effectively handle such situations. To aid in developing crisis intervention skills we have gone beyond the description of specific crisis interventions procedures. The effective operator must possess not only well-developed intervention skills, but also in-depth understanding of specific types of crisis, what causes them, how people tend to respond to them, and how the operators intervention will affect the success or failure of the resolution of the crisis.

The first section presents the applicable principles of a crisis. Within this section, a crisis is defined as *a subjective reaction to a stressful life experience so affecting the individual that his ability to cope is severely impaired.* The psychological dynamics of crises are presented and the role of the emergency operator who responds to crisis situations is specifically explained.

Once a call is identified as being of a crisis nature, the operator is faced with the task of dealing effectively with the crisis situation. Crisis calls have certain important similarities. First, one or more highly emotional callers are likely to be involved, though the particular emotion being expressed will vary accordingly to the type of crisis. In order for the operator to deal effectively with the highly emotional caller, the next important step will be to calm the caller involved in the crisis. Calming an aggressive, confused, or hysterical caller is often a difficult task. Such callers must be calmed, not only for their own comfort, but also to permit the operator to get on with the job of resolving the crisis and restoring order. Once the operator has calmed the caller, he can begin to gather relevant information and take appropriate action. In the second section of this chapter, we present several procedures for quieting highly emotional callers and offer guidelines by way of a chart that illustrates behavior precipitated by the stress of the crisis situation. Listed are the five ways that the operator can make a quick diagnosis of their interac-

tion in a crisis call: tone of voice, verbal expression, physical movement, decision-making abilities, and display of confidence are easily
discernible behaviors that the operator will have little problem identifying.

The text then turns to common situations that the emergency
operator handles that are usually crisis events for the callers involved. Each crisis situation has its own definitive phases and
behavior patterns, however, for the most part, each can be related to
the general crisis theory. Each situation may require a different type
of response from the operator. At the core of each call for help is the
possibility that someone is experiencing a crisis event in their lives,
therefore, a thorough knowledge of crisis theory and the different
behaviors associated with different calls is imperative for the
emergency operator.

Death is a crisis that affects all of us. It is one of the more difficult
aspects of the operator's job that must be faced and understood in
order for the operator to handle such calls effectively. The following
section discusses the role of the operator as it relates to calls involving death, whether it be from natural, homicidal, accidental, or
suicidal causes.

The underlying theme of this entire chapter is that many of the
calls that the operator will respond to are stressful events that profoundly affect the people involved. Knowing what to say and how to
respond to the needs of the caller in such situations can make the
operator's job more effective and self-satisfying. Understanding the
primary behavioral principles in crisis situations rounds out the
basic helping role of the emergency operator. Understanding and
utilizing crisis intervention procedures (i.e. identifying the crisis call, calming highly emotional callers, gathering the needed
information from the callers under difficult circumstances in
order to take appropriate crisis-reducing action, and restoring
order) is a fundamental requirement for effective emergency
operators.

CRISIS THEORY

A *crisis* is basically defined as *a significant upset in the generally steady,
smooth functioning of an individual or situation*. Some people associate
crisis synonymously with stress, panic, catastrophe, disaster,
violence, or potential violence. Others adhering to a medical con-

notation regard it as a "turning point" between a fortunate and unfortunate change in the state of an organism. In decision-making analysis, it is a "one-of-a-kind" situation or event.

The concept of crisis theory is used by historians, sociologists, political scientists, and psychologists to refer to critical events that occur within their own particular frame of reference. For example, a political scientist or historian might use the term to refer to the "economic crisis" caused by an oil embargo, or the "international crisis" precipitated by the violent overthrow of a foreign government. A sociologist might refer to the "urban crisis" and a psychologist might refer to a "personal crisis." For the emergency operator, the term might be used in a psychological sense to refer to people who are having difficulty solving or coping with a personal problem, event, or interpersonal situation.

Despite the wide use of the term "crisis," there are a number of dimensions or characteristics that have been identified as occurring in a crisis, irrespective of the event or happening it is associated with. Crisis, for example, is often a turning point in an unfolding sequence of events and actions; it is a situation in which the requirements for action is high among participants, yet the ability to cope with the situation is lowered. Crisis usually threatens the goals and objectives of those involved and is followed by an outcome whose consequences shape the future of those involved. Crisis may consist of a convergence of events that result in a new set of circumstances. Crisis reduces control over events and the effects of these events and also heightens urgency, which often produces stress in the victims. Lack of adequate information to a crisis victim will usually cause an increase in the level of stress associated with that crisis.

Crisis is acute, rather than chronic, although its length is usually unspecified and limited. There is great difficulty in defining exactly what is a "crisis" to everyone, in that what is a crisis event to one person may not be a crisis event to another. However, a crisis could be any event that reduces an individual's ability to cope with a given situation.

Emergency work today entails responding to sudden, shocking, traumatic events that profoundly effect the people of the city. Correct job performance requires not just prompt responses, services, and reports, but also personal attention to the needs of the individual and to the effects of the crisis situation on the human psyche. A death situation, for example, is a crisis that psychologically affects most of us. Using only prompt response, service, and reports in a death situation does not make for a complete, effectively done job. Adding the so-called "personal touch" (in ways that will become clear as we proceed) will result in highly effective, complete, self-satisfying work. To refrain from adding the personal touch makes for an incomplete response.

FLOW OF CRISIS

By its very nature, a crisis is time limited. That is, it will resolve itself for better or worse in a relatively brief period of time, which may range from a few hours to a maximum of usually about six weeks. The person involved in a crisis may well resolve their crisis by a general discharge of anger directed at the cause of their crisis and arrive at some working agreement, resolving their problem within the time it takes to make the call for help and the arrival of assistance. For others, it may not be so simple. The deciding factor may be the type of crime perpetrated against the caller and the amount of aggression contained therein.

Another characteristic is that a crisis has some stages that are recognizable. These proceed from the initial impact with its highly charged emotions, through a recoil stage of denial, to a resolution stage where some type of solution or accommodation is found.

People will request and accept assistance more readily when they are in a crisis situation. The degree to which they will accept help is dependent upon the amount of distress they feel and the level of helplessness and loss of control they are involved in. Given the concept of balance and equilibrium, it is known that the person in the crisis will do whatever is necessary to restore their former state of equilibrium. This makes the acceptance of outside help easier and cooperation needed for a quick resolution of their problem more readily available. Therefore, the course that a crisis takes may be diagrammed in this way:

Equilibrium→Disorganization→Resolution→Equilibrium restored

CRISIS THEORY FOR EMERGENCY OPERATORS

What is a crisis? It has been defined as *an upset in a steady state*, or as *a disruption of coping ability caused by a sudden, arbitrary, or unpredictable impact of stressful life experience; one that taxes adaptive resources.* Reactions are painful, disruptive, and dysfunctional. Although producing such a response, a crisis may at times afford an unusual opportunity to improve coping ability. Usually, however, people need assistance to cope and the operator provides that assistance. When experiencing crisis most people are more receptive (normal defenses are down) to the skillful, authoritative influence of others offering help than at times of psychological equilibrium. This places the emergency operator in a position to effectively decrease the trauma and aftereffects that a crisis event can have on a caller. Even the most well-adjusted person will find it difficult to deal with the more serious crisis events in life.

When an unpredictable and/or arbitrary incident causes an overwhelming sudden input of stress with which a person is unable to cope, that person is experiencing a crisis, for example: at the scene of a vehicle accident where an infant is seriously injured. The mother of the child, who was the driver of the car, might be exhibiting various behaviors: she might be calm and collected, she might be dazed and unresponsive, or she might be crying, screaming, or physically uncontrollable. No matter what the behavior, it is her reaction to the crisis event and her way of coping with the overwhelming input of stress. Psychologically, she may feel guilty for the injury to the child. Her behavior in a short time could and probably will change as she gradually adjusts to the occurrence. However, if she is not a strong person, and this frustration and guilt produces stress that she can't deal with, then anything you say can affect her adjustment either adversely or favorably. Saying, for example, "Would you like to give me your vehicle registration," or "Would you like us to notify someone?" are favorable statements that respond to her suggestibility. On the other hand, "Why did you pass the red light?" or "Why did you ride with the baby in the front seat?" are adverse statements that can increase the frustration and guilt she already feels, causing stress. This type of questioning may infer that she is to blame, therefore making it more difficult for her to eventually adjust to the occurrence and its aftereffects.

CHARACTERISTICS OF A CRISIS

Sudden and Unexpected Characteristics

A crisis event can be any event that occurs suddenly; that is, interrupts normal life events by blocking the attainment of expected conclusions or goals. Without the opportunity for the individual to "prepare" psychologically for it, these events occur at any time and can enter into any and all situations for no apparent reason. The impact is unexpected; there is no warning. If, for example, a person knows he will unavoidably lose a great deal of money in his business this year or that his wife will die of cancer within the next six months, he can be somewhat psychologically prepared for these events. The stress that will occur from them will not be sudden. However, if his wife suddenly died, or all of his money was lost in a burglary, he might experience a serious crisis because of the suddenness of the events.

Unpredictability

Unpredictable events usually cause this sudden psychological reaction. Events such as accidents, death, crime, and disasters are many times unpredictable events that interrupt normal events and block some of life's pursuits.

Arbitrary

Such events may also be arbitrary. When one feels that an event occurred without apparent reason, is unfair, or defies an explanation, such an event is considered arbitrary. For example, a heavy object may fall from a high building and kill one pedestrian walking in a crowd. Why that particular person?

When an event occurs causing a sudden input of psychological stress, the event is usually sudden, unpredictable, and/or arbitrary.

THE EMERGENCY OPERATOR'S ROLE IN CRISIS EVENTS

The emergency operator must be able to display expertise in dealing with crisis events. Most events with which they deal have crisis implications for someone, and the key to the most effective completion of their tasks is in the nature of the intervention. The knowledge and understanding of crisis behavior and intervention on the part of "who" intervenes is extremely important, and the skill and competence of "how" the job should be done requires insight.

The "how" of doing the job correctly is infinitely more important than the "what." Earliness (immediacy) of intervention is critical. Intervention should begin before the disrupted emergency state "hardens" and becomes a fixed pattern of feeling and behavior; that is, before the susceptibility to outside influence is lost. Authority of intervention is also critical.

Most professionals in our society are seen as authority figures, and their ability to perform their duties is enhanced by this aura of authority. Professional people are expected to be competent; to be able to do their jobs well. Therefore, those seeking their services will listen and follow directions to facilitate this competency.

Similarly, a police emergency operator has considerable authority, both real and symbolic. Emergency operators, because of the nature of their job, have immediacy and authority, and their behavior toward the individual in crisis will have impact upon people's short- and long-term adjustment adaptability. In order to be effective in assisting others, help must come from an authoritative source, however, *authority* must be distinguished from *authoritarianism*.

1. AUTHORITY: This is exhibited by the individual's overall knowledge of his position, competence in his ability to recognize and deal effectively with individuals in crisis, and his understanding of his role in the overall picture of the organization as a *helping system*. These of the authority mode as opposed to the authoritarian give the individual a variety of possibilities when intervening in crisis situations, whereas the power mode (authoritarian) is just one answer to a limited number of crisis situations. Authority then is derived from knowledge and competence.

2. AUTHORITARIANISM: This is exhibited by a display of power (physically or vocally) or status, indicating control over everything because of your position in an organization, and is derived from power and status. Crisis dependency needs to be fulfilled in a temporary and constructive way so that a

sense of order and control can be found in the victim's suddenly chaotic world.

The emergency operator's role in today's society directly leads to the need for expertise in the crisis intervention role. Emergency operators are available twenty-four hours a day and respond promptly when called. In fact, the average call is responded to in approximately four seconds. The public calls when they need help, and the role of the emerency operator grants them the authority to intervene. Because of their experience, the operator can develop intervention competence and become experts in dealing with people in crisis situations.

No matter what the situation, the caller's perception of the incident will determine the support response required of the operator. This response is basically communicative in nature. How the operator deals with each situation and with the callers involved will affect the degree of safety for all concerned, will help accomplish basic tasks of emergency operators, and will help reduce the overall traumatic effect on the individual psychologically.

The proper handling of crisis events by the operator has other advantages for the operator and the caller. In handling crisis situations correctly and competently, the operator gains self-confidence in his ability to mediate conflict and receives job satisfaction from the fact that he has provided meaningful assistance to the crisis victims. For the caller there is a renewed sense of self-esteem and confidence in their own future.

Effective communication while intervening is the key to handling crisis events. If the operator communicates professionalism, confidence, efficiency, sincerity, and empathy, the job will be accomplished. If the operator is calm and concerned, the job will be performed easier. Making a good impression and using common sense will promote confidence in the operator's ability to handle crisis situations. Approaching crisis response with these general considerations will enhance the operator's potential for accomplishing the self-satisfying, supportive, emergency operator's role.

CRISIS BEHAVIOR OF CALLERS

Crisis reaction (i.e. feelings and behavior) may appear in any combination. The emergency operator will hear people who call in for help that are experiencing feelings of:

CHAOS: "Things are falling apart."

CONFUSION: "I can't seem to make a decision."

HELPLESSNESS: "I can't help myself."

DEPENDENCY: "Please tell me what to do."

Characteristic crisis behavior patterns will all also be shown in various combinations, such as:

REGRESSION: reverting to child-like behavior

DISRUPTION OF BASIC FUNCTIONS: eating, sleeping, etc.

DENIAL: behaving as if nothing has happened

REPRESSION: "I can't remember anything."

MISTRUST: "I don't trust anybody to help me."

Even if a person properly adjusts to a crisis incident, its effect is indelibly imprinted on the psyche, as the event will never be forgotten. Proper adjustment to these permanent impressions and the incident itself will depend on the kind of help people in a crisis receive at the outset of their trauma.

The crisis state presents complicated problems for the communications process. Therefore, to further understand human behavior and improve our ability to communicate, a look at crisis behavior may improve our ability to communicate.

We will now consider specific behavior that is usually evident in the many crisis calls the police agencies receive annually. Keep the general crisis principles in mind. Remember that many of the 2,400,000 calls for assistance that the police receive annually in large cities are direct cries for help that are made by people who might be experiencing a critical, crucial moment in their lives. Many of these crisis moments concern actual occurrences. Some, however, may be imagined or completely false. In either case, many of the callers just need some sort of assistance in coping with a problem. These problems may at times seem very insignificant to the operator, but to the callers they may be very real. The help needed might just be a kind word or sympathetic ear; however, if rendered properly and to the best of the operator's ability, it is a job well done. If the operator satisfied the caller and accomplished the basic task of the emergency, the mission was accomplished correctly.

Following is a table displaying behavior that arises from a crisis situation (*see* Table 4-I).

Table 4-I. CRISIS BEHAVIOR

	TONE OF VOICE	VERBAL EXPRESSIONS	PHYSICAL MOVEMENT	DECISION MAKING	DISPLAY OF CONFIDENCE
(Caller) DISORGANIZATION AND CONTAGIOUS BEHAVIOR	Rapid speech Missing words Stuttering Stammering Quivering with emotion Breaking of voice Faltering Hesitancy Smacking of lips Search for words Shortness of Breath	Silence Yelling and screaming Unable to articulate Cursing Referring to God Reverts to second language Argumentative Unemotional Very restrained	Running around Waving arms Hitting Trembling or immobility Grabbing Catatonic	Indecision, "What should I do?" Shifting of decisions Unable to be decisive Difficulty in making choices	Lack of confidence Very sensitive Questioning of previous decisions Self-blame "Why me?" "What next?" Irrational
(Operator) PITFALLS TO SUCCESSFUL RESOLUTION	Blame Ridicule Telling caller to "snap out of it." Arguing with caller "You're acting abnormal." "You shouldn't feel that way."	Complete silence Shouting Use of jargon Use of codes "This guy sounds bad." Joker Humor Out cursing Anger	Threatening posture Strutting Rolling of eyes Negative shaking of head Folded arms	Inappropriate assumptions False expectations Negative first impressions	Shifting of role Placing blame Unnecessary officious behavior

1. Tone of Voice

The tone of the caller's voice may be the first indication to the operator of a crisis event. For instance, a person tends to speak faster when nervous, causing more speech disturbances such as missed words, stuttering and mispronunciation of common words, than one might ordinarily expect in conversation. There may also be quivering in the voice, indicating heightened emotions or the breaking off completely of the voice. Other signs include abnormal amounts of lip and tongue movements, faltering, hesitancy, and searching for words, which should be a clue to the operator that the caller is anxious.

At the other extreme and not to be ignored is the caller who is very unemotional and restrained while relaying information that would ordinarily evoke more anxious responses. These callers may sound as though they don't care about the incident, but the experienced and sensitive operator knows that this is just a defensive response to the overwhelming stress the caller is experiencing at the moment.

2. Verbal Expressions

It must be understood that a person caught in the grips of a crisis situation may be demonstrating various types of verbal expressions. They may be yelling and screaming, cursing at everyone and everything, including the emergency operator offering help, referring to or calling to God for help, or they may even revert to their native language, which may be completely foreign to the operator. This occurs because of the sudden, unpredictable nature of a crisis, which initiates a regressive process. In an effort to restabilize oneself psychologically, emotionally, and physically, a person will regress to that point of their development in which they found gratification or in the case of crises, behavior that the person is most comfortable or most familiar with. If the regressive process does not find a workable frame of reference during this regression, the victim may not be able to articulate what has happened and, in fact, may regress to a completely frozen, silent state (incapacitated). The regressive movement of the crisis situation carries with it a contagious element. The responding operator should be aware of this contagious element of the crisis event and avoid getting caught up in attempting to over-shout the caller. When a caller is very angry, or very anxious and confused, he is usually tuned in to his own feelings of the moment and is often unresponsive and unaware of the feelings and attempts of others to communicate with him. The operator may have to repeat himself several times to "get through" to the caller. The operator who doesn't understand the verbal expressions as a response to crisis may tend to respond to hostile expressions by being too harsh and leaning too hard on the caller with attempts to over-shout and outcurse. The operator then fails to achieve his purpose of calming the caller, getting the required information, and resolving the crisis. The operator has then in fact got caught up in the con-tagious nature of the crisis call, and the opposite of his goal may oc-cur. The disturbance level may then increase and threats and ex-pressions of anger directed at the operator become more possible.

3. Physical Movement

Although the emergency operator will not be able to see the caller's physical movement, this is an important category of crisis behavior to be aware of because physical movement can be heard and visualized over the telephone. For example, in terms of physical movement, the victim may be running around waving arms, grab-bing, hitting, or be completely catatonic (i.e. frozen in an im-mobilized state). The operator will be able to hear the behavioral effects of this kind of physical activity by the rapid manner of speak-ing, the breathlessness of the caller, or in the caller's gasping for air.

The operator should not take personal affront to this behavior, but he should undertake whatever reasonable action necessary to prevent injury or further harm to the victim. The victim is quite vulnerable to influences, negative as well as positive, at this point. Positive, helpful advice will be readily accepted; however, negative responses such as shouting, rolling of the eyes in disgust, impa-tience, or shaking of the head on the part of the operator can cause further victimization of the caller.

Contrary to what may be thought at this point, the rolling of eyes and shaking of the head on the part of the operator may not be visually seen by the caller, but the associated sounds and words may be very much heard. For example, in his attempts to gather information during the expression of crisis behavior on the part of the caller, the operator may become frustrated and exasperated. The sounds and words associated with these feelings of impatience may range from merely impatience in the voice, to sounds such as clucking (i.e. "Tsk, Tsk"), or expressions such as, "Oh for God's sake!", or "This person doesn't understand me," or "What the hell's the matter with this person?"

Body language and facial expressions conducive to listening and empathy that is supportive of the caller's plight can be transmitted across the wires and will assure the successful resolution of the crisis.

4. Decision-Making Abilities

To expect a crisis victim to make sound and rational decisions is asking too much of the person caught in a crisis. Rather, what we are likely to observe is a shifting in behavior. The person in crisis is not able to make decisions and will ask "What should I do?" Responding operators should avoid making inappropriate assumptions based on first impressions of the caller. To help the crisis victim overcome his physical and/or psychological trauma, the responding operator should be decisive and firm when interacting with the victim. These decisions made on the behalf of the caller should be objective and considerate of the psychological effect it has on the victim. In addition, consideration could be given at this time to allowing the victim to make inconsequential decisions. The process of making a simple decisions will help the victim regain his decision-making ability that was lost in the reactions to the crisis.

5. Display of Confidence

The nature of fact-finding, information gathering and report writing has a "blaming element" inherent in it; therefore, be aware that the crisis victim lacks self-confidence and will be sensitive to any display of blame directed towards them. The crisis victim tends to question their previous decisions and will blame themselves for what has happened. Also, without realizing it, the operator in an effort to gain control and initiate orderly behavior may shift from a helping role to a blaming role. The operator may hear the caller state their questioning of their actions leading to the crisis such as, "Why me?"

"What next?" "Why didn't I stay home?" "Why was I out so late?" "I should have locked the door," and so on.

DEATH AS A CRISIS EVENT

As previously stated, crisis principles apply to many of life's stressful occurrences. Death, no matter how or when it occurs, is a crisis event for those who were close to the person who died. Whether sudden or expected, the sense of loss involved creates crisis reactions for those remaining. Just the thought of human death is usually suppressed by individuals. Because of the finality of death, the fear of the unknown, the sadness of the event, and the stress provoked by the thought and the event, people naturally tend to avoid the unpleasantness of death. The reminder that such thoughts evoke assurances of our finite life is a basic reason for such denial.

However, calls regarding death is another important aspect of the emergency operator's job. Just about every human death that occurs in a large city, except supervised death (i.e. those occurring in hospitals or institutions) requires some form of police involvement. Besides the necessary administrative matters, such as cards, reports, notifications and other required duties, the operator should be able to recognize crisis symptoms among those who call to report the death and render proper service consistent with common crisis intervention techniques.

Death has been classified into three categories: natural, accidental, and intentional. These are now briefly defined as they are related to police involvement:

1. *Natural Death*: Heart attacks, old age, and chronic illnesses usually comprised the bulk of non-suspicious deaths that are handled by police and fall under this heading.
2. *Accidental Death*: The range in this category is quite diverse. Traffic accidents account for the greatest number of deaths, although fires, poisoning, and drug abuse have also had their impact.
3. *Intentional Death*: This area includes all homicides (justifiable and criminal) as well as suicides.

For the operator, the human relations aspect in each of the three categories will be basically the same. In each situation, the operator will interact with a concerned party of the victim — a spouse, a close friend, or other relative. An understanding of the trauma that is experienced by these people will help the operator to render a service that will be personally rewarding and self-satisfying as well as beneficial to the caller in a crisis.

Bereavement is the term used to describe people suffering the effects of a loss, by death, of a loved one. The emergency operator should be able to deal with expressions of bereavement by others. They should be able to interact with and offer comfort to those who are closely involved with the situation and call in for assistance.

Not only must the operator efficiently handle the situation, but he must also be emotionally able to handle the call himself. Calls regarding a person dismembered in an auto accident or struck by a train, or an infant death, all manage to emotionally sneak through the staunchest defenses. Becoming too engrossed in obtaining information for reports, and failing to identify with relatives of the deceased over absorption in gathering information regarding the death scene, are common reactions in the performance of the inexperienced emergency operator. These reactions are analogous to the defense of denial.

Prior Conditioning

Prior conditioning and lack of exposure, added to the anxiety-producing thoughts and feelings about death as previously mentioned, produce this avoidance reaction. Regardless of the previous conditioning of the emergency operator, the task of handling calls regarding dead bodies is one in which he or she has no choice to respond to. This part of the operator's role calls for forced exposure. Consider the following calls and examine your own emotional response. Then answer to yourself how well you maintain emotional stability or how you may restabilize in case of emotions regarding these calls as they are evoked:

1. You are on duty and receive a call regarding a head-on collision on a major expressway. The caller states that four of the five occupants of one are dead — one of them having been decapitated. The fifth occupant is lying nearby and alive and requires immediate first aid. How would you feel as the responding operator?

2. You are on duty and receive a call from a hysterical wife,

stating that her husband has committed suicide by carbon monoxide poisoning. He left his car running while in the garage and closed all the car windows and turned the heater on full blast. His wife discovered the car eight hours later, with the motor still running. In the background you hear the screaming, hysterical voices of children crying for their father.

3. You are on duty and receive a call regarding the scene of an apparent homicide-suicide incident. A husband calls and calmly explains how he came home from work and discovered his newborn infant drowned in the bathtub and his wife with her wrists slit, dead on the floor. How would you respond in this situation?

The above cases are by no means isolated incidents. Emergency operators are called to intervene in such crisis situations everyday, and they do with amazing coolness and control.

Conclusion

Death in any form can be considered a crisis incident. To help one understand further the operator's role in death-related incidents, death may be categorized by natural, accidental, and intentional. The amount of involvement required of the operator varies in accordance with the type of death reported.

The two variables that determine the amount of loss felt are our prior conditioning, or cultural expectations, and the sense of loss involved by the death of loved one. Whether intentional death or unintentional death, calls regarding death are always stressful to both the caller and the operator. Yet, the operators are at the other end of the phone when such a call comes in and must be able to emotionally handle the situation themselves and perform effectively the administrative and investigative procedures required, including the empathetic services the relative(s) or caller may need. It is a task that the emergency operator will dislike, yet perform with efficiency as these calls come in.

GATHERING INFORMATION

Whether a person is directly involved or has just witnessed a crisis, the caller of a crisis event is quite likely to be in a highly emotional state. Which particular emotion that is being expressed will depend partly on the caller himself and partly on the nature of the crisis itself. That is, different emotions will be expressed with different crisis in varying intensities. For example:

Type of Caller and Crisis Event	Type of Emotion/Behavior
Tourist	
Child Caller	
The Elderly	Confusion/Agitation
The Intoxicated	
Mentally Disturbed	
Disputes:	
Marital	Anger, Aggression
Between Strangers	
Accidents	Anxiety
Suicide Attempts	Depression
Rape	Hysterical, Anxiety
Assaults	Dazed
Manslaughter	
Fatal Assaults	Fear,
Homicide	Shock, and
Suicide	Disbelief

However, regardless of whether the caller is aggressive, angry, anxious, confused, or hysterical, it is the operator's duty to first calm the emotional caller before he will be able to gather the information needed to provide assistance. It has been demonstrated that inefficiency will be reduced if the operator is adequately prepared in advance for the crisis situation in which he is intervening. In many crisis calls, the operator will be able to successfully calm the caller and gather the information he is seeking that is necessary for intervention. In many other crisis calls, however, the operator will have to use calming procedures throughout the entire call.

Nevertheless, once the operator has calmed the crisis situation so that the caller will give information more readily and reliably, the activity of gathering important information can begin. This can proceed quite calmly and easily or it can proceed with a struggle. In order to facilitate the information gathering, it would be helpful if the operator carefully explains in detail the purpose and need for the information you are about to ask for, and the type of information that is expected. That is, explain to the caller what is needed and why it is needed. In this way, the stage is set for information gathering, the caller is calmed and has been advised of what to expect from the operator, cooperation has been gained, and assistance can be given rapidly and efficiently.

While it is obviously true that the main goal of the emergency operator's job is the gathering of relevant information, we have seen that the job is not quite that simple. As already noted, if the call is conducted in a highly professional manner, with the operator providing the caller with an impression of skill, awareness, sensitivity to their problem, and purposeful and efficient information gathering, the operator will not only obtain maximum cooperation, but will also build goodwill for himself and the organization he represents.

COMMUNICATING EFFECTIVELY WITH THE CRISIS VICTIM

In gathering information or communicating with the victim, the mode of interaction somehow take on one of three styles: interrogation, investigation, and interviewing. If we think about the nature of these three modes and analyze the trauma the victim is experiencing, we would quickly discard all the methods of gathering information. Interrogation is used to take information from an unwilling person. The victim has had enough taken from him already, i.e. pride, dignity and security.

Investigation is also a technique about which the structure and direction is controlled by the investigator. The victim has just experienced being controlled by the assailant or the effects of the crisis, which also causes a degree of impairment.

Interviewing is thought to be and is accepted as a most acceptable method of gathering information. What happens here is that control is shared by both the interviewer and the person being interviewed. This is not acceptable in this case because the victim does not have the physical and emotional stamina to exercise control. Therefore, the victim of a crisis needs to be dealt with via psychological first aid. This process of information gathering gives something back to the victim first (i.e. power, dignity, security) in order to get the needed information. Psychological first aid incorporates the "May I" or "Are you ready to" approach, as opposed to ordering, directing, or waiting for the victim to do it on his own.

PSYCHOLOGICAL FIRST AID

Psychological first aid can basically be described by comparing it to two other common police techniques. In order to define psychological first aid, we should first consider the following:

1. *Interrogation* is the taking of something.
2. *Interviewing* is the getting of something.
3. *Psychological first aid* is the giving of something.

As far as interpersonal skills are concerned, interrogation means the *taking* of information from someone who is capable of giving it, but is not willing to. Interviewing means the *getting* of information, and psychological first aid means the *giving* of something to someone who is willing to give information back but may not be capable of doing so. The giving of psychological first aid is done in order to improve the person's capability of dealing with their situation. The emergency operator must attempt to get the victim to the stage where he was prior to the crisis. Once this is accomplished, it makes the job of information gathering much easier.

What can we give to a crime victim? We want to replace to the victim that which he lost during the crime; namely his power, his dignity, and his security. Psychological first aid simply means helping people when they are in emotional distress. People in crisis are experiencing unbearable pressure on their emotions: their injury is real and the victim needs help. Emotional injuries can cause a victim to lose strength just as blood loss weakens the body. For the operator, learning to cope with victims' reactions is one of the goals of psychological first aid. Objectives of psychological first aid are: (1) to get the victim to function as quickly as possible in their original state (before the victimization); (2) to lessen the emotional intensity of the victim's reaction to the stress of the moment; and (3) to prevent the victim from harming himself further while his judgment is impaired.

Techniques of Psychological First Aid

In order to replace these losses to a crime victim, the operator may employ the same techniques we have already mentioned that are used in any other crisis intervention. In addition, restore these three just mentioned:

1. POWER. All crime victims lose a sense of power. The victim had few choices given to them by the assailant, who possessed all the power, so the police emergency operator can give the crime victim power by:
   a. asking the victim questions leading with:
      "Are you ready to. . . ?"
      "Are you able to. . . ?"
      For example, pertaining to giving a description:
      "Are you ready to give a description now?"
   b. perhaps giving the victim a choice as to where to meet the police.
   When interacting with callers there are certain ways of restoring power, and this will help to do so.
2. DIGNITY. All crime victims lose a certain degree of dignity and often blame themselves for being a victim. The operator can restore dignity by:
   a. telling the victim, "you did the right thing."
   b. avoiding criticism of the victim's actions.
   This can be said about almost any action that the victim has taken; for example, even calling for assistance.
3. SECURITY. All crime victims have a sense of insecurity after the commission of a crime. The operator can restore security by:
   a. telling the victim that everything is all right now.
   b. saying the police or other assistance is on the way.
   c. emphasizing your concern and expressing empathy for what has happened.
   d. shifting blame for what happened off of the victim and on to the criminal, where it belongs.
   All of the above suggestions and techniques are extremely important and go a long way toward making the victim capable of giving accurate and detailed information.

SECURITY FIRST AID

In the area of psychological first aid, the emphasis on the part of the person interviewing should be structured so that responses are primarily supportive of restoring a sense of security. Secondly, allow the victim to recapture a sense of pride and dignity. Once the first two have been accomplished, the victim is ready to regain control by exercising his own sense of power. The following table will better illustrate how psychological first aid is applied (*see* Table 4-II). The first half indicates how supportive behavior, on the part of the operator by way of the five categories, is conducive of a successful resolution of the crisis. The second half of Table 4-II illustrates the crisis caller's behavior when it is restored to equilibrium. After a brief explanation of the operator's role in calming the emotional caller, there is a complete chart of crisis behavior and psychological first aid combined that will enable the operator to get a complete overview of this chapter.

Calming the Emotional Caller

How a caller reacts to the emergency operator will, of course, be determined by his personality in general, his past experience with emergency events, and the effects of the crisis itself. However, the emergency operator's behavior, especially the first impression behavior, will have a lot to do with how aggressively the caller behaves or how cooperative he is with the operator's efforts to calm the situation and resolve their crisis. Therefore, in the initial phases of the operator's dealing with the caller in crisis, the operator should behave in a non-threatening, calm manner.

Demonstrate Understanding

By the use of supportive words and tone of voice, the operator can make it clear to the caller that he understands what the caller is feeling and how intensely he is feeling it. The operator should remain calm, speak softly, and carefully select his words. For example, avoid the use of department jargon and joking. Department jargon such as the use of the word "bus" instead of ambulance is foreign language to the crisis caller in the same way that a native language may be to the operator. The call should be handled in a calm manner, with the operator speaking clearly and remaining respectful towards the victim. With the careful choice of words and the correct tone of voice the operator can make it clear to the caller that he is responding calmly to the crisis situation. This will frequently have a calming effect on highly emotional callers in crisis.

Table 4-II. PSYCHOLOGICAL FIRST AID

	TONE OF VOICE	VERBAL EXPRESSIONS	PHYSICAL MOVEMENT	DECISION MAKING	DISPLAY OF CONFIDENCE
Recommended operator behavior supportive of a successful resolution. RESOLUTION:	Calm Reassuring Gentle Empathetic Interested Compassionate Allow	Clear Free of cursing Polite Free of derogatory words. empathy ventilation to recapture dignity. Ask to relate story without interruption. Do not immediately jump to first name (psychological distancing). Show empathy Encourage caller to talk.	Body language and eye contact and facial expression conducive to listening and all involved. Assign tasks in harmony with harmony with call relatives, comfort another.	Be decisive and show firmness Decisions based on safety of but safely. Objectivity Check emotional state of caller and self. Monitor your own feelings. Provide inconsequential decision-making.	De-emphasize blame of person in crisis. Minimum of use officiousness. Deal with caller in crisis quickly Convey to caller that he did the right thing "We are here to help you." "We'll get you what you need, medical etc." "You did the right thing by calling us for help."

Table 4-II. PSYCHOLOGICAL FIRST AID

	TONE OF VOICE	VERBAL EXPRESSIONS	PHYSICAL MOVEMENT	DECISION MAKING	DISPLAY OF CONFIDENCE
†Crisis caller behavior restored EQUILIBRIUM† RESTORED:	Normal voice restored	Dignity and respect	Physical movement is when successful resolution is arrived at.	Caller is ready to give and information Better able to make minor decisions.	Regain crisis callers confidence by making Caller has the feeling that he has done the right thing.

Reassurance

Use of reassurance aids in calming an emotional caller because it indicates to the caller the operator's concern for their situation. For example, the operator may reassure the caller with statements such as, "Don't worry, we'll take care of it for you," or "Everything will be all right," or "The ambulance will be there very soon, don't worry." Reassurance works particularly well in calming a situation if the operator has established a first impression of concern and desire to give assistance.

Ventilation

Encouraging the caller to talk is often an effective means for calming him down. It is difficult for a caller to continue yelling, screaming, crying, or cursing if they are trying to answer a series of questions at the same time. This procedure serves a double purpose, as in the process of ventilation the caller gives important information that the operator will need anyway. To this end, it will prove useful to encourage talking about the crisis itself. Questions relating to the event, regarding who did what, at what location, and the time involved can be helpful to the operator. However, some callers will remain upset when talking about the crisis itself because of the feelings of intensity of the feelings they are experiencing. In this situation, information that has no emotions attached to it can be sought, such as names of people involved addresses, ages, phone numbers, occupations and so forth. Whichever methods seem suited to the situation, the operator should realize that ventilation allows for the victim to recapture dignity, respect, and control, and the operator should not interrupt while the victim is telling his story.

Psychological Distance

Although we have mentioned this before, it bears repeating that the operator should be particularly aware of the psychological distancing. By this is meant that the operator should not jump to a first name basis, which would position him too close to the caller. To the opposite extreme — the position of acting disinterested in the victim's problem — would position the operator too far away.

Display of Confidence

The operator may help by avoiding blaming responses such as, "You should have locked the door," or "What were you doing out so late?" The operator's role is to de-emphasize blame of the person in the crisis, and all efforts should be towards that end. A quick but safe response is essential before crisis behavior sets in and becomes a permanent part of the victim's character. The operator should exhibit minimum use of officiousness and officious behavior. Finally, the idea that the victim did the correct thing by calling for help should be conveyed with statements such as, "You did the right thing by calling us." It is important to restore confidence and feelings of self-worth to the victim. The emergency operator is, after all, there to help.

Victims of Property Crimes

Restoring power to victims of property crimes is important, and this can be accomplished in many ways. A police emergency operator has a symbolic authority, which includes an aura of power to assist those who are in need. Some of this power can be given to the victim if the operator will do the following:

1. ASK PERMISSION. "May I ask you some questions now?" "Do you mind if I take notes on this?"
2. ACCEPT CREDIBILITY. One can listen discerningly without conveying suspicion.
3. PERCEPTION OF CRITICISM. Realize the forces that generate hostility and do not accept or react to implied criticism such as: "What can you people do for me now?"
   "It's too late, everything's gone."
4. GUILT REDUCTION. Try to help the victim realize that the self-evaluation he might be engaging in is unfair and non-productive.
5. IMPORTANCE. Make the victim feel that his case is important. However, do not make any promises that cannot be kept. Consider all property taken as valuable.

Finally, in discussing the last recommendation, there are certain points that should be noted. The critical point here is that we are in no way implying or suggesting that victims be falsely appeased. Saying to the victim, "Don't worry, we'll get your property back" would be a disservice to all involved. Also, to say "Forget it, you'll never see your belongings again" would be just as non-productive. Once again, the important concern of the emergency operator should be "What does the victim need now in his moment of crisis?"

GUIDELINES FOR DEALING WITH RAPE VICTIMS

It would not be an exaggeration to say that the way an operator handles the initial contact with rape victims could aid or endanger her future mental health.

This is a crucial crisis in the life of the victim. Because of the suddenness of the attack, and the innane invasion of privacy, the operator will frequently encounter the victim in a serious state of shock and hysteria. Therefore, the operator's attitude and approach can be important factors in forestalling any long-term mental effects on the victim.

On initial contact with the victim, the operator should be exceedingly *compassionate*. He must *show understanding* and help the victim feel that he is there to help her. It must be understood that this is a catastrophic event in the victim's life. It impedes all normal functions. The victim may be helpless, and her family may be experiencing a similar shock. The operator must realize the importance of his helping the victim. As the first person contacted, how he acts can be either beneficial or harmful to the victim.

Forcible rape is the ultimate intrusion into a person's privacy and is extraordinarily destructive to the victim's physical and mental being. She may be hard to deal with, and it may take her time to adjust to questioning. Her energies may be drained to the extent that she cannot effectively cope with questioning.

It is critically important that the operator avoid any suggestion of force. Often, in an effort to gather information, the operator may be perceived as aggressive and forceful. In this sense, he would be acting toward her as the rapist had acted.

Further, any attempt to criticize the victim, for whatever reason, should obviously be *avoided*. Statements such as:

- "What were you doing in that neighborhood anyway? Don't you know you were just asking for it by going there?"

- "What can you expect if you're walking around at this hour of night, anyway?"
- "Why did you take the chain off the door if you did not know whom you were talking to?"

Any of these statements would be so callous that no one would say them at a time like this. However, an operator who has listened to rape victims make such mistakes time and time again can become so frustrated by such apparent lack of foresight, and the resultant grief and hurt it causes, that he might be more than tempted to vent such frustrations. And even if he does not express them in words, he should be aware that they can become apparent to the victim in many other ways, such as the tone of his voice and the matter-of-fact way he asks questions.

It is crucial that the operator present himself in a benign, non-judgmental way. The operator must have patience and create an atmosphere in which the caller will be able to convey information willingly and naturally.

General Guidelines for Applying Psychological First Aid for the Rape Victim

1. Establish yourself as a helping person who wants to and can help. Demonstrate an actual potential for helpfulness immediately by showing concern for specific needs. These needs may be related to physical well-being, to the reduction of guilt, or the relief of tension and anxiety.

2. Inquire about the physical state of the victim. If physical health is in danger, the first task is to get medical attention. If guilt and anxiety are present, or the caller is immobilized, then this must be dealt with also.

3. Don't confuse the caller with a lot of details about the problems ahead. Reach out to the caller and get enough information so that an appropriate follow-up can be conducted.

4. Always administer psychological first aid. No matter how disinterested or cool and calm the caller may sound, do not be deterred in giving sound psychological help. Victims sometimes hide their fear and grief behind a mask of competence.

5. Establish trust and rapport with the caller; give understand-

ing and not just sympathy. Let the victim talk and ventilate her emotions, and allow the ventilation. The venting of frustration and rage is helpful to the victim in order to recapture self-respect.

6. Everyone has a right to his own feelings. Everyone is unique and interprets his environment and situation according to his own experiences. Most people who become emotionally disorganized do not want to feel the way they do. They need help to pull themselves together into the normally functioning people they normally are. Psychological first aid implies acceptance and help rather than judgment and blame.

7. Everyone feels some emotional disturbance when injured or involved in a disaster. Emotional injury is just as real as physical injury.

8. Do not become emotionally involved. The irritability and stubbornness of emotionally disturbed people is not a personal attack on the operator. There must be an understanding and acceptance by the operator of the disordered and confusing emotions, the sometimes irrational behavior, and the negative responses that a crisis victim may exhibit. Emotional callers need help and reassurance even though they may appear stubborn, unreasonable, and irritable. Fear and insecurity cause people to react in various ways. These reactions may have nothing to do with the operator, if the call is handled with sensitivity for the crisis victim. Victims sometimes accuse the operator for what has happened to them and express anger at the operator who is trying to help. Acknowledge the caller's right to be angry; however, redirect it at the criminal. Avoid becoming defensive or argumentative. This behavior must all be placed in a rational understanding of crisis behavior.

Additional Guidelines for Rape Victims

1. Expect to hear expressions of clinging behavior. This may be expressed in a physical sense (not wanting to be left alone) or a psychological sense (expressing a need to feel secure).

2. Treat the victims family, particularly, mother, father, sisters, brothers, and husband, who might call as you would the victim.

3. Expect fear of hospitalization or medical treatment. The victim sees this as further abuse and exposure.
4. Expect possible respect for the assailant. This results from a sense of feeling grateful to the assailant for not doing more harm, i.e. "At least my life was spared."
5. Often the victim feels physically unclean, dirty, or soiled. Be sensitive to the desire to bathe, yet at the same time emphasize to the victim the importance of not bathing.
6. In all probability there will be calls from women who were raped in the past. With some of these calls, the operator must realize or become aware of serious emotional problems in the caller. Be sensitive to them.
7. Usual concerns of the victim on the phone include questions about veneral disease and pregnancy. She may have fears of the assailant's return, of those close to her finding out about the incident, or of simply being alone. Allow her to ventilate those fears. Take them seriously. She may be feeling angry at the rapist, or at the situation in general, and this may be sometimes misdirected at the operator. Assure her that she has every reason to feel angry, but keep in mind that she is not angry at you personally. In general, you should encourage her to discuss her feelings fully.
8. Don't jump to first-name basis with the victim. Respect the concept of psychological distancing. To jump to first-name basis would be a further violation of personal space, which has already been invaded and destroyed by the assailant.
9. Don't order the victim around, for example, to the station house or the hospital. Ask the victim if she is ready to go to the hospital or to the station house. The assailant has already done enough ordering around of the victim.

REMEMBER: We are dealing with the *victim*.

The possibility exists that someone the operator knows or a member of his family may call in for help. Be aware of this and your feelings that may come to the fore if you are ever faced with this situation. Some operators feel that they would be unable to respond effectively, while others feel that because they knew the caller they would be extra helpful. If possible, you may want another operator to handle this call. However, this may not be possible. If so, maintain your objectives as much as possible and pursue the call as you would any other. Then, if necessary, call someone to talk to yourself.

CHRONIC CALLERS AND CRANK CALLERS

1. CRANK CALLERS. Phony, prank, and/or obscene calls are to be discouraged immediately as soon as the call has been identified as such. On the other hand there are chronic callers.
2. CHRONIC CALLERS. These are calls received from people who call frequently. Some may be trying to build trust and will eventually reveal their real problem; some simply need a listener on a frequent basis; and others will attempt to manipulate the operator. Most of these callers can be referred to those agencies that are designated to handle people who just need to talk to someone.

The following first-hand account from one compassionate operator demonstrates how the awareness of crisis behavior and the application of psychological first aid aided in the resolution of a callers dilemma.

I will never forget the one call I received in which all of my classes on crisis intervention, victimology, and psychological first aid fell into place. I was working on a 12 x 8 tour and it was a fairly active night when I picked a call about 1:00 AM from a young lady who needed to talk to someone. I asked her if it was an emergency and explained that we only take emergency calls, but she answered that it wasn't exactly an emergency but that she needed to talk to someone quickly. I listened to her voice, and it was quivering with fear and excitement, so I decided that I would at least hear her out.

It seemed that she was alone at home with her father. Her mother and younger sister had gone to Europe two weeks earlier, and she couldn't go because she had just graduated from high school and had begun a new job. That night she told her father to watch a movie on television that she thought he might enjoy. After the movie was over, her father came into her bedroom and said that he wanted to have sexual relations with her and attempted to talk her into it. She became angry and told him that he was crazy and to leave her alone or she would call the police. Her father left the room and went out for a walk. However, she was terrified that when he returned he would rape her.

I began to question her about some alternative solutions to her dilemma. Of primary importance was the need to find somewhere else to stay until her mother returned. After inquiring about friends and relatives, she said she was close to her aunt and was sure she would take her in. She hesitated, though, because she felt embarrassed about telling her aunt what happened, and that her aunt would probably tell her mother. This, she felt, would break up her parent's marriage, which would hurt her, particularly, since it would be her fault that it happened.

It was so obvious to me that this young lady was caught up in the grips of a crisis and not only couldn't see an alternative way out of her situation but was also feeling fear, guilt, embarrassment and feeling somehow responsible for what had happened. After allowing her to ventilate all of her feelings, we talked of the possibility of telling her aunt that she was just fearful of sleeping alone in the apartment at night, since her father worked nights anyway. In this way, no one would have to know anything. She agreed that this would be a good solution and said that she would call her aunt right away and have her come pick her up.

It seemed to me to be an obvious solution, so obvious that I wondered why she didn't think of it herself. I then remembered our crisis behavior classes in which I had learned that when a person is in a crisis, the intense anxiety and confusion that they are feeling doesn't allow them to think clearly. Also that after talking about it with someone else who can be objective about the situation, certain solutions will suddenly become clear.

The interesting part of this job is that in many cases you never even know the name of the person you've helped and sometimes it is not even important. I had a really good feeling after the call. I felt that I had helped another human being through what was a terrible crisis for her. She never even thanked me, and I probably will never speak to her again and if I met her on the street I wouldn't even know her, but somehow even all of that didn't seem important.

My only regret was that when it was all over in thinking of my psychological first aid lessons, I had forgotten to say "You did the right thing by calling us. We are here to help." But, I guess that was understood anyway!

Table 4-III. CRISIS BEHAVIOR AND PSYCHOLOGICAL FIRST AID (continued)

	TONE OF VOICE	VERBAL EXPRESSIONS	PHYSICAL MOVEMENT	DECISION MAKING	DISPLAY OF CONFIDENCE
R (*Operator*) E S O L V E	Empathetic Calm Compassionate Gentle Reassuring Interested	Free of derogatory words Encourage caller to talk. Polite Free of cursing	Body language and eye contact and facial expression conducive to listening and empathy.	Check emotional state of caller and self. Be decisive Objectivity Firmness	Convey to caller that he did the right thing Minimum use of officiousness. De-empahsize blame of person in crisis.
R (*Caller*) E S T O R E D	Normal Voice restored.	Dignity and respect restored.	Physical movement is restored when successful resolution is arrived at.	Better able to make minor decisions. Caller is ready to give and receive general information.	Caller has the feeling that he has done the right thing. Regain crisis callers confidence by making minor decisions.

Table 4-III. CRISIS BEHAVIOR AND PSYCHOLOGICAL FIRST AID (continued)

	TONE OF VOICE	VERBAL EXPRESSIONS	PHYSICAL MOVEMENT	DECISION MAKING	DISPLAY OF CONFIDENCE
R E S O L V E (Operator)	Empathetic Calm Compassionate Gentle Reassuring Interested	Free of derogatory words Encourage caller to talk. Polite Free of cursing	Body language and eye contact and facial expression conducive to listening and empathy.	Check emotional state of caller and self. Be decisive Objectivity Firmness	Convey to caller that he did the right thing Minimum use of officiousness. De-empahsize blame of person in crisis.
R E S T O R E D (Caller)	Normal Voice restored.	Dignity and respect restored.	Physical movement is restored when successful resolution is arrived at.	Better able to make minor decisions. Caller is ready to give and receive general information.	Caller has the feeling that he has done the right thing. Regain crisis callers confidence by making minor decisions.

Chapter 5

CALLERS THAT PRESENT SPECIAL COMMUNICATION PROBLEMS FOR THE OPERATOR

I. THE IMPAIRED CALLER

INTRODUCTION

IN order to respond and function effectively, emergency operators must be trained adequately so that they might be more sensitive to the many social problems related to specific groups in society that need special attention. This chapter deals with those persons within a unique group that present a special problem to the operator. How does the emergency operator communicate with children, for example, whose ability to communicate has not been fully developed? There are also other groups that must be paid particular attention to: the elderly, the mentally retarded, and the emotionally ill all present a challenge to communication for the operator.

Stigmatizing the sick, the disabled, and the deformed is an old story. Primitive people feared and punished the physically afflicted; they considered them witches and purveyors of evil and evidence that the gods were angry. This mystical, religious interpretation particularly pervaded the attitude toward birth defects. In medieval times, the blind and deaf were avoided, especially by a pregnant woman, whose child might be similarly afflicted by her sight of them. Whenever evil befell a community, the physically disabled were the first to be blamed. Although little was known of contagion, communities in which lepers lived were not content to isolate them, but treated them with hatred and contempt.

Even in this era of rationalism and science, superstition has not disappeared from society's attitudes toward the disabled and the ill. People continue to be uncomfortable in the presence of those with physical defects. (It has not been too long ago since an aura of shame surrounded the victims of tuberculosis and cancer.) This unwill-ingness or inability to interact normally with a physically disabled person and accept him as an equal is probably one of the more serious discriminatory practices. It often suggests a prejudice that in turn reflects a perpetual fear and anxiety about losing one's own physical integrity and becoming disabled. The non-disabled, as a result, may feel repulsion and disgust for the disabled in different degrees of intensity about different types of disabilities, and then usually a guilt reaction because of these "unacceptable" feelings. Because of this emotional conflict, the non-disabled either avoids coming into contact with the disabled altogether, or, when they do interact with them, do not allow themselves to get angry with or to insult the disabled person, regardless of how irritative his personality or offensive his behavior. Since the non-disabled have to watch their every gesture and word so clearly in order not to make a negative slip or show their aversion, and since the norms regulating disabled/non-disabled social interaction are quite ambiguous for both parties, such interactions are usually uncomfortable, rigid, and strained.

Because of the limitations of this particular group, and the un-comfortable feelings on the part of the operator when interacting with these callers, there may be a tendency to deny assistance or a tendency not to take these calls seriously. Because of the limitations in their ability to communicate, they are also at times mistakenly disregarded as unfeeling and incompetent, misunderstood, and denied assistance on the part of the general public.

The emergency operator should familiarize himself with the characteristics of this unique group of callers. Thus far, we have ex-plored many environmental and psychological problems involving the communicative process in dealing with most callers. Yet, there are still variables in the communication system that we have not discussed. These variables are found in various people, placing them in a separate group. You will note that the following groups of peo-ple have a common quality when it comes to reponding to emer-gency situations or asking for help via the telephone. These people are:

1. Children

2. Tourists   } Impaired

3. Intoxicated persons

4. The elderly

5. Mentally retarded

6. The emotionally disturbed

Frame of reference

and

boundaries

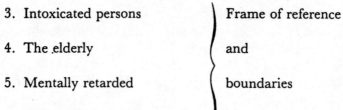

With these callers it may be necessary for the emergency operator to extend himself a bit more than in their usual calls. Since the procedures for dealing with these callers is somewhat modified from the normal operational procedure, it is important that an emergency operator be able to recognize what he is confronted by. This will help in determining and identifying the mode of communication necessary to most effectively provide assistance.

Upon discovering and determining that the caller fits into this particular category, the operator will have a need to avoid words and phrases that will create problems when trying to gather information. The operator will have to establish a unique framework that substitutes simpler words in the information-gathering process that will enhance rather than inhibit the already complex process of gathering information. If we consider each particular type of caller within this group, and consider their specific characteristics, this will become clearer.

Child Callers

The child has not established a mature frame of reference of past experiences in order to draw upon to communicate effectively. There is not yet a rich vocabulary, and the ability to give accurate and pertinent information is still underdeveloped.

Tourists

Tourists are like children, in that they are not familiar with their surroundings, and, therefore, their frame of reference for their immediate surroundings is limited. Every tourist in a strange city has no boundaries or frame of reference for that city, so they too cannot rely on past experiences in order to communicate within that setting. A person in a strange place has difficulty connecting their past experience in a strange environment. It is difficult for a tourist to read landmarks and signs because of a lack of familiarity with the areas. As a result, they too are limited in their ability to communicate accurate information from that environment. The operator will experience difficulty, in turn, in getting vital information from this person.

Unfamiliarity with their surroundings, and being in need of assistance, the tourist can experience feelings of helplessness. This sense of helplessness is the same kind of helplessness that is associated with child behavior. The child depends on others, such as parents or other parent/adult replacements, so there is a sense of dependency in his helplessness. This dependency limits movements — the ability to move about freely without need for restraint — and limits the ability for one to find their own way and to take care of themselves.

Intoxicated Persons

The intoxicated person is childlike in his behavior and communicative ability because alcohol impairs his ability to reason and his memory. Therefore he too responds very much like a child and the tourist. Alcohol is not a stimulant. It acts upon the brain as a depressant and inhibits a person's mental efficiency and level of alertness, rather than stimulating them. Some of the effects of alcohol consumption upon the nervous system are:

- Deficiencies in sight and hearing
- Loss of muscular coordination
- Stumbling, because of loss of control
- Tremors that affect equilibrium
- Passouts
- Memory blackouts

Usually these symptoms, which is the nature of alcoholism, take years to develop. Judgment deteriorates as the drinking habit increases, and this contributes to the lack of control. There may be a lowering of restraints and inhibitions and other internal social controls.

The operator may hear the results of this behavior in the calls made by intoxicated persons. Calls regarding physical injuries caused by these symptoms are common. In addition, the intoxicated person may become the victim of a crime. "Rolling a drunk" and assaults is often a source of income for some, which may cause injury to the vulnerable, intoxicated person.

Alcohol has a toxic effect that causes a lack of judgment, delayed reaction time, which can result in changes in value judgments, and attitudes, brought about during intoxication and carried over into the remainder of one's life. An "I don't care" and "Everything's rosy" attitude can often be heard by the operator, in the caller's singing voice, while calling for assistance because of an assault.

The problem drinker is the group of intoxicated persons with whom the operator must concern himself. It has been estimated, for example, that 40 percent of all victims of homicidal assaults are intoxicated at the time of the fatal attack, as are 50 percent of their attackers. In fatal automobile accidents, available research would indicate that about 60 percent of the responsible drivers had been drinking heavily.

These statistics cannot be ignored. It would not be uncommon for an emergency operator to hear a caller with a slurred, practically incoherent speech attempting to communicate to the operator, "I just ran over a little kid on a bike. I think he's dead."

In addition, the drinker who has been using heavy doses of alcoholic beverages as a psychological crutch may hallucinate wildly when deprived of his drug. A person suffering from the "DTs" may tremble and shake violently and uncontrollably. Worse, he may see persons and things that simply do not exist, such as pink elephants and blue snakes.

As mentioned, while excessive consumptions of alcohol may distort reasoning ability, it simultaneously lowers inhibitions and normal social restraints. Thus, the so-called "quiet type" who would not dream of raising his voice at anyone while sober, becomes the screaming, hostile, abusive caller while intoxicated.

A very important concomitant of the intoxicated person who calls for assistance for the operator is the poor understanding of things explained to him. Research has indicated that when simple instructions were given to intoxicated persons, they oftentimes did not seem to understand what was said to them. His ability to recall certain words, pronounce certain words, and his ability to logically connect ideas and thoughts has been impaired, therefore hampering effective

tive communication. His ability to respond has been reduced to childlike behavior because of alcohol, and his ability to give accurate information as to his location, for example, has been impaired. Therefore, the operator has to deal with this caller with a simple, step-by-step mode of communication.

The Elderly

The elderly are similar to the previously mentioned callers, in that the elderly sometimes suffer from loss of memory, slurred speech, and loss of the ability to connect logic to reason. These can be due to certain illnesses that are commonly found among the elderly. Older persons often lose the ability to recall the immediate past of a few days ago, but they may have vivid recall of things from their childhood. This is often the result of brain damage — senility — brought on by hardening of the arteries in the brain. Other types of memory loss can follow emotionally or physically painful experiences.

An older caller may also suffer from a form of paralysis that impairs a person's ability to form their lips properly in order to form certain words properly. This can be a particular problem in communicating over the telephone. Concerning the attaining of the location of the elderly caller, there may be some difficulty. An older person who has kept to himself or has isolated himself because of fear may not be familiar with some of the more modern terms for surroundings. As mentioned already, the elderly person may remember a location of a building, but has since been torn down. They have lost their frame of reference through what may appear to be to them a constantly changing community with which they have not bothered to keep current with.

In addition, hearing is another factor that may be impaired in the elderly caller. Even if the caller could understand what the operator is saying, it would be the same as with the child caller, who hears a word and doesn't know the definition. The elderly because of hearing loss may know the word but not hear it in full and therefore will not be able to understand.

The senile person has difficulty getting along with people; therefore, he becomes childlike in his habits, quarrelsome, and hoards strange objects. He also has a tendency to wander and becomes forgetful. He may leave his house, walk a short distance, and forget where he was going or where he is. He may not remember what he ate for breakfast, but can vividly describe events in his youth. As the illness progresses, his speech becomes rambling and incoherent, and he may tell convincing lies to compensate for his inability to remember recent events. In some instances, he may even fail to recognize relatives.

RECOGNIZING THE DISTURBED CALLER

A caller suffering from severe mental illness will exhibit one or more of the following symptoms:

CHANGES IN BEHAVIOR PATTERNS: A normally quiet person may become suddenly very belligerent or over-talkative; the happy, outgoing person may become quiet and moody. At times, the same caller will be raving and screaming at the operator that he is "singling me out for abuse and harassment," while at other times he will be calm and quiet.

LOSING TOUCH WITH REALITY: The emotionally disturbed individual may become disoriented and be unable to recall who he is and the date or the time of day. He may withdraw completely from reality to the extent that he becomes totally unaware or unresponsive to his surroundings.

LOSS OF MEMORY: Temporary or permanent memory loss are clear symptoms of mental disturbance.

DELUSIONS: He may have false beliefs that his family or people in general are plotting to kill him.

DELUSIONS WITH HALLUCINATIONS: This disturbed person may not only believe that people are plotting against him, persecuting him, or depriving him of his rights, but he can "hear" them or "taste" the poison in his food. He "sees" them lurking at his window or under furniture and can "feel" the electricity or radar waves that are being directed at him by his enemies.

It is not unusual for a mentally ill person to hear voices from space or from the woodwork, and to see, smell, taste, or feel imaginary things. Persons suffering from such hallucinations actually feel or sense things that are not really present. This type of person is suffering from one of the most severe forms of mental illness and must be given immediate medical attention. Because they really believe what they see, hear, or taste, they may react to them, and the results are often fatal.

A mentally ill person may have fantastic ideas about the body and its functions. He may believe that he has cement in his stomach, his heart has stopped beating, or that mice are eating his brains out. These symptoms and illnesses are very real to this person. He suffers from them as if they were actually due to some disease. If he is convinced that he has an incurable disease he may even attempt suicide.

The Mentally Retarded Caller

The mentally retarded caller is childlike, in that the person's intellectual development was arrested during the developmental stages and, therefore, their intellectual functioning is subaverage. This results in some degree of social inadequacy or impairment in one or more aspects of maturation, such as learning, social adjustment, and of general adaptation to the achievement.

Basically, mental retardation means an intelligence quotient (IQ) score below 75 or 80 on valid, repeated administrations of an individual intelligence test. However, there are several levels of retardation. The mildly retarded individual has an IQ range of 50 to 70. This indicates a mental age of 7 to 11 years after reaching adulthood. He is considered educable and capable of achieving social and vocational skills and basic academic skills.

The moderately retarded individual has an IQ range of 30 to 50, indicating a mental age of 3 to 7 years at adulthood. He is considered trainable and has the capability to communicate orally, to care for himself physically, and to become economically productive in sheltered environments. He can participate in simple recreation and travel alone in familiar places. The severely retarded deficient has an IQ below 30, indicating a mental age of 3 years or below. He is capable of performing daily routine and repetitive physical activities under close supervision in a protective environment. He generally requires continuing directions and may even need nursing care. It is not the premise of the giving of this information on retardation that operators should be therefore trained as mental health therapists. However, the role of the emergency operator in recognizing and handling the mental retardate caller is one of importance. The need of assistance in this area is understandable when one realizes that the mental age of the caller ranges between 3 and 11 years of age. Therefore, the operator must remember to handle this caller with simple, step-by-step directions and guidance.

Interviewing a retarded person is a difficult task. You will need patience to overcome a communication barrier and to alleviate the persons exaggerated fears. If the caller is allowed to set the pace, he will feel less frightened and the situation will seem more understandable to him. A rapid firing of questions at the retardate will generally cause confusion and withdrawal. If he withdraws, he may not respond to any further questions. At other times, he may respond in a way that he thinks you would like him to answer, rather than offer, the factual information that you need. Therefore, the operator should be constantly on the alert. An objective, patient, and understanding manner is the best approach to elicit a factual account of events from the retardate.

Common Situations Involving the Mentally Retarded Caller

Missing person cases are common situations in which the operator will encounter the retardate caller. Often they may wander away from their custodians and are then reported missing. They may aimlessly wander the streets until they realize that they are lost, then call in for assistance. Retarded adults are just as likely to become lost as retarded children. This is not to imply that retarded persons cannot learn their way to different places or even to travel by themselves. Retarded persons can travel to familiar places in unfamiliar locations but may not be able to reason how to find their way.

Some retarded persons realize their differences and try to compensate for them by acting bold and tough on the streets. They can also be easily influenced by others to act unlawfully and to get them into situations in which they can be injured. Some people will deliberately exploit a retardate and instigate them into doing something they would not ordinarily think of doing by themselves. In addition, it is not uncommon for a retarded person, because he is vulnerable, to be cheated or forcibly robbed of his money.

The Emotionally Disturbed Caller

This type of caller is perhaps the most difficult of this group of callers because, in their conversations, logic may be apparent at one moment and the next moment it is gone. Within one sentence, the operator may find logic in one phrase, and in the next phrase of the sentence the caller will be illogical and immature. This can be confusing to the operator who is trying to come to some conclusion about the call. We will discuss only those forms of mental disturbances that the operator will come into contact with, namely, psychosis and neurosis.

Psychosis

A psychosis may be defined as *a severe form of mental illness in which a noticeable and progressive disintegrating change occurs in the personality*. It is usually characterized by serious changes in thought, feeling or behavior, withdrawal from reality, persistently false or distorted beliefs (delusions), and imaginary sights, noises, tastes, etc. (hallucinations). The basic problem is that this person is overwhelmed with fear that may be unrealistic but very frightening and may sometimes be completely out of control.

Neurosis

A neurosis is a less severe emotional disturbance. Some neuroses are more disabling than others and can prevent people from leading useful lives. This caller is characterized by irrational or unreasonable fears, rigid thought and behavior patterns, and by his inability to adjust to life's problems. He suffers tensions and emotional strain, constant instability, some depression, and a somewhat pessimistic view of life. Neurotic persons often behave in unusual ways when they become overly anxious or excited. These symptoms become a problem when they overwhelm and control thinking and behavior.

Manic-Depressive Psychosis

This form of psychosis is marked by emotional extremes that are exhibited as mania (overactivity) melancholia (depression). In its lesser form, mania may range from a feeling of well-being, over-enthusiasm, and a talkativeness, to extreme confidence and boastful self-assertion. In a more acute case, the speech of the disturbed person may become disjointed and endless. He may talk about a variety of topics and be continuously shifting from topic to topic. His prevailing mood is that of elation and overconfidence. He is always busy, but never accomplishes anything, and is seldom tired and requires little sleep.

If he is overstimulated, he may use his energy by shouting, singing, or smashing furniture. He is inconsiderate of others and is easily aroused to anger and fury if his activities are curtailed. He may display a domineering arrogance, especially towards authority. The total effect is that of a person highly speeded up, totally disorganized and not intelligible.

The symptoms of the opposite end of the manic-depressive continum is one of underactivity and depression. In the mildest form, they are discouraged, feel inadequate, and there is slowing of movement and speech. When such a person is interviewed he speaks slowly, in a low tone, and with as few words as needed. The more serious cases of depression assume forms of overwhelming sadness and morbidness, with an outlook of gloom and utter hopelessness. He may believe that he is suffering from an incurable disease or that his insides are disintegrating. A person in deep depression is a potential suicide caller. He groans, moans, and squirms and tries to hide from others because of his shame and feelings of unworthiness.

In summary, some of the signals to look for in order to recognize the emotionally disturbed caller are:

1. Rapid changes in attitude during conversation. (Unusually soft and sweet one moment, then abusive and hostile the next moment)
2. Unusual or bizarre disclosures. ("I was ordered by a voice to put my baby in the oven.")
3. An increase or decrease in activity. (Rapid, disjointed speech, shifting from topic to topic, to a slow, sad hopeless speech.)
4. Argumentative and uncooperative with uncontrolled outbursts of anger without provocation.
5. Pervading hostility. ("I can never get any help in this damned city," or "You operators don't know what you're doing, that's why.")
6. Disorganized thinking. ("I can't think, I don't understand.

Tell me that again. What did you say?")

7. Hallucinations and delusions. ("Operator, please send help. The man in the next apartment is sending waves of radar through the walls. I tried to stop them by putting up aluminum foil on the walls, but the waves are still coming through. He is trying to kill men.")

This group of special callers is unique because there is a common theme of behavior that is displayed in each of the callers ability to communicate. In each there is a childlike response, thinking is not systematic, and there are problems with thinking in abstract terms. Because of this impairment, their thinking process has been reduced to a simple, basic state, and information must be elicited in the same manner. The operator must understand that in order to gather information from this special group, he must develop a method of breaking down complex messages into simple, step-by-step components in a manner so that the caller might understand them. In order to do this, the following suggestions might be helpful.

HANDLING THE DISTURBED CALLER

The operator must rely upon his patience, tact, and reasoning abilities in an attempt to provide assistance to this particular and unique group of callers. In order to establish an appropriate mode of communication for dealing with this type of caller, the operator must first determine that the difficulty he may be experiencing with the caller is due to the fact that the caller is one of the persons named in this category. As such, the operator needs to be able to quickly diagnose the caller and establish his mode of communication needed to handle this call. As previously mentioned, the operator needs to approach the problem caller with a step-by-step, simplified approach, in order to discourage *circular interactions*. Circular interactions occur when the terminology used may have alternative meanings for the caller and the language then becomes circular; that is, it takes you around in circles. For example:

Operator: Where are you?
   Caller: Home.
Operator: Where is home?
   Caller: Where I am.
Operator: Yes, where are you?
   Caller: I just told you I was at home.

Instead of using terms that waste time and gather no information, such as in the example given above, the operator needs to develop an approach in which the language is exhaustive in meaning. One of the first things that the operator may want to do in developing a method of communicating with this special group of callers is to first think in terms of a framework. In his own mind, the operator must establish a model or framework that can be used in this type of setting. The range-finder model is one approach that may be helpful in determining the exact location of a caller within the group.

THE RANGE-FINDER MODEL

Initially, the operator needs to solicit a point of location from the caller where assitance is needed. In order to establish this point — the location or range within which the caller will be located — we must have an abstract model of how to establish it. In order to do this, one must simply understand that any two lines intersecting creates a point. What the operator can do then is substitute streets and avenues and/or directions for lines. He may then gather information that would show or illustrate where streets or avenues intersect in order to define the point. To illustrate further, consider the following diagram and operator/caller dialogue. The caller is located on Green Street at the corner of Fourth Avenue (*see* Figure 5-1).

Operator: What is the name of the street you are standing on?
　Caller: Green Street.
Operator: What is the name of the other street crossing Green Street?
　Caller: Fourth Avenue.

The name of one constitutes one line. The next piece of information the operator needs is the other line. The other line is the other street that crosses the first. Where the two streets cross constitutes the point. By this interchange, the operator can establish that the caller is standing nearby or on the point where Green Street crosses Fourth Avenue.

To further pinpoint locations within a range, the operator may ask for other types of information, such as:

• Names of stores located nearby
• Any landmarks, such as monuments, statues, museums, theatres, or special names of well-known large buildings

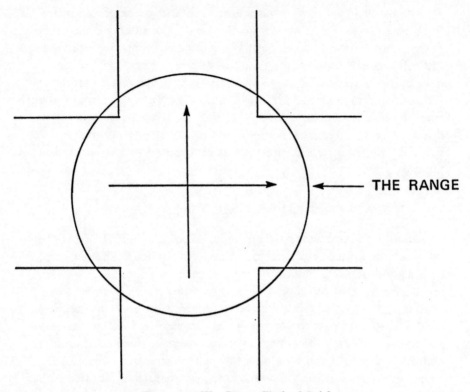

Figure 5-1. The Range-Finder Model.

- The color of buildings
- Any parks that may be nearby

This kind of information that the operator can elicit from the caller helps clarify misunderstood transmissions.

In addition, asking for a house number rather than the caller's address is an exhaustive method of attaining the correct location. The operator may ask for the caller's address, which may not be where the caller is presently located and in need of assistance. For example, Mr. Jones lives at 2525 Green Street, but he calls for assistance from 3000 Main Street. The operator may ask "What is your address Sir?" and Mr. Jones replies, "My address is 2525 Green Street." Help is sent to his home address, as opposed to where he is located in need of assistance. Remember, the person seeking help does not necessarily have to be at home.

The operator should also be mindful of calls from subways or apartment buildings. A necessary piece of information is whether the subway is elevated or underground, whether one is in the basement of the apartment building or on the fifteenth floor hallway or the roof. The numbers of apartments or letters designating apartments and floors of the building is needed. Much time can be lost in responding to an apartment building of 300 apartments divided among 20 floors, without having first pinpointed the floor and apartment in which the caller is located. Also, be aware that apartment numbers are not necessarily reflective of the floor that the apartment is located on. Apartment five is not always on the fifth floor, nor apartment fifty-two always on the fiftieth floor.

Department Jargon

The operator should avoid using department jargon. This type of language further confuses an already confusing situation. For example:

1. The use of *Cross Streets*, as opposed to "What is the name of the street that intersects your location?"
2. The use of *Call Back*, instead of "What is your telephone number at which I can reach you if I need to call you back?"
3. The use of *Bus*, instead of "An ambulance is on the way."

Digital Form

Numbers should be repeated back to this group of callers in simplified, digital form. When numbers are phrased together they become more conducive for errors to be made. This would be for confirmation of addresses and telephone numbers. Digital form is exhaustive in its terminology, and, therefore, there is opportunity to correct an error if one has been made. The following dialogue illustrates this more fully:

Operator: What is the telephone number of the phone from which you are calling, sir?

Caller: Seven forty-nine, eleven hundred. (Phrased)

Operator: Is that, seven, four, nine, one, one, zero, zero? Digital form)

Guidance and Support

The type of caller that fits into this particular category also needs continuing guidance that is supportive of the gathering of information. For example, the child caller who calls because his grandfather has fallen, is unconscious, and cannot get to the phone will need simple, step-by-step guidance and support if assistance is to be given to his grandfather.

Child Caller: "Operator, Grandpa just fell down the stairs and I can't wake him up."

Incorrect Approach

Operator: "What is your address?"

Correct Approach

"Are you and Grandpa in a house or an apartment?"

"Do you know the number of the building where you and your Grandpa are now?"

"Do you know the name or number of the street where you and Grandpa are now?"

Operator: "What is the apartment number?"

Child Caller: "I don't know."

"Could you go look at the front door of the apartment and tell me if there is a number or letter on it?"

Operator: "What is your

"What do Grandpa's

Incorrect Approach	Correct Approach
Grandpa's name?"	friends or other people call him?" What name do
Child Caller: "Grandpa."	they call him by?"

Operator: "What is the telephone number where you are calling from?"	"Look at the part of the telephone that is on the wall. Are there any numbers there?"
Child Caller: "I don't know."	"Look at the part of the telephone that is on the table. Are there any numbers on it?"
	"Look at the part of the telephone that you are holding. It is called the receiver. In between the part that you are talking to me into, and the part that you are listening to me from, look and see. Are there any numbers there? If so, please give them to me, so that if I have to call you back I will have your telephone number."

In addition, continuing reassurances, as to the reasons you will be needing this information, is helpful. Keep the caller supported throughout the call:

Operator: "I know this is difficult for you to do, but please. We need this information to get help for your Grandpa."

For the intoxicated caller, listen to specifics, so that extra information can be picked up. For example:

1. "I need help. Someone is beating me up."
2. "My arm is broken. I'm bleeding."

Because of their inability to articulate clearly, information that would indicate a need for an ambulance, besides a radio car, may be missed. Therefore, careful listening and probing is essential. All of these "special callers" discussed here should be important to the operator. The assistance that the operator renders them, however, temporary in nature it might appear, does give them the awareness that someone does care and is concerned for their welfare. The emergency operator does have his ordinarily difficult job compounded by the addition of these variables that are evident in these special callers. However, the sensitive, patient handling of these callers, reflecting compassion and understanding, not only gives the callers hope and confidence in their futures, but can reap the operator his greatest rewards.

In concluding this section on the impaired caller it might be helpful to summarize some practical suggestions on how to handle these calls. The following suggestions will make the performance of your job easier and more efficient.

1. Take time to consider the caller, as to whether he fits into this unique group of callers.
2. Never rush these calls or make assumptions. Talk to the caller, ask questions, and find out all you can about the caller.
3. Tell the caller that you are there to help him. Soothe him with your voice, your manner, your understanding, and your patience.
4. Keep reassuring him that he will be well taken care of.
5. Avoid excitement in your voice. Do not abuse the caller with words or threats. Besides being discourteous and unprofessional, such behavior will only make your gathering information more difficult and take longer.
6. Speak slowly and distinctly. Let the caller set the pace. Practice asking questions, gathering information, and giving directions and instructions in a simple, step-by-step manner that will be understood by this group of callers.
7. Use words and language that is exhaustive in meaning. This means that there is only one meaning that could not

be misunderstood by the caller.

8. Ignore verbal abuse. Be aware that some callers that fit within this group will frequently verbally abuse the operator. If you are wise and understanding, you will know that this person is confused and frightened.

9. Do not deceive. Lying to a confused and frightened caller may not only strengthen his belief that no one really cares. Never resort to lies in order to gain cooperation from the caller.

10. Continually re-evaluate the situation. Has the caller's mood changed? Adjust your approach and your mode of communication accordingly.

Although these callers require sensitivity on the part of the operator, the caller contemplating suicide requires an even more delicate approach. This person has also lost his sense of logic and must be dealt with in a childlike manner. In addition, the operator must be particularly aware of the caller's psychological needs. In the next section, we will discuss techniques and procedures for handling the caller contemplating suicide.

II. THE SUICIDAL CALLER

The problem of suicidal callers permeates the area of the emergency operator's responsibility. Its practical importance requires that this type of call be considered separately. Suicide is now almost the only direct psychiatric cause of death and usually, although not always, can be avoided. The prevention comes from first suspecting that there may be a risk, then assessing this risk and arranging adequate changes in the mode of communication accordingly.

For the emergency operator, calls from those persons contemplating suicide presents perhaps the most frightening and challenging of all calls received and possess many complex questions:

- What state of mind drives people to the point that life is no longer worth living?
- What is the operator's role in preventing suicides?
- How does the operator recognize suicidal tendencies in the depressed caller?
- How does the operator interact with the caller comtemplating suicide?

What the questions are really asking is:

- Does the operator have the necessary insight to recognize the potential suicide?
- Can the operator successfully interact with the suicide caller in such a way so as to play a major role in the prevention of that caller carrying out his plans?

Ideally, the role of the emergency operator in suicide calls is to prevent the suicide from occurring. Many operators somehow miss this point and don't see it as part of their job. Although they may respond to thousands of calls each year, they fail to recognize their potential for preventing suicides. Unless the caller actually manifests psychotic or bizarre tendencies, the call is not handled as a possible suicide. The operator should realize that it is not only the obvious "jumper on the bridge" who is desperate and wants to die. Suicidal calls are received from less obvious, but as equally intent callers.

It is wise of emergency operators to become acquainted with

techniques and procedures for handling suicidal callers. The material that follows will provide you with a basic knowledge of the many different aspects of suicide. This knowledge should help you improve your skills in dealing with suicidal people and, hopefully, increase the probability that a call from a person contemplating suicide will be successfully thwarted. In addition, knowledge about suicide and its causes may tend to reduce the distress and anxiety in dealing with a problem that usually causes discomfort for everyone involved.

We will cover three areas that relate to these goals. They are:

1. The reasons why individuals attempt suicide.
2. A description of the people and methods usually involved in suicide.
3. The actions which the operator can take in the various suicidal situations.

We will treat each of these areas separately, and each area will have its own unique contribution for improving the operator's effectiveness and will help the operator make a more accurate assessment of this and other situations. The goal is to provide a service that will accomplish prevention and be performed in a professional, understanding manner. Specifically, the object is to provide guidance and support for those persons involved that will see them through the critical period so that they can adequately adjust to and deal with the present problems and learn to cope with future ones without resorting to self-destructive behavior. This can be accomplished through proper action and understanding on the part of the emergency operator.

The operator at this point may be thinking: "How can I detect those tendencies, I'm no psychiatrist!" However, in fact, most people overtly threaten suicide before they actually kill themselves. It is the rare occasion for a person to commit suicide without giving some prior indication of his intent. Thus, the emergency operator equipped with some basic understanding of the psychology of suicide should be able to identify certain clues that might indicate suicidal behavior. From this point, questioning might reveal a past history involving suicide attempts. Then, the operator is in a position to make a proper diagnosis and proceed with the correct method.

In this role, the operator is rendering a true service to the community. He is seen as showing concern and true involvement rather than merely performing a routine task, requiring only a gathering of information and dispatching of assistance. The operator who sincerely understands the emotionally disturbed potential suicide caller realizes that his most important action is to take all suicide attempts and threats seriously, and this can be done by responding as if that person's life depended upon his demonstrating concern. This concern for the person may be all that is necessary to prevent the suicide from occurring. This point may become more clear by understanding some of the different types of suicides.

TYPES OF SUICIDE PATTERNS

Researchers have delineated three basic types of suicide patterns. They are as follows:

1. SYMBOLIC SUICIDE. This type of suicide involves displacement of personal hostility on to some neutral object or person. If this hostility (usually resulting from internal frustration, conflict, or pressure, in general) is focused inward, personal harm or self-destruction may occur.

2. ACCIDENTAL SUICIDE. This type is characterized by the occurrence of an accident that results in an individual's death and appears to contain some element of an unconscious desire for death. This might be evident in automobile accidents in which the car serves as the instrument for self-destruction. Sometimes alcohol might serve as the catalyst and give the person courage to commit the act. The same internal forces are at work here as in symbolic suicide.

3. OVERTLY INTENTIONAL BUT UNSUCCESSFUL SUICIDE. This type of suicide comprises the majority of operator involvement. Here, the operator is dealing with a suicide attempt that has failed for various reasons. The reason for failure may have been intentional or unintentional. It is not so important to know why the suicide attempt failed. The operator must instead threat these cases seriously, even if the "intended victim" made a very shallow attempt. The operator should be aware that most successful suicide victims have had a history of one or more prior unsuccessful attempts. With this in mind, he must also be aware of the effect the suicidal attempt has had on either close friends or relatives. These persons may very

well experience much guilt and feel responsible for the person's actions. Remember this last desperate cry for help may bring the necessary attention, sympathy, and perhaps hospitalization and therapy needed to enable this person to cope with life.

MOTIVES FOR SUICIDE — SUICIDE ATTEMPTS

The average suicide victim does not exist. Self-destruction is a problem of the young, the mature, and the aged of both sexes in all walks of life. Sometimes an individual finds himself bereft of all support, perhaps without accommodation, and deprived of close relationships. A suicidal act may occur out of desperation. For example, a suicidal act commonly occurs as an appeal when a close emotional attachment is endangered. The person hopes that, as a result of it and the subsequent medical attention, affection may be rekindled in the loved one.

Adolescents quite often reach a point of crisis after a phase of increasing rebellion, perhaps against intolerant parents. He hopes that in the resulting emotional upheaval of a suicide attempt, attitudes are reappraised, with a possible improvement in his relationship with his family.

Each person has feelings that need to be satisfied (e.g. love, affection, dependency). In order to satisfy these needs, the person reaches out to others and develops and sustains relationships with these others. If a conflict develops in a relationship between two people in which affection or dependency played major roles, suicidal thoughts may develop.

It is important to remember that suicide is not a solitary act that occurs in a vacuum. The suicidal person operates in a family or a social setting that influences and sometimes causes him to consider suicide. For years the prevailing feelings were that an attempted suicide was an unsuccessful try to end one's life. On the contrary, a number of studies indicate that while a suicide is generally a final solution to one's problems, the attempt is usually aimed at improving his life. Many suicide attempts occur because the individuals feel powerless or incapable of effecting a change in those around them or their situation. Attempts are generally made by people who in their own minds have little intention of actually dying, but rather are attempting to force a change in an intolerable or overwhelming situation. For example:

- A wife who feels that her marriage is undesirable because of her husband's insensitivity to her needs may attempt suicide as a way of overcoming the communication gap that exists between them.
- A well-established businessman in his forties who is angry with his wife and who feels she is emotionally and physically rejecting him.
- A young girl recently jilted or a wife facing a divorce she does not want. Both are filled with intense anger and overwhelming feelings of rejection and worthlessness.
- A teenager may feel angry with his father for giving more attention to his brothers and sisters. He may not be able to express the angry, aggressive feelings towards his father because of respect and, therefore, may turn them inward on himself.

These attempts are ways of communicating some message to another person to change their behavior, rather than to die. It may be an attempt to make a spouse, a parent, or a lover change his actions in some way. It may be an angry effort to strike back at someone or to persuade him not to take an unwanted action, such as a divorce, a separation, or other change.

Other Motives for Suicide

Besides anger at significant others turned inwards, there are other motives for suicide attempts. These may be the fear of being punished for a real or imagined wrong that has been committed. For example:

- A respected business person being arrested on a morals charge.
- A student faced with final examinations and fearful of failing and disappointing his family.
- An older person suffering from an incurable or serious illness.
- A widow or widower who feels lost, a burden to others, or not needed by others.

A typical suicide attempt may be made by any person of any age group who is motivated into an act of self-destruction by a variety of factors.

Some statements that the operator may hear the caller make are as follows:

- "My family would be better off without me."
- "Things just haven't been going right."
- "I just can't sleep anymore. I can't eat. I don't go to work anymore. I'm just not interested in anything."
- "I gave away all of my jewelry yesterday."
- "I've been so unhappy lately. I have no energy for anything."
- "A voice inside my head is telling me to take 150 pills. Should I listen to the voice?"

Generally, the danger of suicide is present when a person perceives his life situation as overwhelming, hopeless, or unsolvable or his suffering is unbearable. Thoughts of suicide may occur in many persons, but the common factor is depression. Probably everyone at one or several points in their lives has been depressed. However, approximately 60 percent of people who attempt suicide have shown some signs of being depressed prior to the act.

The signs of severe depression an operator should be aware of are several. First, the person contemplating suicide may report that he has been feeling "sad." He may say that he has been "feeling blue" or "down in the dumps." He may be crying or may indicate that he has been crying frequently lately. The individual's speech will be soft and slowed down. He may indicate a loss of interest and motivation to do certain things, e.g. work, household chores, recreation, etc. His conversation will center around his feelings of inadequacy, hopelessness, failure, unworthiness, and guilt. He may report inability to sleep, loss of appetite, and feeling "tired all the time."

Any recent change in social conditions should be noted, and these may include a move of house, loss of job or or a relationship, death of a loved one, disappointment in love, an accident, some occupational setback, or feelings of guilt concerning failure.

With the mentally disturbed, because of severe disturbances of motivation and behavior that are found, it may be impossible to determine reasons for attempting suicide. In schizophrenic persons a suicidal episode may be produced by delusions or may be the result of hallucinatory instructions, and the person responds without insight and therefore with no capacity to control the impulse. Quite often it is difficult to obtain adequate explanations as to what has happened, in which case it may well be part of a general and motivational abnormality. In addition, it has been noted that schizophrenics on medication for long periods sometimes develop typical depressive symptoms, which may lead to suicidal acts. Giving these examples is not meant to suggest that each attempt can be identified with a specific motive. The mixture of feelings involved is nearly always complicated.

METHODS OF SUICIDE

Contemplating suicide, as well as actually committing the act, is not limited by race, age, or socioeconomic class. Suicide occurs in all levels of society, and the methods that people use to end their lives are as equally diverse. Within these diverse categories and methods, however, certain patterns do emerge regarding who takes their live and how. Knowing these patterns can help an operator who is developing communication techniques designed to circumvent suicide threats.

The choice of suicide method is influenced by sex differences. Women and men tend to choose different methods. While women may choose more non-violent means, men usually choose more violent means, such as the use of firearms, jumping from high places, cutting or piercing vital organs, hanging themselves, or throwing themselves in front of vehicles.

Those persons whose personalities are the type that deal with problems orally — the alcoholics and drug abusers — are very likely to make suicidal attempts usually by increasing their intake or adding other substances, which is an extension of their familiar means of relieving distress. In addition, impaired self-control while under the influence of alcohol or drugs may be another important factor. Whatever the reasons, alcoholics form a large group with a high risk of death by suicide. Drug-dependent persons may become disturbed or depressed and make a suicidal attempt, but they sometimes kill themselves without suicidal intent as a result of increasing their dose of drugs or as a result of abnormal behavior.

Alcohol is frequently taken together with an overdose of tablets, which may cause potentiation (one poison combined with another chemical, intensifying the strength). Statistics indicate that excessive drinking and attempts at self-destruction are sometimes related. Add alcohol to the despair and low self-esteem that a chronic alcoholic may feel, and the stage is set for a suicidal encounter. It has been stated already that excessive consumption of alcohol suppresses human inhibitions and weakens self-control. Inasmuch as the impulse to engage in self-endangering or reckless behavior may be one of the factors kept in check by normal inhibitions and personal controls, it should come as no surprise that their absence may lead to dangerously suicidal actions.

TALKING ABOUT SUICIDE PLANS

Most suicidal persons are willing to talk about their suicidal thoughts or intent, since most, if not all, persons who are suicidal continue the struggle over whether they should live or die right up until their last moments. Therefore, the operator should not hesitate to ask questions concerning their plans. The operator may hesitate to inquire about suicide thoughts because of the fear of suggesting what has not already been considered by the caller. However, if a caller has not contemplated suicide as a solution, the asking of the question by the operator will not place the suggestion in the caller's mind.

An effective and sensitive way of inquiring about intentions is to say, "Often when people feel the way you feel, and have gone through some of the things you have gone through, they think about taking their life. Have you been thinking about this?" Approaching the subject in this way indicates understanding on the part of the operator and will open communication more readily to the subject. On the other hand, the insensitive operator may be heard to say, "Wow, if I had so many problems, I'd think of jumping off the closest bridge!" This type of statement could only make the caller defensive and uncooperative towards the operator.

If the caller states that he has not thought about suicide, the operator should accept this, unless he has a reason not to. However, if the person states that he is considering suicide, it is very important to ask certain follow-up questions. These may include:

- "How long have you been feeling this way?"
- "Have you thought about how you would end your life?"
- "Have you made plans?"
- "Have you acquired the means?"
- "When do you plan to do this?"

- "Where do you plan to do this?"

These questions do not invade privacy (as the caller is often quite willing to share this information) and is important information for the operator to have.

If the caller responds by saying he has feelings of "being better off dead," with no specific plans made as to the carrying out of this statement, there is no need to pursue this type of questioning. This caller is not as highly suicidal as the person who gives specific information and may be just reaching out for a reassuring word or someone to talk to.

Chronic Illness

Many times the caller will mention the presence of a severe, recent, or chronic medical problem. The presence of medical difficulties, such as cancer, or severe heart problems, increases the risk of the person carrying out a suicidal act. The other area that is often mentioned is a recent loss. The loss can be due to any one of a number of events: death of a loved one or close family member, loss of a loved one or close family member, loss of a job or other financial setback, or rejection by a partner through a divorce, separation, or quarrel. The presence of any of these or other losses increases the risk of a successful suicide.

An inquiry may be made as to previous attempts at suicide. The absence of any previous experience is a positive indication; the presence of previous efforts is a negative indication.

DEVELOPING A LANGUAGE THAT IS
SUPPORTIVE OF THE SUICIDAL CALLER

Initial Contact

A person seriously contemplating suicide is undergoing an emotional crisis in which he has lost the ability to consider an alternative method of dealing with his situation. A mild suicide attempt, or even a threat to end life, is an indication that the caller is in desperate need for sympathetic understanding and compassion.

The operator receiving the suicide call must immediately show an interest in the caller's situation. He must take immediate efforts to establish the caller's name, address, and telephone number in case the line is disconnected. Maintaining communication with the caller is critical. The caller must be reassured from the start that you want to help him. Most callers are reluctant to reveal this information immediately. In these cases, the operator may direct his efforts at establishing rapport with the caller and attempt to get the location after the caller has placed trust in him.

From the onset, it is very important that the operator project a certain attitude to the caller. This attitude can be best described as one of concern and caring. The operator's first verbal contact should be to introduce himself by name. Often it is helpful to give your full name, such as, "I'm Barbara Peters." This allows the caller to respond on a more personal and informal basis if he chooses to use his first name. Ask the caller what he prefers to be called. Most callers will respond with just a first name in order to protect their identity. This does not present a problem but rather will allow for a more personal communication relationship to develop, which should be the operator's goal.

Avoid any sudden aggressive comments or display of impatience, and refrain from using abusive language. These reflect your hostility and a lack of understanding and may be just the impetus the caller needs to follow through on his plans. When a person is threatening to jump from a high place or talks about taking 200 pills, the operator should be cautious and thoughtful about what is being said. Make every effort to engage the caller in conversation. Once the operator has established trust with the caller by speaking calmly and non-judgmentally, and has been able to communicate a non-threatening position, he will usually receive positive responses to questions. He can then move on to problem areas that are more emotionally charged.

Vocalization

This term refers to the volume, speed, and pacing of speech. It is generally a good idea to speak to callers in a soft and slow voice, while allowing a few seconds to lapse between questions. People who are upset tend to speak loudly and quickly. The operator's soft, slow voice will lead them to speak in a similar fashion. People who hear themselves speaking in this manner are likely to be better able to control their own emotions than people who hear themselves talking loudly and quickly. Pacing questions slowly gives an impression of patience and concern. The rapid firing of questions leads to an impression of impatience and adds a note of interrogation, which can lead the caller to feel blame.

Self-Disclosure

Following this initial interaction, the operator can begin to establish rapport and find a common ground. Establishing rapport and finding a common ground is very important for building trust, and this can be accomplished with the technique of self-disclosure. People tend to be more open with those who are open with them. We tend to be more disclosing about our own thoughts, feelings, and backgrounds when others first reveal such information to us. For example, the operator can very easily find a common ground with the caller around the following topics:

- Age group
- Ethnic group
- Familiarities in family settings, number of children, brothers, sisters
- Troublesome parents
- Background experiences
- Schools attended
- Other interests, sports, movies
- Area that the caller lives in

If the operator offers information concerning himself, the caller will begin to build trust in him. For example:

- "You know, we're the same age."
- "I'm Italian too."
- "I have six brothers, I know what you mean."
- "Yes, my parents have gotten older and are more dependent on me now also."
- "My friend went to the same school you did."
- "My aunt lives in Brooklyn. She lives in Sheepshead Bay. Which section do you live in?"
- "I understand. My wife walked out on me last year. It was a difficult time for me also."

Communicating with the caller through conversation about various topics is an effective deterrent to most suicide callers. Talking distracts the person, as they more or less have to pay attention. It also allows time for him to consider his actions and for help to arrive. Try to give hope to the caller while at the same time respecting his predicament. Moralizing over the telephone to someone you do not know and cannot see is seldom effective. Inquire about friends, relatives, or neighbors. Attempt to establish if there is anyone he can trust and has confidence in. Loved ones, family members, and friends may be in a position to give emergency assistance. Offer to contact them if possible with the caller's permission. However, don't attempt to pass off the caller to someone else, as this may be interpreted as disinterest. The understanding and interest you display towards the caller and the speed in which you react can all be instrumental in preventing the distressed or disturbed person from ending his life.

Active Listening

When another person is talking, we may simply be present or we may communicate that we are interested in hearing what is being said. The latter process is called "active listening." Some of the main features of active listening are as follows:

CLARIFICATION. We clarify when we repeat to the speaker something he has just said, but in our own words or ask a question about what was just said. Using this procedure serves to show the caller that you have been listening and paying attention and also encourages him to go on and provide further details. It also serves to indicate to the caller that what he is saying is important to the operator. It is best to clarify when the person has finished a complete segment rather than to interrupt repeatedly to ask about details.

SHARED FEELINGS. Whereas clarification stresses repeating back some facts to the caller, this procedure focuses on expressing to the caller an understanding of his main feelings. Some operators are rightfully taught to be *impartial*. Unfortunately, as noted previously, this is often translated into *impersonal*. When dealing with callers contemplating suicide, a personal expression of concern and shared feelings, such as, "I'm sorry this has happened to you," can be very comforting to the caller. Rather than try to conceal the emotions, the operator will convey to the caller that they are present. To reflect the caller's feelings accurately, the operator must pay attention both to what the caller is saying and to how he is saying it. The suicidal caller might know his feelings are being shared with an operator who says, "Everything seems dark to you right now; there doesn't seem to be hope anywhere."

PERSONALIZED STATEMENTS. Emergency operators do not differ from other persons in large organizations in their tendency to make impersonal statements, such as, "It's probably a good idea for you to see a psychiatrist!" When dealing with potential suicides, it is far more effective to personalize statements by prefacing them with, "I feel" or "I think." This conveys personal concern and involvement with the caller.

STATING THE OBVIOUS. Persons contemplating suicide are usually confused and thinking slowly. In many respects, their emotional level has reverted to that of children, in that things are not clear to them. Therefore, the operator can reassure the caller with what may seem to be obvious statements. These are, for example: "I am here to help you," "I want to help you," or "I can see that this has been an upsetting experience for you." These types of reassurances may seem condescending, but are in reality very important messages for the caller to hear.

RESPONDING NON-DIRECTIVELY. This technique is used when one wants to help the other person in a conversation to continue talking. It is especially effective in situations when the topic is sensitive and you want to give the other person control over what may be said. Responding non-directively allows the other party to cover a topic in psychologically satisfying sequence and to feel that he has made the decision about the hows and the whats of the discussion. Responding non-directively is grounded in the theory of positive reinforcement. People like to talk to those who support them, or at least to those who do not deny or reject them. If you react or respond in a supportive manner to something the other person said, he will feel the comments have been reinforced.

HOW TO REACT TO THE SUICIDAL
CALLER IN A SUPPORTIVE MANNER

In order to utilize the above techniques, the operator must have a sincere concern for the caller and an interest in listening to what he has to say. Although each type of response can be used individually and independently, the techniques of responding non-directively, clarification, shared feelings, etc., are cultivated most effectively when they are used in conjunction with one another. The caller will usually open the conversation with a statement, after which a clarification or an "uh-huh" response is given (responding non-directively). Thereafter, as the conversation runs through a sequence of interactions involving shared feelings and personalized statements and "uh-huh" responses, an open question is asked. The following dialogue will make this clearer. The caller may begin the conversation with a statement or question.

> Caller: Will you please help me? I have an urge to jump out of the window and I'm on the twentieth floor.
> Operator: Yes, certainly I'd be happy to help you. My name is Joan Mason, what's yours?
> Caller: My name is Pat.
> Operator: Okay, Pat. How can I help you? What's going on?
> Caller: I'm seventeen, and I'm having all kinds of trouble.
> Operator: Uh-huh.
> Caller: My parents have been really pressuring me lately, and my boyfriend just called it quits.
> Operator: Uh-huh.
> Caller: And I'm failing in all my classes in school.
> Operator: How have you been getting along with the folks?
> Caller: I really appreciate all they do for me.
> Operator: Uh-huh.
> Caller: They really seem to care about me.
> Operator: Uh-huh.

The "uh-huh" responses provide support and indicate that the operator is following the conversation.

On the other hand, you might want to secure more information about a topic. In that case, clarification and shared feelings would be appropriate responses.

> Caller: But I simply can't stand living here any longer.
> Operator: You can't stand being there any longer!
> Caller: You said it! They're constantly picking at me about my boyfriend and my grades.

Operator: Well, how do you feel about your teachers and school?

Caller: I can't stand them either. I can't get anywhere with anyone.

Operator: I understand. Everybody's on your back, and everything seems bleak right now. There doesn't seem to be any hope anywhere.

Responding non-directively is a basic technique that shows support and encourages the other person to continue talking. Non-directive responses are essentially non-evaluative — they avoid expressing approval or disapproval — and require careful listening.

In using the "uh-huh" response, focus on the other person and verbalize your support by saying "uh-huh," "hmmm," "I see," or some equivalently non-judgmental comment.

Clarification responses are provided by echoing or mirroring back the content of what the caller said. Avoid using a question in reflection sound like a challenge to and an evaluation of what the other said.

The open question involves asking a free-response inquiry that requires a statement or explanation, rather than a simple yes or no answer.

Although the evidence is strong in support of the effectiveness of these techniques, in some cases, if not used sincerely, they might be seen as a gimmick. In those instances, the other party usually recognizes what is happening and refuses to cooperate, as the other's attention is focused on the technique rather than on communicating, and the technique fails to help the other to express himself. If this happens, the operator should discontinue use of the technique and just let the caller take full control of the content of the conversation. Then, gradually reinforce the other's comments by using the "uh-huh" response. Introduce new topical areas through the use of the open question and self-disclosure, but refrain from the use of clarification until they can be worked into the conversation unobstrusively.

In a majority of suicide calls, one of two major themes will be present: either a feeling of hopelessness and helplessness, or a feeling of anger and disgust. The latter feeling may be prompted by wanting to get back at someone the caller feels may have hurt him.

Once the general theme becomes obvious, the operator can respond appropriately. In the call where the person is feeling hopeless or helpless, the operator's responses should be one of providing hope. The operator can provide hope by mentioning that other people he has helped in similar situations have handled their problems with the proper help. He can also indicate that there are specially trained people (psychologists, psychiatrists, social workers, etc.) who are concerned about people, as he is, who can also help.

If the call appears to be one which reflects mostly anger and disgust, the responses should be different. In these situations, the suicide attempts may be a way of getting back at or hurting another individual. The person contemplating suicide may be justified in his rage toward these other persons. The response of the operator in these situations is twofold: (1) recognizing the caller's anger so as to legitimize it and allow ventilation, i.e. "You're really feeling very angry and upset at him," and (2) offering the possibility of more effective alternatives than suicide for dealing with such feelings. Because one feels hopeless, they are unable to see alternative solutions to their problems and tend to have a narrow focus. Most suicidal people will say that they have tried all other options. However, upon questioning, the operator will discover that only a few solutions have been thought of and tried. Just the opportunity to discuss the problem or difficulty with an individual who is trained and who is objective will often produce new, more realistic solutions.

Which particular emotion is being demonstrated will depend partly on the person calling and partly on the motive for attempting suicide (loss of a loved one, family fight, shame, intoxication, drug addiction). However, regardless of whether the persons involved are highly aggressive, angry, confused, dazed, depressed or hysterical, it is the operator's responsibility to first gain the caller's trust and confidence in order to appropriately help the person in need.

An effective operator is a flexible operator. The operator must be especially flexible in dealing with this type of caller. The type of questions asked and the areas of discussion must be varied, depending on the circumstances and the attitudes of the person calling. A single approach is not suitable for all circumstances, but, instead, the operator varies his behavior, depending upon the caller and the nature of the call. In order to be flexible, one must know a variety of approaches well and develop the knowledge of which one to apply at which times.

The caller will be most likely to continue conversation with the operator if he is shown that the operator in a variety of ways understands him. These include the methods described earlier: active listening, clarification, shared feelings, personalized statements, and stating the obvious to the caller. As a general rule, it is usually a good practice to begin asking questions in those areas that are not as emotionally charged, and slowly work toward the person's more troubling concerns. Remember, what may appear to be insignificant to you may be overwhelming to the caller. If you indicate that you feel his problems are minor issues, you lose your opportunity to understand what really is occurring in the situation.

Bluffing the Caller

A frequently heard comment among emergency operators is that the suicide caller is "only trying to get attention." This type of thinking among operators only supports the impersonal feelings about suicide and may, therefore, cause the operator to ignore suicide callers or even to ridicule them. Don't belittle their actions or minimize their attempts. Under no circumstances should the operator attempt to bluff the caller with statements such as the following:

- "Go ahead, kill yourself, who cares!"
- "Hey pal! If you want to end it all, go ahead. Why are you bothering me?"
- "I know what you're up to: you just want attention. Nobody cares if you kill yourself. Go ahead."
- "Listen, if you really wanted to kill yourself you'd go and do it. You wouldn't call me, so stop putting me on."

Approaches such as these often signal the caller to carry out their intentions, as the operator is seen as giving approval to their actions, which has all too often ended in tragedy.

Actually, there is an element of truth to the statement that the attempted suicide is a bid for attention. It is an attempt to call attention to the person's problem or state of mind. It is a cry for help. If it is not answered, another, perhaps more serious attempt will follow. Any indication that someone is considering suicide is a cry for help and a call to action. The concern of the operator here is in developing language and responding in a supportive manner to the potential suicide victim.

- Be supportive
- Be empathetic
- Achieve rapport immediately
- Talk freely
- Open lines of communication
- Ask questions:
  What do you think is going on?
  How do you see this situation?
- Talk calmly
- Don't be judgmental
- Don't bluff the caller

By asking the caller questions, the operator can accomplish many things. He can keep the conversation flowing at a steady pace, and this indicates to the caller that he is interested. He is also gaining information about the person, which just naturally flows out in conversation, and is gaining insight into the person's problem. The caller, on the other hand, is getting an opportunity to ventilate some of his feelings, which helps to reduce the stress of the situation. Also, the caller will feel that the operator is concerned and will tend to cooperate with whatever the operator says.

As the caller is talking about his difficulties and his situation, the operator should be alert and responsive. The operator should be gently probing with questions so that he can gain as much factual data as possible in order to evaluate the person's actual intentions. In addition, by gaining the caller's trust, the operator will gain cooperation to the point that the caller will offer his location so that help can be sent to him.

In order to trace calls, in which the caller is reluctant to disclose his location, the average time needed is approximately forty-five minutes. This time may vary in different locations. Most operators who have handled these types of calls report that it is an extremely rewarding experience to be able to talk to a caller contemplating suicide out of acting on their threats. It is also rewarding to be able to hold on long enough to a caller until help arrives. There is nothing like the feeling of speaking to the police officer who has arrived at the caller's home to provide assistance.

The operator may also be called upon to respond after a suicide attempt has occurred. The operator's first responsibility in such circumstances is to insure that the caller's needs are met. The operator must ascertain the extent of injury and call for the necessary medical assistance immediately. All attempts must be made to keep the caller on the line and talking as long as possible. For example, a person may call for assistance after he has taken some pills or after he slit his wrists. In terms of the person's personal response, the operator will note that the subject is more cooperative, less agitated, and, at times, almost serene. It is as if he accomplished his goal in the attempt and the conflict is over. The operator should focus on his concern for the caller, his willingness to help him, and the speedy sending of medical assistance.

Handling the Successful Suicide

The emotional responses to suicidal behavior shown by other individuals are also complex. The rejecting attitudes that are aroused in some operators may prejudice their judgments in dealing with these callers. These attitudes are probably associated with the fact that attempts at suicide run counter to established feelings about life. A successful suicide will evoke stronger attitudes.

The operator is often puzzled and astonished at the confrontation of a call for assistance concerning a successful suicide. It might be incomprehensible to the operator as to why a successful businessman with a beautiful home and a loving family would take his own life. Why would a child who had "everything" take an overdose of drugs? What made a husband kill his wife and then take his own life? Why would a mother kill her own child and then commit suicide? These questions often baffle and confuse an emergency operator. There is nothing that can be done for the victim, as this situation has gone beyond the preventative stage, and the operator may be left with many questions.

The operator's first actions should concern those who are overwhelmed with grief or distress. Whether the caller who reports the successful suicide is a member of the family, a neighbor, or friend, the operator should use tact when obtaining information for dispatching help. Realize that these same rejecting attitudes may be expressed by family, friends, or anyone who had a close relationship to the deceased that will cause guilt and shame. At the same time, these members, particularly a spouse, may experience a number of reactions and feelings and may show contempt for the victim. It is not uncommon for the operator to hear:

- "Why did he do this to me?" (rejection)
- "What am I going to do without him?" (loss)
- "If only I had been home, this wouldn't have happened." (guilt)
- "That louse, leaving me with all these kids." (anger)
- "I could have helped him. I thought he was faking." (feeling responsibility)
- "I tried to help him. It didn't work." (sense of failure)
- "Why didn't I believe his threats?" (inadequacy)
- "It's all my fault." (guilt)
- "I hope no one finds out about this." (shame and embarrassment)

Such statements will be intermixed with expressions of guilt and grief. The operator may be required to continually reassure the involved persons that the suicide was not their fault.

It is not necessary for the operator to respond to all of these feelings, but he should be aware of their existence and be sensitive to them when they are expressed. This will allow him to complete his responsibilities more quickly and avoid any unnecessary confrontations with callers.

In short, the following seven steps should be followed when talking to the suicidal-prone person:

1. SHOW UNDERSTANDING. By your words and your tone of voice, you can make it clear to the caller that you accurately understand what the person is feeling and how strongly he is feeling it. Do attempt to understand the person's view.

2. DO CREATE RAPPORT WITH THE CALLER. The operator may indicate legitimate agreements between himself and the caller in as many areas as possible. Some examples of this might be agreement on the difficulties of raising a family, the hurt involved in a loss, the problems of not having enough money, personal likes and dislikes in such areas of interest such as food, movies, sports, etc. This helps to develop the relationship and allow the caller to feel that the operator can understand him since they have some similar background.

3. DON'T BE JUDGMENTAL. Criticizing, judging, and giving advice is rarely helpful to the person contemplating suicide. This only increases their feelings of failure and inadequacy and heightens their suicidal intent.

4. DON'T CALL THE PERSON'S BLUFF. Attempts to shock the caller back to reality by minimizing their attempts and calling their bluff never helps the caller.

5. KEEP THE CONVERSATION FLOWING. Respond non-directively so that the caller will continue talking.

6. DON'T BE AFRAID TO SHARE FEELINGS. Being impersonal only turns people off. Personal expressions of concern are necessary in these situations.

7. BE FLEXIBLE. Vary your approach according to the caller and the nature of the call.

CONCLUSION

Suicide and suicide attempts are always tragic and unsettling situations. Confronting and dealing with the individuals and families involved is uncomfortable, even for the most experienced mental health professional. However, the reward of knowing that you have helped a person back to life is, likewise, very rewarding. In this chapter we have attempted to provide certain fundamental information so that emergency operators may experience that reward.

However, the personal experience of one emergency operator may perhaps say it better. One operator got a call recently from a woman who said that she was about to commit suicide. Her boyfriend had deserted her, she said, and she didn't want to live anymore. The operator talked with her for more than an hour while the call, made from a public phone, was traced. Finally, help got to her, and the suicide was averted. "I felt like I had done something extraordinary for a fellow human being," he said. "It was a nice feeling that has sustained me in times when I have hated this job."

Chapter 6

CRISIS, VICTIMOLOGY, AND TRANSACTIONAL ANALYSIS

THUS far, we have discussed communication theory, barriers to effective communication, and bridges to effective communication. We also introduced transactional analysis as a method for analyzing various modes of communication and to diagnose interactions between the caller and the operator in order to minimize conflict and continue understanding. "Victimology," the following chapter, introduces the study of victim behavior, focusing on various attitudes that surface as a result of victimization. In crisis behavior, the various responses to a crisis situation is delineated by way of five separate categories of behavior.

In this chapter, we integrate all of this information with the concepts of T.A. in order for the operator to achieve a better understanding of how T.A. can work for them. A simplified explanation of the application of T.A. to the operator's role is offered. Further, how positive stroking can be utilized most effectively for operators is explained, in addition to examples in order to clarify application of positive, nurturing, or supportive strokes to callers in crisis.

The various T.A. styles are also combined with the operator's role so that an operator's individual style can be recognized and changed, if needed.

THE EFFECTIVE USE OF POSITIVE
STROKING FOR OPERATORS

As we have learned already, an OK positive stroke can be verbal or non-verbal and is designed to enhance others. They can be *given from* any ego state and *sent to* any ego state. They can be simple, unconditional messages such as a look that says,"I'm glad you're you," or a sudden "Let's have lunch together," or a sincere, "I'm glad we're working together tonight.

Since strokes are necessary for survival, a person will do whatever he thinks necessary in order to receive the strokes needed.

A person will develop a style of giving and receiving strokes based on their life position. Persons who feel OK about themselves and others tend to seek out exchanges of positive strokes. Persons who feel not OK about themselves and/or others tend to seek out negative strokes, which will increase their not OK feelings. When unconditional positive strokes are not given to or accepted by an individual he will seek out others kinds of strokes.

One of the best ways to receive positive strokes is to give them. When you receive plenty of positive strokes, you build a stroke reserve and, therefore, have a ready supply to give to others and enjoy for yourself. Being open to positive strokes you get more and have more time and energy to be a tolerant Parent, a competent Adult, and a fun-loving Child.

Yet, each persons' stroke needs are different. Some people want to be stroked for Adult rational thinking, and some people want Parental strokes of approval instead of straight Adult feedback. There are also Nurturing Parent or supportive strokes that are most effectively used by the operator in crisis situations.

NURTURING PARENT OR SUPPORTIVE STROKES

The Nurturant Parent is an ego state that is part of every emergency operator, but, unfortunately, its presence is rarely seen and rarely acknowledged. The fictional stereotype of the cold, critical, impersonal operator in his Critical Parent ego state is most often thought of as the average operator. The supportive side — the Nurturant Parent — is not seen very often or publicized. Yet, many of the calls received are direct calls for help made by people who are experiencing a critical, crucial moment in their lives: crisis moments. Many of these moments concern callers who require some sort of assistance in dealing with a problem. The problem may concern a crime (past or in progress) a need for medical assistance, a conflict situation, or a petty annoyance. The help needed may range from just a kind word or a sympathetic ear to the nurturing of the family of a successful suicide, a rape victim, a child at the scene of an accident in which no family is near, or an elderly person who was mugged. In these situations, it is not the Critical Parent who is responding, rather, this is where the Nurturing Parent stroking is needed.

From their positive OK side, these types of strokes may encourage those who are confused or helpless to become more competent. They are strokes of emotional support that help others only until they become self-supporting. The message accompanying these types of strokes is "I'm OK, and I am willing to help you get through this crisis. I'm willing to work with you."

The emergency operator's role in today's society directly leads to the need for expertise in the supportive nurturing aspect of their job. As was previously stated, this profession is fundamentally people oriented, and whether an operator is in an information-gathering role or in a support role, dealing with people is an essential element of their job. The primary function of this people-oriented profession is *service*. This human service system is unique in that it is inevitably involved in stressful events or crisis situations that profoundly affect the people involved. During the course of one tour of duty, an operator may encounter many types of crisis events.

Under normal circumstances, most people are able to cope with and adjust to minor upsets and events that they may encounter. However, when an unpredictable, sudden, or arbitrary incident occurs, and that person is unable to cope with the overwhelming stress and the resulting emotion produced by the incident, that person is experiencing a crisis and is often unable to function as they would normally. It is at these times that supportive strokes by the emergency operator are of most value.

SUPPORTIVE BEHAVIOR IN A CRISIS SITUATION

Basically, crisis behavior is behavior associated with the Child ego state. The Child responds emotionally and is our emotional self. In a crisis, it is not unusual to see someone regress or revert to a state of helplessness or dependency and rendered completely powerless. A quick review of crisis behavior, as noted in Chapter 4, will assist the operator in relating crisis behavior and the Child ego state. The operator's first actions should concern those who are overwhelmed with grief or distress. Nurturant Parent strokes of emotional support from the Nurturant Parent ego state are necessary to the victim in a crisis situation. Conveying to the victim your empathy and support of them and their dilemma can help the victim overcome his physical and psychological trauma. Avoid Critical Parent behavior.

It is not uncommon for the victim to turn their anger into blame and direct this blame at the responding operator as criticisms for not getting help when they needed it. The operator may hear "I've just been mugged, and you operators are just sitting on your butts taking all this casually!" or "Listen mister, I already give you my name. What are you stupid or something?" (*see* Figure 6-2).

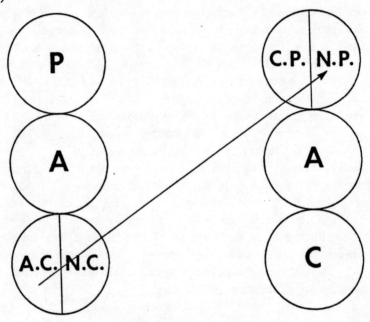

Figure 6-1. The Victim needing help.

While it is obvious that the investigator must be flexible in his approach to an interview situation, there are certain basic elements of interviewing skills that could be developed and integrated with T.A. in order to more effectively gain the required information. Let us consider the following examples of dealing with victims. Coming at the victim from the Critical Parent ego state by criticizing, expressions of cynicism, challenging the victim's credibility, or any indication or suggestion that the victim was at fault in some way contributing to his own victimization can have a devastating effect.

The impact of the crisis, its shattering effects, and the regressive tendency of the victim combine to form the victim's need of a firm,

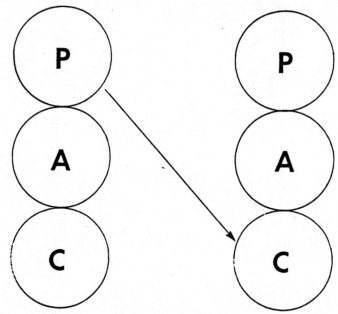

Figure 6-2. The Victim expressing anger.

yet gentle, and knowledgeable authority who, by his actions, can satisfy the need for support, strength, and compassion.

In the case of female victims, there is nothing gained by criticizing the victim for accepting a ride with a stranger, for example, or for her manner of acting. This type of criticism imposes guilt feelings upon her that heighten her anxiety and deepen her crisis. The operator must be patient, tactful, and non-judgmental about any conduct or behavior that the victim may exhibit.

Statements appearing in Figures 6-3, 6-4, and 6-5 should be avoided. In general, the theme of these questions is aggressive questioning of the victim, and these questions generally take the form of implying that the victim's injuries could have been prevented or avoided.

In contrast, words of kindness, support, and understanding may be of enormous value. There is a need to provide sensitive, professional service to victims, to display a positive supportive attitude, a need for sensitive professional behavior, and show of compassion (*see* Figures 6-6 and 6-7).

The emergency operator is most effective if he is compassionate and reassuring and indicates to the victim that he will help her,

"What were you doing in that neighborhood anyway, don't you know you were just asking for it by going there?"

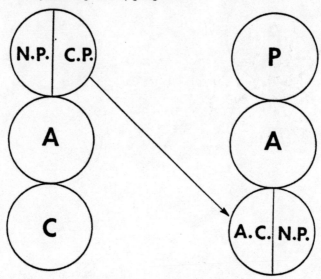

Figure 6-3. Criticizing the Victim I.

"What can you expect if you act flirtatious like that?"

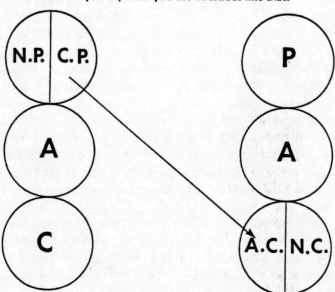

Figure 6-4. Criticizing the Victim II.

"Why did you take that chain off the door, if you did not know who you were talking to?"

"Didn't you know that that neighborhood is dangerous to walk in after dark?"

"Didn't you have your door locked?"

"Weren't you suspicious of that man in the elevator?"

"Why didn't you scream?"

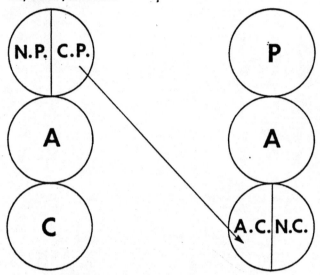

Figure 6-5. Criticizing the Victim III.

without being overbearing. The operator's role of reassurance includes the information that all will be done to find the suspect, and that a number of questions will have to be asked concerning the incident. Once the caller has been reassured, the Adult can be "hooked" for information (*see* Figures 6-8 and 6-9).

Many emergency operators, because of the pain and suffering they listen to daily, have become immune to expressions of empathy for others. However, in dealing with injured children or elderly victims, the Nurturing Parent gets hooked, and it is certainly understandable. The same kindness and compassion that would be utilized in reducing anxiety in injured persons at the scene of an accident should be demonstrated to someone in crisis.

It is also important to avoid any suggestion of force. Your behavior should not be so overzealous as to cause you to be perceived by the caller as aggressive and forcible. If the operator hopes to

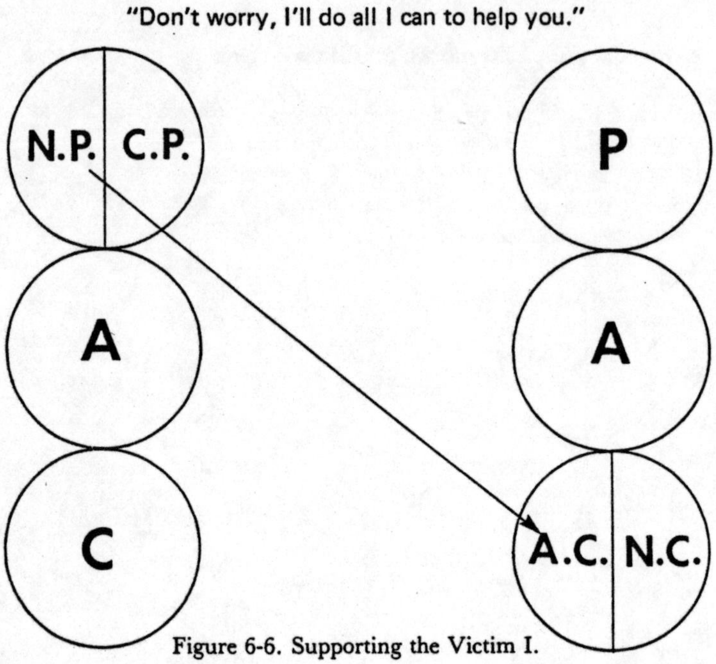

"Don't worry, I'll do all I can to help you."

Figure 6-6. Supporting the Victim I.

"I am here to help you. You are safe now!"

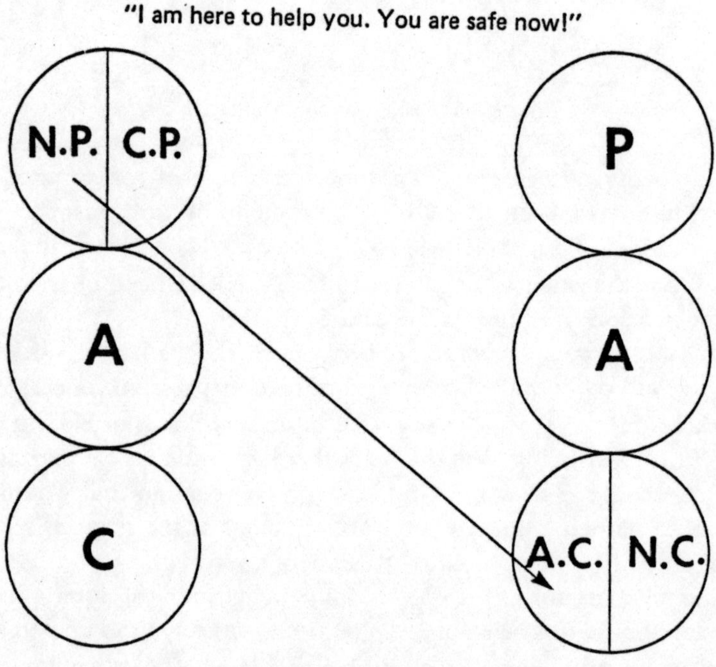

Figure 6-7. Supporting the Victim II.

"I know this is difficult to talk about, take your time."

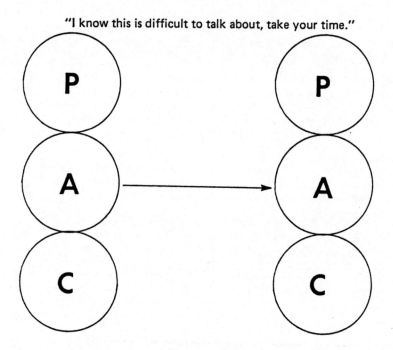

Figure 6-8. Hooking the Adult in the Victim.

"I'm going to ask you some questions now about exactly what has happened."

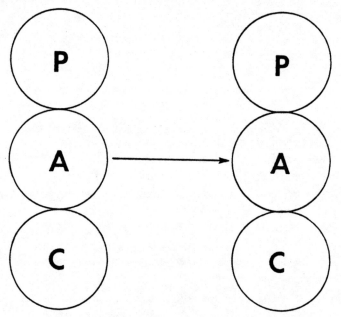

Figure 6-9. Adult-Adult transaction.

gain the caller's confidence, he should be non-judgmental and patient. Avoid the Critical Parent ego state. Put the caller at ease and create an atmosphere that will allow the person to relate his/her story willingly and naturally.

PRESSING FOR INFORMATION

The operator realizes that the sooner he can get information the quicker he can send the required help to the caller. Hence, there is a natural tendency to want to press the victim for all pertinent information. However, he has a responsibility to help the victim, which frequently means the operator may have to postpone questioning until the person calms down and the shock wears off. Being too anxious to get information can actually deter rather than aid the ongoing interview.

CONFLICT AND HOOKING

When an Adult request for information fails to draw forth an Adult response, conflict results. The request may be a discount, which would come from someone's Critical Parent, or someone's Adapted Child. Because crossed transactions can hurt others, they restrict communication and destroy the cooperative relations necessary for the effective interacting that is necessary for the investigation of calls and generally the gathering of important information. Conflict causes crossed transactions and inhibits communication.

Crossed transactions are sometimes OK and necessary for getting information. However, it is necessary first to satisfy the stimulus, with the expected response to relieve the frustration of the crossed transaction. For example, consider a caller who initiates the transaction with a pleas from her Adapted Child in an attempt to hook the operator's Nurturant Parent (*see* Figure 6-10).

If the operator responds from his helpless, pleading Child in return (*see* Figure 6-11) with "Oh God, how horrible! I don't know what to do. I don't like this any more than you do," or from his Adult (*see* Figure 6-12) with "I see, what is your name?" both parties will feel frustrated and angry, and the goal of the transaction will remain unmet or unsatisfied.

However, if the operator will recognize the need for the Adapted

"Operator, please help me! My baby is caught in the high chair and is choking!"

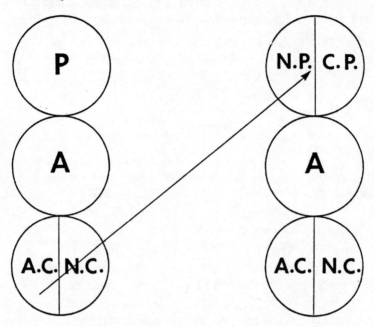

Figure 6-10. Hooking the Nurturant Parent.

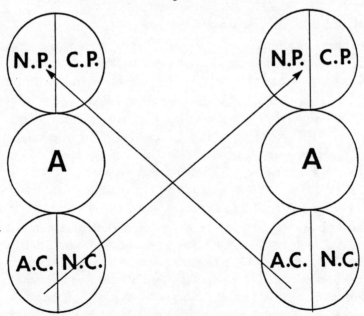

Figure 6-11. Adapted Child-Adapted Child transaction.

Child to be satisfied with a Nurturant Parent response and then send a hook to the Adult, communication can continue. For example:

> Operator: Yes, of course I'll help you. You just hold on to the baby, and make sure he doesn't choke, and give me your address. I'll send help immediately to you and your baby (*see* Figure 6-13).

HOW TO HOOK

Satisfy the Parent . . . parallel it. Don't cross the transaction. Then, hook the Adult for the information. In this way you have allowed for the ventilation of the anger, appeased the frustration of the Parent, and hooked the Adult for the information needed.

Consider the following interaction.

> Operator: Hey Boss, I'm sorry. I can't finish this report. I've got to have some help. Can you help me?
>
> Supervisor: Yes, of course I'll help you. What can I do to help you?
>
> Operator: I can't get all the information I need.
>
> Supervisor: You might call headquarters. They should have all the information you need.
>
> Operator: Oh yes, that's a good idea.

What has transpired in this example? The supervisor has responded to the operator's Child from his Nurturing Parent. In consciously choosing this course of action, he has accomplished two things:

1. His response satisfied the needs of the Adapted Child, in that the supervisor has avoided putting the operator off and has resisted the hook to step in and take over the job for the operator (*see* Figure 6-15).
2. His response kept the relationship on an objective basis and gave the operator a chance to try again, this time from his Adult (*see* Figure 6-16).

Crossed transactions occur when the expected response is not given. The lines between ego states cross and communication breaks down. The person who is crossed often feels misunderstood, surprised, and confused. Be alert for the times when you or the other person gets angry or hurt or changes the subject. Someone doesn't like what is being said; someone doesn't want to listen to what is

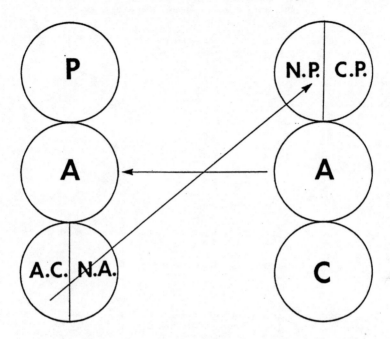

Figure 6-12. Adapted Child-Adult transaction.

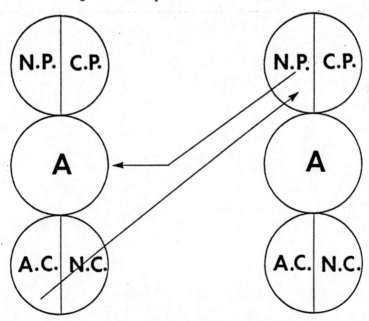

Figure 6-13. Hooking the Adult I.

Caller: Where the hell are the police, I called over an hour ago and nobody is here yet. This dammed city, a person can't even get help when he needs it.

Operator: I'm sorry for the inconvenience, Sir. May I have that address again?

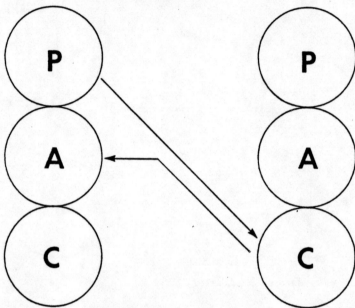

Figure 6-14. Hooking the Adult II.

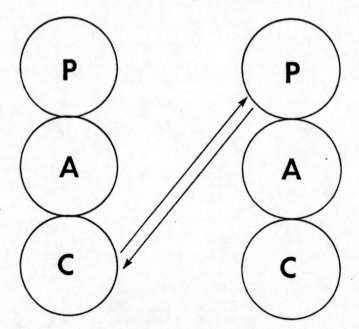

Figure 6-15. Child-Parent parallel transaction.

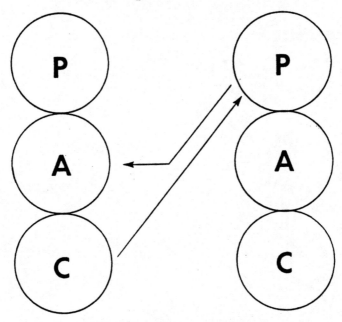

Figure 6-16. Hooking the Adult III.

being said. When two people are arguing it is often because the Critical Parent in either one is coming on strong, trying to take control of the situation and making the other into a bad Child, hooking the Adapted Child.

Sometimes, the other person just refuses to be the bad Child and instead gets angry and verbalizes it. Communication has then stopped. One person has pushed the Parent button, putting the other person in his Child, but he refused to be the Child. This is an example of a crossed transaction.

Look for a crossed transaction when one person doesn't answer the other but switches the subject (*see* Figure 6-17).

IS IT OK TO CROSS A TRANSACTION?

As we have already noted, crossed transactions often cause others to feel put down, misunderstood, and not OK. When this occurs, frustrations set in and communication breaks down. However, the ability to recognize the need to cross a transaction can be a valuable conflict management tool that can be effectively used in some situa-

Operator: May I have your address, please?

Caller: What address, you fool!? I just told you I was in the lobby of the Georgian Hotel!

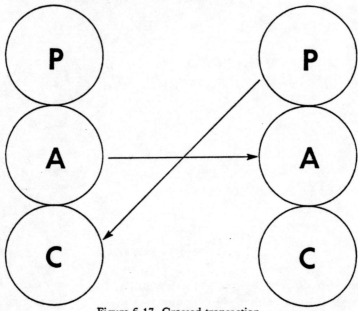

Figure 6-17. Crossed transaction.

tions. In a situation when you may need information in a hurry, and the caller is just rambling on or speaking in a confused manner and using generalities or unclear terminology, an OK cross may be used (*see* Figures 6-18 and 6-19).

The not OK use of the crossed transaction often leaves others feeling put down, misunderstood, and generally not OK. When this happens, the cooperative atmosphere of communication is destroyed and effectiveness drops. However, the OK use of a crossed transaction as a conflict management tool can help operators and others to work together more effectively and efficiently.

The professional operator is expected to remain in his Adult in most situations. When the operator is in the Adult there is a good chance that the Child and Parent ego states will recognize that stimulus for what it is and move to the same position. However, there are times when commitment to an ego state is too

"Is there something you would like to say but can't find the right words?"

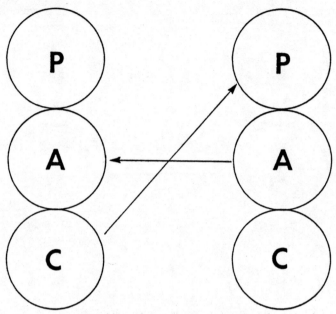

Figure 6-18. An OK crossed transaction.

"I think it would speed up our information gathering, if you could clarify some important points first."

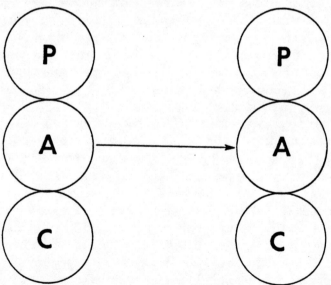

Figure 6-19. The OK crossed transaction II.

"Yes, you've told me that", when someone talks on and on indefinitely.

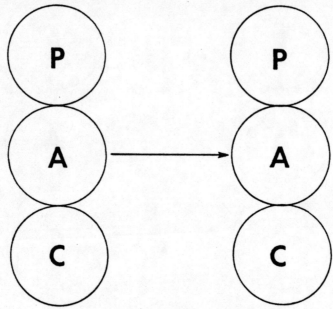

Figure 6-20. The OK crossed transaction III.

strong to shift.

The persistent use of the Adult in such a situation encourages the other person to do likewise. When this happens, communication is open and it can be productive. Initially, of course, the transaction is crossed. Although there is a possibility that this may stop communication, it is more likely to improve communication if the Adult is used persistently. For the important, information-gathering aspect of the operator's job, this is essential.

At this point, you may conclude that one should always stay in the Adult and never come from the Parent or the Child. It is not humanly possible, nor is it desirable, to always remain in the Adult. There are times when personal judgments are necessary. There are times when the situation needs a Critical Parent. There are many examples that could be stated to support the Parent action. The Adult ego state, however, is the manager of the entire personality and sometimes may direct the person to behave in the Parent ego state. Just remember to let the Adult moderate so that the Parent responses are appropriate to the reality of the encounter.

OPTIONS WITH NEGATIVE STROKES

Since each person in a transaction is free to exercise options regarding the strokes he will give and receive, the ultimate responsibility for how a person feels lies in himself, e.g. negative strokes can be accepted, in which case bad feelings may result, or they may not be accepted, in which case there will be no bad feelings (*see* Figures 6-21 and 6-22).

THE TRANSACTIONAL ANALYSIS OPERATOR STYLES

As already stated, we use our different ego states at different times and for different reasons. In learning the basic concepts of T.A., and by understanding the three ego states, as well as the benefits of stroking and OK and not OK attitudes, we can begin to see many different ways in which the operator role is expressed. There is no such thing as a specific operator personality. Rather, there is a variety of behavior, both OK and not OK, connected to the different ego states. Describing them in T.A. terms can demonstrate to us how we use our ego states in different situations, and provide the option for changing any behaviors we're not satisfied with, in order to increase our effectiveness and professionalism. A knowledge of T.A. behavior possibilities makes change easier.

Our operator style can be described as the way an operator relates to others in getting his job done. It is demonstrated in how he gains cooperation from others, how he gets along with others, and how he handles his responsibilities. In essence, it's his own method of operating. Change can be undertaken if you find, after careful analysis, that your predominant ego state behavior is not working most effectively for you.

The point is to become aware of the style you are using, and the impact that particular style is having on the situation you are involved in and on others, and whether or not you are satisfied with that style. The following styles are based on the use of predominant ego states in the performance of your job.

THE CRITICAL PARENT STYLE

The operator who operates from the Critical Parent style mainly

Caller to Operator: "You're a poor excuse for an operator."

Option A
"I'm not OK, he's right. I am a poor excuse for an emergency operator, and I feel badly."

Option B
"I'm OK, and I feel good about myself, regardless of what that person said."

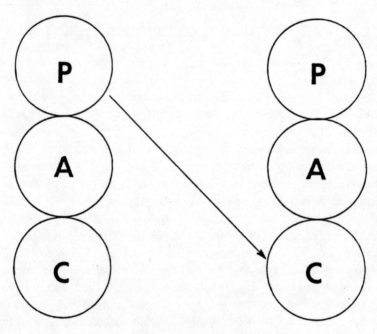

Figure 6-21. Negative-stroking caller to operator.

communicates with others from Critical Parent to Child ego states. He uses threats and intimidation to gain cooperation, frequently puts people down, and seldom gives praise or positive strokes. Any positive stroking on his part is brief, not sincere, very conditional, and frequently discounted, such as, "Not bad for a woman."

This operator handles conflict by controlling and oppressive methods. The direction of his communication is primarily downward and one way. He is constantly evaluating and judging, using phrases like: "You should know better," or "You are wrong." He says things like: "I'm in control here," "I'll do the thinking," and

OR:

Caller to Operator: "Only a jerk would do your kind of work. Couldn't you get another job?"

Option A
"I'm not OK, they're right. I'm nothing but a dumb operator."

Option B
"I'm OK and I feel good about myself regardless of their comments."

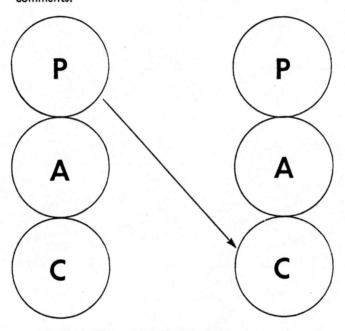

Figure 6-22. Negative stroke.

"You do just as your told."

This is the superiority style that is typified by the need for power. Superior people are not even interested in anyone else's needs or comfort, unless the situation can be exploited to satisfy their own needs (*see* Figure 6-23).

Coming from the Critical Parent style has some undesirable consequences. The operator is regarded as someone to fear and, therefore, someone to avoid. Complaints frequently result when an operator communicates with callers with exaggerated notions of his

Caller: You can't talk to me like that. You can't treat me like that, it's against the law.

Operator: I am the law around here.

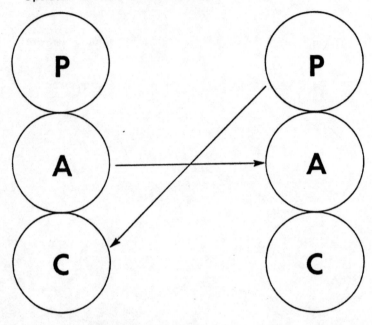

Figure 6-23. The Critical Parent M.O.

importance and his authority. Emotional displays of disgust and contempt are common to this style. The operator constructs barriers between himself and the callers by misconstruing his role or by continually focusing on that which distinguishes him from them. He thinks in terms of "we" and "they" and uses expressions such as "your kind" or "those people," which can be highly offensive to many people. These operators are not socially popular as other types because of their critiquing ability and are usually "caller overcritical."

This type of style generates in others feelings of accusation, guilt, anger, and resentment. A person's hostility tends to be contagious, stimulates defensiveness and counterhostility, and raises barriers to communication. No one wants to be talked down to, and no one likes to be made to feel inferior. The dictatorial or authoritarian attitude impairs communication and cooperation. Cooperation simply does not exist in an atmosphere of laying down the law of "take it or leave it" or "I know a lot more about this than you do." This attitude will cause the listener to react emotionally (from the Child ego state) and not rationally (from the Adult ego state). In understanding the pitfalls of the Critical Parent ego-state style, defensiveness will be reduced, and we can more easily solve the problems that face us in communicating with others.

THE NURTURING PARENT STYLE

The operator in the Nurturing Parent style is supportive, caring, and encouraging and often takes pleasure in caring for others. A positive Nurturing Parent cares for another person in a loving way when the latter needs it. They do everything possible to help others, by encouraging them, and are pleased with their successes. Supportive operators are often concerned over the physical and emotional health of others. They are usually patient when they give instructions and will repeat if not understood clearly. They listen well, are comforting, and give appropriate advice and sympathy. As a consequence, others tend to feel understood by him, and, because they feel understood, often respond with strength and confidence.

He likes people and wants to be liked in return. These types of people usually give advice using phrases such as "You'll feel better if," "It would be best for you to," or "My advice to you is." They may pat others on the back, look sympathetic, and say things such as "Don't worry, it will be all right. I'll take care of this for you."

The use of the Nurturing Parent style is most often seen in crisis situations. As we have mentioned previously, many of the callers that the operator will encounter in the course of his work are victims and persons in crisis. They are most likely going through an emotional crisis. Any consideration and understanding the operator can offer them at such a time would be of great help. By expressing the Nurturing Parent styles, the operator will be able to show that he is concerned about what has happened to this caller and that he is going to do all he can to help him. By showing compassion, the operator conveys that he is understanding, and this will help the caller feel that the operator is there to help.

THE NATURAL CHILD STYLE

The operator who uses the Natural Child style may be very effective in working with young people or young children. They enjoy parties, having a good time, and giving gifts. The strokes they give others come from their Child ego state and may be directed to the other person's Child ego state. Statements such as, "Wow, great idea!" or "Fantastic, wish I had thought of that!" are typical. This encourages further creativity, and most people enjoy receiving these kinds of strokes. Since the Child in people is creative, they are great joke tellers, creative clowns, the life of the party, and love to entertain others. They can usually be counted on to dream up new solutions for old ideas, new designs for outmoded equipment, and new policies, programs, and procedures for others to implement.

Their behavior is very friendly and they can easily make friends. A good sense of humor is an asset to the person dealing with emergency calls. The ability to see humor in some situations can help ease tension, lessen the burden, and keep many incidents interesting that might otherwise have become difficult and frustrating. The ability to laugh at oneself is one indicator of a well-developed sense of humor and a well-developed personality.

THE ADAPTED CHILD STYLE

In the Adapted Child style, the operator tends to be conforming and seeking acceptance from everyone. He exercises great skill in avoiding conflict or offending anyone. He is very secure without changes, and he dislikes change. He tends to be conservative and accepting of everyone. He is generally agreeable, obedient, compliant, and aware of everyone's feelings and views. They dislike conflict and will go to great lengths to avoid confrontation by saying such things such as "Let's not get upset" or "It'll all work out in time" or "Arguing won't get us anywhere."

The agreeableness of his actions is positive. It has a strong healing quality, as he will spread calm everywhere he goes. This is the crucial characteristic of a fair person. He tries to please everyone in a conflict and can be counted on not to upset anyone. Because of their willingness to consider both sides in a dispute, people with whom they interact often feel as if they can relax and let down their defenses in their presence. Consequently, there is more opportunity for misunderstandings to be clarified, conflicts to be negotiated, and problems to be solved.

On the negative side, the cynical person is in this style. The extreme cynical attitudes is usually accompanied by depression or anger. A depressed or angry person cannot function as efficiently as a calm, optimistic one. In addition, this attitude is communicated to others and influences the outcome of the interaction. An operator like any other person is entitled to his private biases and personal feelings. However, when these attitudes determine the manner in which he approaches and deals with persons on the phone, then his effectiveness is diminished. Narrow-mindedness and prejudice are partly related to a lack of information and education, as well as a need to overvalue what is familiar and thus "true." In this style, since change is avoided, what is familiar will tend to be comforting and what is familiar will tend to be comforting and what is unfamiliar tends to produce anxiety and thus seem a threat. For example, ethnocentricism is an attitude characterized by the belief that one's own race or ethnic group is superior to others. The ethnocentric is incapable of evaluating other cultures logically and unemotionally. Intolerance, prejudgments, and the inability to evaluate and change are handicaps that must be examined, acknowledged, and controlled.

CHANGING YOUR STYLE

The styles described here are not likely to exist in such extreme, pure states. Like everyone, operators have three ego states, and their behavior shifts from one state to another according to the demands of the situation and their best interpretations of what is appropriate behavior under the circumstances. However, taking a look at the various styles described will make it easier to understand the different types of operator behavior.

Many operators have a favorite or habitual style that is based primarily on use of one or two of the styles discussed. A style is useful to the degree that it accomplishes the objective intended and produces satisfying human relations. If either is lacking, then you may decide that some change is in order. Change can start with more concern for your relations with others and more concern for getting your job done more effectively, or both. This would involve examining the style you have been using in various situations for strengths and weaknesses and making the appropriate change in order to be more effective. Effectiveness and efficiency go hand in hand. Both are essential for OK operators. Having the idea for change, and actually implementing the change, is two different things.

For example, an operator who habitually uses his Critical Parent to meet objectives does so at a high cost to his relationships with others. Change for him may mean exhibiting more trusting and more nurturing behavior when needed. He may be willing to make this change, yet be reluctant or resistant to expressions of this behavior in an actual situation calling for more nurturant behavior.

There is no ideal style, though some are obviously more suitable to some situations than others. Neither is there one "real" ego state, as all of them are real in the sense that they are different presentations appropriate to different environments or situations. Most people can and do alter their behavior in different circumstances, however, some people do not or cannot. Their rigid behavior stems from their almost exclusive use of Parent, Adult, or Child. On a day-to-day basis in a single setting, such people tend to present themselves in a habitual way. This is why there is value in studying different styles of acting in the operator's job. When an operator's style becomes rigid, his effectiveness diminishes.

If you like your style and are satisfied with your effectiveness, then just keep on doing whatever you are doing to achieve your goals. It has evidently been productive for you. However, if you do not like your self-evaluation and you think there is any cause for change, you can make changes. Based on the information you have processed thus far, get into your Adult and consider your options. You could consider trying out one or another style. For example, if you were to proceed from a Nurturing Parent style and act accordingly, would others feel more at ease with you? Does the style that you have been using interfere with your message? What do your tone of voice, gestures, words used, and emotions expressed convey? You will probably find that as you act more and more OK others will respond in like manner. You will also find that certain styles are more appropriate for one situation and not another.

THE ADULT STYLE

The operator who uses the Adult style is one who can interact with many types of individuals or groups effectively, with as much concern for them as persons as with getting a job well done. He can communicate with people on a variety of levels, he is a good provider of strokes, and he knows when to joke and how to empathize with others. People like him because he is capable of accepting them as they are, while urging them on to further growth and development. He does not play roles; he does not "put on." He levels with others and asks that they do so with him. People feel free to approach him, because they know from experience that he will not put them down or put them off.

He does not foster dependency, but encourages people to deal with problems with their Adult. He expects each person to perform to the degree that he is capable of and is the only style in which deliberately straight strokes are commonly and honestly given.

Such a person in the Adult style has an I'm OK — You're OK position. This person is humanistically oriented, i.e. people are important. This responsive person works on speaking and writing clearly and is not repetitive, vague, evasive, or inconsistent. They do not get caught up in psychological games. They know that there is a time for work and a time for play and how to distinguish between the two. He conveys the idea, "I respect you and will consider your feelings." He is not upset by the occasional person who acts superior and is able to demonstrate authority when it is appropriate.

The operator using the Adult style may use his Adult to filter and assemble his thoughts before he speaks or acts. When he does act, it is in a way appropriate to the needs of the situation. He may act from any of his ego states, but he will do so only after consulting his Adult.

WHO WILL RESPOND?

Changing a style of transacting is not always easy. Habits developed over the years are difficult to change and often seem right to us. In learning and utilizing the basic techniques and theory of T.A., you will have begun your understanding of your ego states, how they function within you, and how they function in your transactions with others. You have also begun to analyze where other people are coming from when they interact with you.

The types of situations that the emergency operator will encounter are many and varied. Transactional analysis is not a perfect solution that is effective in all stress situations, but it can be a most effective tool that can be applied to many caller/operator transactions.

Now that you are aware of the ego states, transactions, and stroking, remember that they are all useful when expressed properly. If you can identify when another person is trying to hook you by coming from a particular ego state, there are several alternatives open to you. You have the option to decide from where you want to respond. Special situations call for special decisions. Your response can reduce friction and head off trouble before it begins. Before you can prevent a crisis from getting out of hand, you must learn how to identify the warning signals. You must be able to accurately identify the ego state that is confronting you, and then you can choose from where you will respond.

Remember: each response become a stimulus for the next transaction, and, if you analyze the transaction accurately, you can wisely choose a response that will hook the other person's Adult, in order to maintain an Adult-to-Adult transaction. From this, you no longer will get hooked into reacting, but, rather, you will respond from deliberate choice. Your transactions with others become professional rather than personal.

Chapter 7

OPERATOR STRESS

FACED with a threat, a cat arches its back, a snake coils to strike, a rabbit darts away, but a human being has taught himself to hide his reactions and to bottle up his anxiety. After a while, the bottling up of anger and frustration causes internal stresses, leading to physical breakdowns . . . the bottle cracks, and the built-up strain makes us sick. Doctor Hans Selye, of the University of Montreal, is the world's leading authority on stress. In his book, *The Stress of Life*, Doctor Selye (1956) says, "Mental tension, frustrations, the sense of insecurity, and aimlessness are among the most important stressors."

Up until this point, we have dealt primarily with the effects of a crisis on the victim and the correct manner in which the operator will handle these calls. However, an added factor is apparent that could effect the outcome of many calls for assistance. This is the emotional impact of the crisis on the operator himself. An operator must be prepared to effectively and productively deal with the emotional aspects of the details of the crisis scene, both for himself and for the victim.

There is no doubt that the police emergency operator's job is a tough one. It is one of the most stressful jobs in any large city that is made more difficult by the intermixing of non-emergency calls with real crisis calls. The operator doesn't know if the next call coming in will be for a complaint about rowdy teenagers or someone threatening to assassinate the mayor of the city at a luncheon that afternoon. The work is highly stressful with the ambiguity and conflicting values surrounding the job, the responsibility for other people's lives and their well-being, and the long hours of inactivity mixed with unpredictable crises.

It is generally accepted that some occupations are more likely to cause stress-related maladies (e.g. high blood pressure, cardiovascular disease, gastric ulcer, mental disturbances, etc.) than others. Being an emergency operator could be considered as one job that is likely to cause these types of illnesses. Being an emergency operator automatically involves shift work, long hours sitting in one position, screaming, hysterical voices coming at you, first-hand details of disturbing events, anticipation of the next crisis call, as well as prejudice and hostility by the callers, which invariably causes disillusionment and disappointment in the job itself. For example: "I get these calls and they hear my accent and ask me if I'm black" states one operator. "I don't understand. What difference does it make? I'm there to help them. This job really gets to me sometimes."

Over time, a person working in such a constantly stressful situation suffers from emotional exhaustion and cynicism, which frequently occurs among individuals who do "people work" or who spend considerable time in close encounters with others under conditions of chronic tension and stress. They begin to distrust and even dislike people they should be helping. This detached and even callous response is, in part, a protective device. It reduces the amount of emotional involvement and consequent stress, but it also seriously impairs the quality of the human contact.

One operator who handles emergency calls every night, then types the information into the computer, takes pride in the reassuring way he takes charge and gets the callers to slow down to repeat their address. He feels that every so often, when someone is in danger, he can do some good. However, he readily admits that, "This job takes a lot out of you."

KINDS OF STRESS

There are varying degrees and different forms of stress (mental, emotional, and physical), all having some impact — sometimes good, sometimes harmful — upon health. Stress can often be the spice of life, or, depending upon circumstances and a person's capabilities and reactions, it may have damaging side effects that may lead to disease, cause us to age prematurely, or sometimes even shorten life.

Strong emotions, too, cause bodily changes, because emotions, in general, are meant to make us act. Fear, for example, makes us tense. When this happens, nerve impulses and hormones (adrenalin) speed through the system, causing the heart to beat rapidly. Blood vessels of the stomach and intestines contract, shunting the blood to muscles for quick action. Breathing speeds up, and other changes occur that help to fortify us to meet an emergency or cope with a difficult situation.

Normal emotional stress is useful in many ways. We can't and wouldn't want to live like vegetables without any feeling or responsiveness. You may get "worked up" over an important or interesting assignment and, as a result, be able to handle the work more effectively. Pleasurable emotions involving stress and tension can be exhilarating. You may get excited and tense while watching a tennis match or a football game. This type of tension can pep you up and then produce healthy relaxation.

All of us, at one time or another, have experienced some of the effects of emotions on bodily functions. We can recall blushing when embarrassed, or having a tight feeling in the chest or a weighty feeling in the pit of the stomach before a physical examination, or having our heart pound and our hands perspire when excited or afraid. These are normal reactions of the body of specific situations. Once the cause is removed, they generally disappear quickly. Knowing how these emotions influence bodily functions, we are better able to understand how strong and persistent mental and emotional conflicts may, over a period of time, disturb the working of body organs, such as the heart or the stomach.

In the contrast to healthy stress, however, intense and persistent anger, fear, frustration, or worry, which we may tend to "bottle up" inside ourselves, can threaten health. It is this buildup of stress, with no release of tension, that leads to trouble. As a result of steady strain, people may experience a variety of symptoms. They may become very irritable, have frequent headaches, or perhaps have digestive distress. These are warning signals, indicating a need for relief.

One exceptionally bright and capable young operator had just this type of problem. She did very well in the training classes, passed the exam with flying colors, and was a most understanding and sensitive operator. However, after one week of working she began to develop severe stomach pains. A medical examination revealed nothing organically wrong, which led her doctor to question her job. After several sessions it was obvious that a change of job would be to her benefit. It was unfortunate that such an able person should be lost to this type of job, and all of her supervisors felt her loss, but in her best interests it was absolutely necessary. Although she loved the job and was liked and accepted by all, her body was signalling another message that had better be listened to. This was one warning signal that was indicating to her a need for relief. Even though we sometimes consciously do not realize the stress we are under, our body will let us know otherwise. This was one situation in which the operator's body was letting her know that this job was too much for her.

BODY REACTIONS TO STRESS

Regardless of the sources of stress, states Doctor Selye, your body has a three-stage reaction to it, which he called the "general adaptation syndrome." These are the alarm stage, the resistance stage, and the exhaustion stage.

In the alarm stage, your body recognizes the stressor and prepares for fight or flight. This is done by a release of hormones from the endocrine glands. These hormones will cause an increase in heartbeat and respiration, elevation in blood sugar level, increase in perspiration, dilated pupils, and slowed digestion. You will then choose whether to use this burst of energy to fight or to flee, i.e. to get away from the stressor.

In the resistance stage, your body repairs any damage caused from the stress. If, however, the stressor does not go away, the body cannot repair the damage and must remain alert.

This plunges you into the third stage: exhaustion. If this state continues long enough, you may develop one of the "diseases of stress," such as migraine headaches, heart irregularity, or even mental illness. Continued exposure to stress during the exhaustion stage causes the body to run out of energy and may even stop bodily functions.

OCCUPATIONAL ILLNESSES

Besides the physical illnesses brought on by stress caused by pressures of the operator's job, there are other illnesses that are brought on because certain parts of the body are overtaxed or pressed into some unusual service. There is, in fact, a dictionary published in 1978 under the title, *Folk Name and Trade Diseases*, in which Doctor E. R. Plunkett (1978), who practiced occupational medicine, made a complete listing of maladies related to the work place. Among the various illnesses listed pertaining to the emergency operator's job are:

- TELEPHONE EAR. This malady is caused from telephone overuse. Symptoms are: headaches, dizziness, and insomnia.
- LISTENING-IN-DERMATITIS. This is a skin disease that comes from excessive contact with the earpiece.
- DESK NECK. This problem is caused by incorrect posture and the constant adaptation of the neck to the headset.
- TYPIST'S CRAMP. This is caused by the pressure of trying to get the information into the computer quickly, especially on busy days.
- EXECUTIVE'S DISEASE. This is a duodenal ulcer that has resulted from the stress of the job itself.

This information shouldn't come as any great surprise to any operator who has experienced the constant battering of hysterical, excited voices on his eardrum hour after hour, or who has sat for eight hours with a headset around his neck. In addition to these occupational illnesses, there also are the problems of varicose veins and hemorrhoids caused from sitting in one position for too many hours.

INDIVIDUALITY OF STRESSORS

We all might agree that noise, air, and water pollution, traffic jams, crowding, and other elements of our environment are irritating, discomforting, and stressful. Yet, scientists have trouble agreeing upon just what is a source of stress (i.e. a stressor). The fact is that almost anything that one person finds stressful, someone else might find enjoyable, or not stressful.

For example, the atmosphere in the emergency room is always charged with a sense of action: the radio speakers are always on, the teletype machines always clatter, and the calls are always coming in. Thus, while some operators may be busily forming committees to establish a "quiet room" in order to relax in, other operators are happily content with the noise level and generally unsettling atmosphere of the emergency room and never even consider the need for a quiet room.

Every emergency operator must learn to measure the stress level at which he personally can function best and then not go either above or below that level. By careful self-observation, he can gradually develop an instinctive feeling that tells him when he is running above or below the stress level that corresponds to his own nature.

It is important to learn how to handle emotional tensions and to know and accept physical and emotional limitations. All this is "easier said than done," but understanding is the first step. We all have strengths and weaknesses, and we all function better in some situations than in others. When possible, we should direct our activities to those areas of life where our function is effective and comfortable and away from those areas where we are ineffective and uncomfortable. We may then reduce the possibilities of developing ailments that arise from inner conflicts. Each of us needs an outlet for pent-up emotions of anger, frustration, hostility, and discouragement that develop from life's situations. Too often ill feelings are passed along in epidemic fashion. For example:

1. The supervisor has a fight with his wife.
2. He then bawls out the operator.
3. The operator screams at the caller.
4. The caller wonders why he is being further victimized by someone to whom he has turned for help.

EMOTIONAL CONTROL

No one would dispute that emotional control or stability is a desirable characteristic, but what can be done about achieving it? Following are some suggestions that can be used for alleviating stress:

WORK OFF STRESS. If you are angry or upset, try to blow off steam physically by activities such as running, playing tennis, or gardening. Even taking a walk can help. Physical activity allows you a "fight" outlet for your mental stress.

TALK OUT YOUR WORRIES. It helps to share worries with someone you trust and respect. This may be a friend, family member, co-worker, clergyman, teacher, or counselor. Sometimes another person can help you see a new side to your problem and, thus, a new solution. This is not admitting defeat. It is admitting you are an intelligent human being who knows when to ask for assistance. AVOID SELF-MEDICATION. Although there are many chemicals, including alcohol, that can mask stress symptoms, they do not help you adjust to the stress itself, and many are habit-forming, so the decision to use them should belong to your doctor. Medication is a form of flight reaction and can cause more stress than it solves. The ability to handle stress comes from within you, not from the outside.

GET ENOUGH SLEEP AND REST. Lack of sleep can lessen your ability to deal with stress by making you more irritable. Most people need at least seven to eight hours of sleep out of every twenty-four.

BALANCE WORK AND RECREATION. Schedule time for recreation to relax your mind. Although inactivity can cause boredom, a little loafing can ease stress. This should not be a constant escape, but occasionally, you deserve a break.

GET AWAY FROM IT ALL. When you feel that you are going around in circles with a problem or a worry, try to divert yourself. As simple a thing as going to the movies, watching TV, reading a story, or visiting a friend may help. There's no harm in running away from a painful situation long enough to catch your breath and regain the composure you need to come back and face the problem. When possible and practical, a change of scene can give you a new perspective. There are times when we need to "escape," even if it's just a brief letup from the usual routine.

All of the above suggestions are helpful to practice after working hours; however, during working hours there are other suggestions for relaxation that will help alleviate stress. What follows are some of the techniques that can be used while actually working to help offset some of the effects of stress.

RELAXATION TECHNIQUES

There are several relaxation techniques that an operator can use to offset the stress and strain of the type of work being done, and many of these exercises can be practiced during the day, even while at the console. Basically, if you really want to relax, you must learn to counteract some biological "coping" mechanisms that readied early human beings for fight or flight when their lives were threatened. Among these are a racing pulse, a spurt of adrenal hormones, and a bracing of the neck and back muscles. Today, our lives are rarely threatened, but we still react in these same ways to change in our lives. The body is ready, we feel the quickened pulse as palpitations, and we have that "keyed-up" feeling, often accompanied by indigestion. There is no physical outlet for this, so often the person will maintain the appearance of being calm, while hiding suppressed fear, rage, or other pressure that has no outlet except against himself.

Because we encounter so much change in modern life and have so many social demands, we too often tense our bodies, clench our teeth, breathe shallowly, tense our necks, and set in motion a physical chain reaction that can lead to a headache, backache, or chronic fatigue. Furthermore, the physical tensions set up a vicious circle. They cause worry about the discomfort they induce and their harmfulness, which perpetuate the tension.

A large number of people seek relief by drinking or taking pills prescribed by doctors, who don't know of any other way to calm their patients. Other professionals have been trying to counteract the trend by teaching systems of relaxation. Since the early 1920s, for example, the physiologists, Doctor Edmund Jacobson, has been teaching progressive relaxation. By tensing and releasing different muscles in the body, a person slowly contrasts the sensations of tension with that of letting go. Evenutally, the subject learns to tense and release body muscles from head to toe like a ripple down the whole body.

Another method, known as *autogenic training*, has been used by doctors since about 1910. The procedure, developed by the physician, Doctor Johannes Schulz, is based on autohypnotic methods that induce certain types of body changes that occur when we get very quiet, such as a heavy feeling, warmth, regular heartbeat, regular breathing, warmth in the diaphragm, and coolness in the forehead.

The first step in learning to relax is a very short exercise. Read the instructions several times before you begin. Assume a comfortable position, and find a stationary object to fix your attention on. This object could be anything, even a spot on the wall or ceiling, positioned just above eye level that produces tension in the eye muscles when you stare at it. Therefore:

1. Pick out a point or spot.
2. Take five deep breaths.
3. Hold the fifth breath; count back from 5 to 1; close eyes and relax.
4. Count back from 50 to 1 (take 1 count for each breath). Allow your mind to go blank, while you say to yourself that you will enter a state of relaxation and calm.
5. At the count of 1, count from 1 to 5 and open your eyes.

You should feel relaxed and comfortable after this exercise. Practice this three times per day, preferably at the same time each day.

This exercise requires taking deep breaths, which aids in reducing tension if they are done properly. How do you breathe? Do you involuntarily tense up before speaking and find yourself taking hurried, shallow breaths? In childhood nobody ever taught us how to breathe correctly, even though breath is the essential energy of life, since oxygen must be sent to every cell.

Breathing can stop tension. If you are serious about changing the tension-creating habits of a lifetime, you will need to introduce relaxed breathing into all of your daily life, practicing every day. In all of these exercises, give your full attention to the sensations and sounds of breathing, trying not to think of other things. Since you breathe all of the time, it might as well become a pleasure, and nobody else will notice anything unusual.

The only way to relax is to begin to reverse your habits of reacting tensely and recognizing what causes your automatic reactions. Although it is not easy, these exercises can help. The following exercise can be done during coffee breaks:

Sit on the edge of a straight wooden chair, your knees about twelve inches apart, and your legs slanting forward at an angle of greater than ninety degrees. Sit up very straight. Now, let yourself collapse like a rag doll, your head forward, your spine rounded, and your hands coming to rest on your knees. Check yourself to be sure you are comfortable and then say to yourself. "My right arm is heavy, my right arm is heavy." Repeat this for about twenty seconds, while concentrating on your arm from the armpit to the fingertips. Then make a fist, flex your arms, taking a deep breath, open your eyes. Repeat this procedure three or four times a day.

After you become adept at making your right arm heavy, you can extend the heaviness to your legs and then to the whole body until you can relax from head to toe.

Another breathing exercise that can be done while at the console is as follows:

Draw deep breaths into the stomach and let it rise. The chest should hardly move at all. When this becomes easy, smile slightly, breathe in through your nose and out through your mouth, whispering a sound like "aaaaah" (which should sound like the wind), while the jaw, tongue, and mouth are dropped slightly open. Think about the sound and the feeling of the breathing as you are taking long, slow breaths down into your stomach. Do this for five to ten minutes at a time.

Sigh deeply, making a sound of deep relief. Let all of the air out of your lungs. Then simply permit the air to come back in. You do not have to force yourself to inhale; it will happen naturally. Do this ten times.

When it becomes natural and pleasant to breathe deeply, practice it at odd moments during the day, taking three or four deep breaths and putting all your attention into the relaxation of breathing. When you have learned to get that relaxed feeling from breathing, you can practice it every time you start to feel tense. Sometimes it helps to follow the breath mentally, as if you could see it entering at the nose and flowing down the throat into the lungs and diaphragm. When you inhale, the energy of oxygen is carried by the blood to all parts of your body. When you exhale, you can feel the air going out the nose like wind with a pleasant sound.

Walking can be a good form of relaxation and meditation. On your breaks or lunch hour, walk for about twenty minutes. Pay attention to how you walk, what parts of you are moving, and how the parts feel. Feel your shoulders, knees, thighs, calves, heels, ankles, and toes. Feel your heartbeat, and pay close attention to your breathing.

Perhaps you may perfer a meditative exercise. Enjoy twenty minutes of uninterrupted quiet. Sit comfortably with your eyes closed. Chant aloud the word "calm" or any other soft word until you hear your own voice. Then let yourself chant mental repetition of the chant. If you begin to daydream, or fantasize, gently guide your attention back to the chant. Stay with it daily, and in a few months you will notice a new calming relaxation about yourself.

Once you have achieved a comfortable feeling about relaxation, you are ready to give yourself suggestions that will assist you in reducing stress. You may say to yourself:

- "I am always calm, relaxed, and in complete control."
- "As each day goes by, I will feel more relaxed."

Another meditative exercise known as *staring* or *pinpointing* involves contemplating on some favorite object, without having any thoughts. A flower is particularly pleasant to stare at. If you find your attention straying, gently bring it back. Just caress the object with your eyes. You do not need to talk to yourself about it, just enjoy it. When you still your mind, it focuses upon the object, which becomes endlessly interesting and pleasant. A few minutes of such contemplation, even during lunch hour at a desk, can provide more refreshment than an nap. This is the important point about these relaxation exercises: they can be practiced right at the desk or terminal while you are working. During a lull in phone calls coming in, take thirty seconds to do a relaxation exercise. Most times no one will even realize what you are doing, and the rewards for practicing relaxation are many.

In conclusion, there are some suggestions that can be followed to alter working conditions that can help reduce some of the stressors of the operator's job.

1. REST PERIODS. Frequent rest periods should be scheduled during the day for the emergency operator. Most positions have a twenty-minute break and a one-hour lunch scheduled into an eight-hour day, and, indeed, this schedule is followed in many communications divisions of large corporations. However, this schedule might well be followed on most jobs where the person may get a drink of water, use the copy machine, check a spelling in the dictionary across the room, etc. The operator, though, is limited to his console and cannot get up to stretch his legs or change his surroundings, even temporarily. Therefore, it is necessary to have frequent rest breaks scheduled during the day in order to increase concentration and efficiency and reduce physical ailments that affect the lower part of the body when one is forced to sit in one position for any great length of time. It is not unreasonable to consider a fifteen-minute break every one and one-half hours, instead of a twenty-

minute break every three and one-half hours.

2. QUIET ROOMS. The establishment of a "quiet room," in which the operator can go to on rest breaks, does much to relieve the stress of the operator's job. The room itself does not have to be fancy, just a softly painted and softly lighted space away from the noise and rush of the communications room. It is up to the operator to convince administration of their responsibility in providing stress-alleviating outlets for their operators, and it is up to administration to accept this responsibility. After all:

> It is difficult to be humane
> to others,
> When you are not being treated
> humanely yourself.

Good Luck!

Chapter 8

HANDS-ON ROLE PLAYS

THE purpose of role play is to practice for crisis events and other situations that the operator is likely to encounter. It has been shown that operator anxiety will be reduced and operator efficiency will be heightened if he is adequately prepared in advance for the various types of calls he will be responding to. It would be simple enough to just read about crisis calls and procedures for handling these calls and learn something valuable. And one could also watch some videotapes or make personal visits or field trips to a communications room on a busy night to get some first-hand information concerning job expectations. However, this is learning by watching. In order to truly learn the operator's role, and develop skills in an effective and flexible manner, the future operator must be actually engaged in hands-on role playing, in which the operator is answering realistic training calls at the console.

After each of the chapters there are a series of practice calls that will reflect the material previously covered in that chapter. The task for the operator is to handle the call effectively by following the chapter's major learning points. All other operators in the group may serve as observers, or, if there are enough computer terminals, may practice processing the same information at individual consoles.

Each role play is based on a real incident, which has been selected from both recorded and live incoming calls involving special and/or stress situations for the operator. In order to effect realism in these role plays, the caller must be able to simulate the special characteristics of that caller, as described in the material in the preceding chapter. This may include hysteria, depression, anger, confusion, calm, and apathy, as well as acting out alcoholism, speech impediments, hearing deficiencies, and a wide range of foreign accents.

Preparing through rehearsal is even more effective if there is in-

249

structional feedback on performance after each role play. After completing each role play, there should be a debriefing session in which the observers may provide feedback on the performance of the caller and operator who participated. The goal of this activity is to reinforce the major learning points of the chapter and to determine whether the participants actually utilized the material learned to effectively complete the call. In order to elicit constructive feedback from participants and observers, the following points can be covered:

1. - FOR THE OPERATOR: "How did you feel about the caller?" "What were your thoughts during the call?" "What kind of mind image did you have of what had happened?" "Do you feel you handled the call correctly?" "If you could make some changes, what would you change about the way you handled the call?"

2. FOR THE CALLER: "How did you feel about the operator?" "Did you feel confident that all was being done to help you?" "Was the call handled correctly by the operator?" "If you could make some changes, what would you change about the way the call was handled?"

3. FOR THE OBSERVERS: "How well was the call handled by the operator?" "Was the caller realistic enough?" "Were the major points of the chapter followed in order to accurately dispatch this call?" "Did the operator adhere to the human skills involved?" "Were human skills coordinated effectively with the technical skills?" "Was there much difficulty for the operator in gathering the necessary information?" "Did the operator form the questions correctly and were they asked in proper sequence in order to elicit all the necessary information?"

In addition, the role plays should all contain information on the average time in which an operator should be required to handle the call and pass on the necessary information to the dispatcher. These time constraints may vary in different localities. However, the operator should be alerted to this important training point when they input the calls.

One final point related to the realism of hands-on role play is that of training stress, i.e. the stress experienced by the operator due to the pressures of initial handling of realistic calls. Trainers should be aware of their responsibility for their students. Although hands-on role playing is an excellent training device, it imposes further stress on an already stressful situation. The importance of debriefing sessions to alleviate much of the bad feelings, guilt, embarrassment, and heightened feelings that will surface during role plays cannot be overstated. An observant trainer will become aware of the excitement that will pervade the training room because of the contagious nature of crisis. It is the trainer's responsibility to help the students deal with their own feelings concerning the calls and what is happening in the room during the debriefing sessions. In addition, it is important that the trainer see to it that feedback is constructive and that the tendency on the part of some students to become destructively critical of their peers be curtailed. In this way, training will be a positive experience reflecting growth and learning for effective emergency operators.

Chapter 1 — Communication

The role plays in Chapter 1 will look at the complexities of communication, i.e. points of misunderstanding, the dynamics of encoding and decoding, cultural differences, and the necessary fusion of human and technical modes.

1-1. Background Information

The caller is a young black male. You realize from the address that he is living in a multiple dwelling, located in a socially and economically deprived area of the city. From his opening comments you recognize that this is a street-wise person with limited formal education.

Opening Remarks

Hello, is this the police? Send some help, there's a cat been stabbed out here in the hallway and he is bleeding!

Analysis of Information Input

This is an example of an encoding communication problem in

that there are two meanings of the word "cat."

Encode: cat stabbed in hallway
Decode: 1. four-legged animal
2. street terminology for a man.

1-2. Background Information

The caller is a young, single, working female, living alone in a working-class community. She is excited and speaking faster than a normal rate of speech.

Opening Remark

Hello, police? I've been robbed. I went to work at 8 AM this morning and returned at 4 PM. I found my door open and my television set is gone.

Operator's Response

Calm down honey and repeat that again!

"Calm down honey" is an example of a disrespectful mode of address and may initiate a defensive reaction on the part of the caller. This is detrimental to the successful resolution regarding the trauma experienced by the caller.

Background Information

The caller is of the upper middle-class, living in an area of the city noted for its social and economic wealth. He is a middle-aged man, an executive type who calls to report a strange car blocking his driveway. His attitude has a demanding quality to it.

Opening Remarks

Listen you, send a policeman here to remove this derelict car from my driveway, immediately! I can never get my tax dollars worth from any of you people!

Analysis of Information Input

"You people" is a term that initiates on the one hand, a defensive reaction and further is a sterotypical term. In addition, the tone of voice is denoting a superior attitude, which is a communication barrier.

Chapter 2 — Transactional Analysis

2-1. Background Information

The caller is critical and demanding.

Opening Remarks

Listen, this is the third time I've called. I have a sick child here, so get a policeman here right away or I'll have your job. You should have had a car here already! I demand to know your name, operator!

Analysis of Information Input

The caller's attitude is typical of the Critical Parent ego state. The Critical Parent is spontaneous and increases of probability of conflict. There is a judgmental quality to the caller's remarks that is an attempt to tell the operator how to do his/her job. This approach tends to create resentment on the part of the listener. In order to avoid this conflict the operator must construct a parallel transaction, therefore, moving to the appropriate ego state. This movement enables the operator to gather information and not take personal affront to the caller's criticism, in spite of being criticized.

2-2. Background Information

The caller is a teenage female who is excited, emotional, and crying intermittently.

Opening Remarks

Please, please help. My mother and father are fighting. They're killing each other.

Analysis of Information Input

This caller is in the Child ego state. Emotional behavior impairs one's ability to encode information with an adequate degree of accuracy. For example, fighting and "killing each other" may or may not convey the message realistically. Here, the operator must control the interaction and response so that accurate information may be extracted from an emotional person. This is accomplished by initiating mind-set in the Adult ego state and completing the parallel transaction via the Parent ego state.

2-3. Background Information

A uniformed police officer on traffic duty calls in to report an automobile accident, a situation that would normally elicit excitable behavior. The officer calmly states the conditions of the accident, giving the operator the location and number of injured with the same calm and assertive temperament.

Opening Remarks

Operator, I have a three-car accident with four injured at 204 East Main Street, Northeast corner. Ambulance needed with oxygen.

Analysis of Information Input

This example poses no problem because the information is given without emotional involvement or subjectivity of the Parent or Child ego states. Although, the information is in reference to a critical incident, it is given objectively with a sense of logic and responsibility that is indicative of Adult ego state.

Chapter 3 — Communicating with Victims

3-1. Background Information

A young female college student who lives in a coed dorm calls in to report a rape that occurred two days prior to the call, after a midsemester party. Her voice is clear, concise, articulate, and seemingly unemotional.

Opening Remarks

Hello, may I speak to the police? I want to report a rape. It happened two days ago.

Analysis of Information Input

The possible attitude of society regarding coed dorms, that is society's resistance to this type of living arrangement, may assist one in drawing conclusions about the innocence or guilt of this victim, therefore determining the way this caller gets treated. The fact that the time of occurrence was two days prior to the call may initiate a spontaneous reaction from the operator, i.e. "Why did you wait so long?" This statement is unimportant and irrelevant at this time and does damage in terms of placing blame on the victim caller.

3-2. Background Information

The caller is a young, male assault victim approximately twenty-five years of age.

Opening Remarks

Operator, I was beat up by a man wearing dark clothes. He was taller than me. No, no he was shorter than me. Wait a minute operator, I'm not sure what he looked like. Well, anyway, could you send a police officer here to protect me?

Analysis of Information Input

As the result of trauma, the victim loses his ability to recall detailed information, and the victim may not be able to articulate important information about the assault. Fear is a phase of the victims behavior. To ask for protection is an example of the victims clinging behavior, which is one of the ways in which fear is expressed.

3-3. Background Information

The caller is a forty-year-old, Spanish-American female who is a burglary victim. She speaks conversational English and fluent Spanish.

Opening Remarks

Oh my God, police, I have been robbed! I went to work this morning and come home and my house is robbed. My mother's necklace has been taken. She gave it to me when I was a little girl before she died.

Analysis of Information Input

"Oh my God!" is a typical phrase expressed by crisis victims. It is an indicator that one may be in a crisis. The crisis situation has a regressive quality to it, thereby influencing behavior as it regresses. People in crisis will regress to that behavior that comes easiest and gives them a better sense of control. For example: a bilingual victim will regress to their native language.

Chapter 4 - Crisis Behavior and Intervention

4-1. Background Information

The caller is an hysterical young male who lives in the basement of a two-family house. His voice is shrill and he is screaming.

Opening Remarks

Operator, please, please! Quick, quick send the police, send an ambulance, send help! The water broke! My wife was in bed and now she is all wet.

Analysis of Information Input

Be aware that excited behavior carries a contagious element. The operator should not respond in the affirmative before verifying information. One may assume in this instance that his wife is about to give birth; however, the man is complaining of a burst water pipe that is over the bed in which his wife was asleep. This unpredicted event initiated a crisis reaction in this caller, thus displaying crisis behavior.

4-2. Background Information

The caller is a female approximately thirty-five years of age, who calls to report that she was driving her station wagon with her young child in the rear seat and was involved in an accident. The young child is seriously injured.

Opening Remarks

Hello, police? Could you send an ambulance or a doctor? I was in a car accident and my child is seriously ill, maybe fatal. (Her voice is calm, clear, and free of excitement.) I am at the corner of Fourth and Main. My car is a 1979, blue and white station wagon.

Analysis of Information Input

A crisis has various effects on people, ranging from calm to logic to excited behavior. In this situation the caller expresses a clear, concise tone of voice and calm and controlled behavior, even though her child has been seriously injured. The operator should recognize this response as a coping mechanism and should not be misled by her calmness and disbelieve this callers crisis situation.

4-3. Background Informaiton

The caller is the owner of a small grocery store who calls to report a robbery. The assailant used a shotgun and took money from the cash register.

Opening Remarks

Hello police, I don't know what happened. I don't believe this happened to me. I've been in business for forty years, and nothing ever happened like this. Why me? I feel so numb! He held that big gun right up to my face!

Analysis of Information Input

Operators should be aware that this type of language and expression is typical of Stage 1 of Victimology. The victim's behavior is reflective of shock, disbelief, and denial.

Chapter 5 — Special Callers

5-1. Background Information

The caller is a six-year-old boy who calls to get help for his mother who has been injured and is semiconscious on the bathroom floor.

Opening Remarks

Hello, hello, hello. My mommy is hurt. She can't talk. She can't get up. Her leg is bleeding.

Analysis of Information Input

A six-year-old boy lacks an extensive frame of reference to articulate problems in a detailed way. The operator must direct this six-year-old and make him an extension of her, so that he becomes her eyes and ears, where help is needed. The operator should be aware that communication with the child is special in the language must be simple and exhaustive in meaning.

5-2. Background Information

The caller is a thirty-year-old male who is calling from the Rose Hill Bar. He has been robbed and assaulted, his speech is slurred, and he is unable to state what he is calling for.

Opening Remarks

Hello, police? Ah, ah, ah, I've been robbed. You know, I was just minding my own business, having a few drinks and these two guys came in and took my wallet and my money.

Analysis of Information Input

It should be noted that the intoxicated caller has similar behavioral qualities to that of a child caller. The intoxicated caller has lost his frame of reference, and the child caller has not developed one yet. Therefore, this necessary quality for the giving of information must be compensated for in this caller as it was for the child caller. That is, the intoxicated caller must also be directed. The tourist, also, has no frame of reference because of unfamiliar surroundings, and the elderly in addition must be treated with this same direction in order for this call to be completed successfully.

BIBLIOGRAPHY

Berne, Eric: *Games People Play*. New York, Random House, Inc., 1964.

Birdwhistell, Ray: *Introduction to Kinesics*. Louisville, University of Louisville Press, 1952.

Drapkin, Israel and Viano, Emilio: *Victimology*. Lexington, Massachusetts, Lexington Books, 1974.

Drapkin, Israel and Viano, Emilio: *Victimology: A New Focus, Society's Reaction to Victimization*. Lexington, Massachusetts, Lexington Books, 1974.

Gunther, Bernard: *Sense Relaxation, Below Your Mind*. New York, Collier Books, 1968.

Harris, Thomas, A.: *I'm OK — You're OK*. New York, Harper & Row, Publishers, 1967.

Jacobson, Edmund: *Progressive Relaxation*. Chicago, University of Chicago Press, 1938.

Plunkett, E. R.: *Folk Name and Trade Diseases*. Stanford, Connecticut, Barrett Book Company, 1978.

Romano, Anne T.: *Transactional Analysis For Police Personnel*. Springfield, Thomas, 1981.

Schultz, J., and Luthe, W.: *Autogenic Training: A Physiologic Approach in Psychotherapy*. New York, Grune and Stratton, 1959.

Selye, Hans: *The Stress of Life*. New York, McGraw-Hill Book Company, 1956.

INDEX

DATE DUE